PRACTICAL BOATING

Practical Boating

INLAND AND OFFSHORE POWER AND SAIL

W. S. KALS

ILLUSTRATED BY VICTOR MAYS

GARDEN CITY, NEW YORK
Doubleday & Company, Inc.

Library of Congress Catalog Card Number 69–13027
Copyright © 1969 by W. S. Kals
Printed in the United States of America

"Lifeboat Drills" © 1966 by Ziff-Davis Publishing Company
"Buoy-to-Buoy Navigation" © 1968 by Ziff-Davis Publishing Company
"Navigation Tricks" © 1965 by *Popular Mechanics*
"Towing and Being Towed" © 1968 by *Popular Mechanics*
"Out of the Mouth of Babes" © 1962 by The Skipper Publishing Company
"Winter Weather in the Palm Belt" © 1964 by *Yachting*
"Going Overboard for Maintenance and Fun" © 1965 by *Yachting*
"What Do You Know About Coral?" © 1966 by *Yachting*
"Wind and Weather" from *Yachtsman's Guide to the Bahamas* © 1966, 1967, 1968 by Tropic Isle Publishers, Inc.
"Drownproofing" condensed from *Drownproofing: A New Technique for Water Safety* by Fred R. Lanoue © 1963 by Prentice-Hall, Inc. Published by Prentice-Hall, Inc., Englewood Cliffs, New Jersey
"Starfinder" © 1968 by The Hearst Corporation
"Visibility at Sea" © 1967 by The Hearst Corporation
"And a Star to Steer Her By" © 1966 by The Hearst Corporation
"Tidal Currents" © 1966 by The Hearst Corporation
"Polynesian Navigation" © 1965 by The Hearst Corporation
"Make a Compass Check at Sunrise and Sunset" © 1962 by The Hearst Corporation
"Learn to Float" from *Today's Health* © 1968 by American Medical Association

For all hands
and the cook,
that is Trudy

STOP—I HAVE SOMETHING TO COMMUNICATE.

In this book I'll talk about matters usually not mentioned in the polite pages of boating magazines, such as wrecking and falling in the drink.

You'll also find tips from that most advanced of all sailors (or the most complete of idiots)—the single-hander.

I also cover cruising in southern areas—the Florida Keys, the Bahamas, the Islands.

If in this book you don't find some wrinkle you've used since you were eleven years old, or do find something that sends you up the bulkhead—here is my answer: Other vessels, other long-splices.

W. S. K.

Contents

List of Illustrations	xi
PART ONE / OPERATION	
1. The Skillful Skipper	1
2. Postgraduate Anchor Work	8
3. Dinghy Management	21
4. Advanced Weather Lore	29
5. Sailing for Powerboat Skippers	47
6. Work on the Hull between Tides	58
7. Skin Diving for Boat Work	67
PART TWO / NAVIGATION	
8. Tools for Pilotage and Navigation	77
9. Lines of Position	88
10. Fine Points of Pilotage	97
11. Piloting in Coral Waters	107
12. Master Mariner's Compass	114
13. Tides and Tidal Currents	129
14. Navigation without Instruments	140
15. Using a Star Finder	155
16. Celestial Navigation	163
PART THREE / EMERGENCIES	
17. Running Aground and Getting Off	177
18. Towing and Getting Towed	184
19. Hold Regular Drills	192
20. Learn to Float	201

CONTENTS

21. Distressproofing Your Boat 208
22. Successful Wrecking 215

PART FOUR / LIVING

23. About Comfort 227
24. The Gimbaled Cook 237
25. Hints for Boat Living 243
Glossary of Terms 253
Index 263

List of Illustrations

1. Any alternate plan?	5
2. Entrance to Hopetown, Elbow Cay, Bahamas.	6
3. A world record?	9
4. Reducing shocks on anchor rode.	11
5. Chain ground tackle.	14
6. Dropping two anchors under sail.	17
7. Signals between helm and foredeck.	20
8. A dinghy has many uses.	22
9. Bringing aboard or launching a dinghy.	23
10. Dinghies designed to solve stowage problem.	24
11. Good dinghy towing rig.	27
12. Curbing dinghy in anchorage.	29
13. Winter weather in the Islands.	33
14. Pressure distribution, southern North Atlantic. Predicting wind direction in Northern Hemisphere.	34
15. Summer weather in the Islands.	39
16. Barograph trace in the Islands.	40
17. Easterly wave over the Islands.	42
18. Wind strength around a hurricane.	46
19. Wind and sails: square-rigged and fore-and-aft-rigged.	49
20. Points of sailing.	51
21. Sailboat close-hauled.	52
22. Tacking.	53
23. Jury sailing rigs may help a powerboat.	57
24. Careening.	62
25. Drydocking against seawall.	63
26. Poor man's marine railway.	64

LIST OF ILLUSTRATIONS

27. Trimming vessel with water-filled dinghy for work below waterline. 66
28. Skin-diving gear. 69
29. Skin diving is useful around a boat. 73
30. Resetting binoculars quickly. 81
31. Leeway. 83
32. Single-handed dividers. 84
33. Finding magnetic course. 86
34. Fix on lines of position. 91
35. Lines of position can be straight, curved, circular. 94
36. Area of uncertainty smallest at intersection of two lines of position at 90-degree angle. 95
37. Area of uncertainty smallest at intersection of three lines of position at 120- or 60-degree angle. 95
38. Dead reckoning deteriorates rapidly with time. 96
39. Geometry of visibility problems. 98
40. Range of visibility. 99
41. Proper helm order to keep off foul ground. 106
42. Coral reefs: general locations. 109
43. Shadow as depth finder. 113
44. Hand bearing compass has several navigational uses. 116
45. Heeling error. 119
46. Lubber's line to convert true to magnetic. 127
47. Memory aid for compass correction when applying variation. 128
48. Tidal current does not reverse at high and low water. 136
49. Rotary tidal current. 139
50. Hopetown–Nassau course. 141
51. Big Dipper and Cassiopeia are at opposite sides of celestial north pole. 144
52. Finding celestial north and south poles. 145
53. Stars on celestial equator rise due east, set due west. 146
54. A stick lets you find latitude. 148
55. The stars as a clock. 154

List of Illustrations   xiii

56. Your hand measures angles in the sky.   156
57. Finding and identifying stars.   157
58. Marine sextant for measuring altitudes of celestial bodies.   165
59. Lines of position from angles.   166
60. Circle of position from observation of the sun.   167
61. Plotting celestial line of position.   168
62. Working up the sight in Figures 58, 60, and 61.   172
63. Walking out an anchor.   181
64. Getting a sailboat off by using an anchor.   183
65. Getting a line to a disabled boat.   186
66. Bridle distributes strain over large areas of hull on boat to be towed.   188
67. Tips for towing astern.   189
68. Alongside towing.   190
69. Safety harness.   198
70. Natural floating position of man in fresh water.   203
71. Learning to float, using face mask and snorkel.   206
72. Downward push of forearms will give extra lift when needed.   207
73. Ketch *Santa Cruz* starting on her last voyage.   209
74. Lengths of copper tubing make eyesplice in wire rope.   212
75. Rope clamps and rigging wire let you repair rigging under way.   214
76. Schooner *Lucina* on a reef.   218
77. Labyrinth of the ear.   229
78. Waterproofing a hatch coaming.   233
79. Improving ventilation below.   234
80. Improving ventilation by anchoring across the wind.   235
81. Safety in the cabin.   236
82. Galley with gimbaled cook.   239
83. Garbage, anyone?   251

PRACTICAL BOATING

PART ONE / OPERATION

1 The Skillful Skipper

Reading won't make you an able seaman, able to cope with all that the sea, weather, and failure of gear may throw at you. But reading about seamanship is buying experience without getting wet. Not only the author's experience, but that of everyone who has sailed before him. When you get into a pickle, you may remember how the author—an expert on getting into pickles—got out of it.

Of course you can't read Article 2625 in Bowditch while trying to land a boat through the surf. But surely you can remember one simple rule. Use of this one rule separates expert skippers from fair-weather sailors.

I take no credit for it. I got it from an old freighter-captain. We sailed from the West Coast of Canada, through the Panama Canal and the Windward Passage, to New York, talking a good part of the day. At seven knots there were many days. Finally, north of Hatteras, he boiled down a lifetime of seagoing into that one rule.

I have since seen other skippers apply it, and for years have tried to use it myself. But hoping someday to write about it for other small-boat skippers, I kept asking questions. What makes a good skipper? Why are some captains so often in trouble, while others operate for years without a scratch to their topsides? I asked these and similar questions at after-race banquets, in cockpits of charter boats, on the bridge of interisland freighters in the Bahamas, and on docks where the smackboats tie up.

Nobody had a better answer than my freighter captain: Have an Alternate Plan. In plain English: Leave Yourself an Out.

In basic seamanship you have been drilled to plan everything you do. The wise skipper goes one step farther. He has already planned what to do if the original plan doesn't work.

Say you had planned to go to Rockhaven. Halfway there, you

find that the weather, ignoring the forecast, is turning sour rapidly. Or on a sailboat the wind suddenly heads you. It's not the kind of place you'd care to enter at night, and beating to windward you'd never get there before dark. On a power cruiser the oil pressure suddenly drops. You find the leak. Pouring in more oil you can steam on for a few more miles, but you can't repair the leak under way, rolling in the trough. How about going to Beachport instead? But did you bring a chart that shows the unfamiliar and tricky entrance channel? If someone in Rockhaven expects you, have you told him about your alternate destination, or will he have the Coast Guard out looking for you?

Don't be ashamed to change destination. Remember Captain Joshua Slocum's long tack. In *Spray*, thirty-six feet over-all, he had just crossed the Atlantic from Yarmouth, Nova Scotia to Gibraltar. He had planned to sail up the Mediterranean, through the recently opened Suez Canal and on, around the world, eastabout. In Gibraltar he slightly changed his plan. His trouble was not weather, head wind, or oil leak (he had no engine), but . . . pirates. He shaped a new course for Cape Horn, recrossed the Atlantic, and sailed around the world—the first man to do so in a small boat and single-handed besides—westabout.

You won't have to decide on course changes until you start cruising. By that time you'll be an old hand at the alternate-plan approach.

You can start practicing it right after you have bought the boat. You may expect always to carry one or two fairly able-bodied volunteers. But what if some day you can't muster a crew, or if under way your crew gets sunstroke or snake bite? Or perhaps the strapping, salty fellow you met on the dock turns out to be a lubber who bumps into himself, and can't tell a squall from a square knot. Then you'll be single-handing surrounded by company. Will you be able to handle her all by yourself?

A change in rigging, or a gadget that lets you drop the anchor from the helmsman's seat can make a boat that requires a crew into one that—at least in a pinch—can be worked by one man.

I have seen an Alden schooner, certainly not intended for single-handing, run aground every time her owner soloed her out or brought her in. Invited aboard, I found out why. The helmsman had a panoramic view of the whole ocean, except he couldn't see the water directly ahead. A raised platform to be dropped in place when needed would have made him an effective lookout and let him steer with his feet, as the bare-toed natives do when sailing in close quarters.

Let's look at a common maneuver: You are coming to a dock. There has always been a dockmaster, and volunteers to catch your lines. But what if for once there isn't a soul around? Simple. You have your crew posted, fore and aft, with docklines that end in eyesplices or bowlines. Their orders are not to cowboy it, but to wait until you are so close that they can drop the eye over a pile.

When wind or current make it difficult to lay her alongside the dock, what's wrong with approaching head-on and dropping an eye from the bow? You can then safely back off, and using the first line for a spring, bring her alongside without squeezing a fender.

When successful docking depends on the throw of a single line, be ready for your crew to miss the throw or the bystander to drop the line. Big ships use a light heaving line with a monkey fist at the end. A good sailor can throw that line an amazing distance, and a heavy hawser already bent to the heaving line can be pulled ashore quickly. I happened to be on a Channel steamer in a cross tide with a stiff breeze blowing when an unfortunate bosun missed the throw to the dock. What made the experience memorable was the microphone that had been recently installed to relay the captain's orders. The microphone was open when the monkey fist splashed into the water. Everybody on the ship and the pier—including some maiden-lady schoolteachers—then learned some words that would have brought a blush to the cheeks of a parrot in a sailor's grog shop.

Anchoring can become a debacle. Crews have gone off to dreamland, have been caught in the bight, or fouled the anchor before they even dropped it. Anything can happen. Also an anchor may just skid along the bottom without biting. Under power you should be able to avoid disaster. With the mainsail still up, you can perhaps quickly hoist the jib again and sail off for another try. But at the very least you should have a second anchor ready, on deck, and with the bitter end of the rode belayed.

Sometimes sleep becomes a problem. A passage takes longer than expected, or you are sailing short-handed and have to get back on watch before you've been properly asleep. First backstop against sleep is strong coffee or pills. (You had better try the pills when it doesn't matter; on some people they act as sleeping pills.) Next, you could set an alarm clock to wake you in fifteen minutes, if that's how long you could safely steer in a circle. If you are alone and have to have sleep, better have it in daytime and keep watch at night; chances for getting run down are less in broad daylight.

Off Guilford, one winter day, my schooner sprang a leak. Alternate plan: put into Guilford. Unfortunately the buoys I saw and the ones on the chart didn't jibe at all. There seemed to be rocks all around. I anchored, pumped, and tried to locate the leak. It seemed to be low down under the inside ballast. I pumped some more and removed ballast from one section of the bilge after another. I pumped and moved iron pigs. As long as I could keep up the work at the pump, I'd be all right. No one had seen my distress and it was now late at night. Beaching amid the rocks, without local knowledge, in the dark was out of the question. So I kept pumping. Finally I had to have some rest. Once asleep I'd never hear an alarm clock. So I took off the right shoe and sock, stretched out on my bunk, letting my right leg dangle. When the first drops of icy water hit my heel, I'd go to the pump again. Between stints at the pump—two hundred strokes at a go—I got quite a bit of sleep that night.

The list of problems you can run into is endless. That's what makes boating fun for some of us. The way to cope with them is always the same: Have a standby plan.

By now undoubtedly you have dreamed up a maneuver that can't be backstopped.

Every afternoon, while refitting in Moorehead City, I watched a professional captain bring in a high-speed sport fisherman. His tie-up was a fourposter against a concrete pier. He'd come in, full ahead on both engines, throwing spray. At a place he knew, he'd throw both engines in reverse and come to a beautiful stop, dead center of the four piles. What possible alternate plan had he if his hydraulic system failed? Buy a farm?

The prudent skipper, faced with a situation that allows no foulup, still finds an alternate plan: He does something different altogether.

Some cruising men delight in entering a harbor under sail. If ever there was a maneuver that needs a secondary plan, that's it. Say you are cruising through the Abacos in the northern Bahamas. Sooner or later you'll want to get into Hopetown's landlocked harbor. And you may want to try it under sail. The entrance channel, which carries about four feet at low water, first tends about SE—the road leading to the water's edge serves as a range—then turns rather sharply to a little west of south. The wind has been steady out of the

The Skillful Skipper 5

ENE. Simple: At the turn you free the sheet and you'll have it made.

But once you are past Eagle Rock the land and the trees may steal your wind, and sometimes abeam of the lighthouse the wind changes direction. In either case you'll gently run aground. You can backstop this maneuver in several ways. If you have an engine, start it well before entering the channel proper, and let it tick over

1. *Any alternate plan?*

ready to put it in gear if needed. If you have no engine, but have a dinghy with an outboard motor, you can still avoid making a spectacle of yourself. Have a member of the crew-power nearby ready to tow you past the critical spot if you give the signal.

Lacking both engine and outboard, how can you backstop your plan? Anchor off and wait for a fair current that'll carry you in. Even wait for high water—another three feet or so—and you'll have a little more room for error. You may even wait until someone offers to tow you in. (There's a real alternate plan!)

Even in a powerboat, anchoring off and waiting for more water, or for someone to show you the way in, is a good idea for the first-time visitor.

Forget all about Hopetown. What matters is not some specific trick, but the skipper's attitude, the always-have-another-scheme.

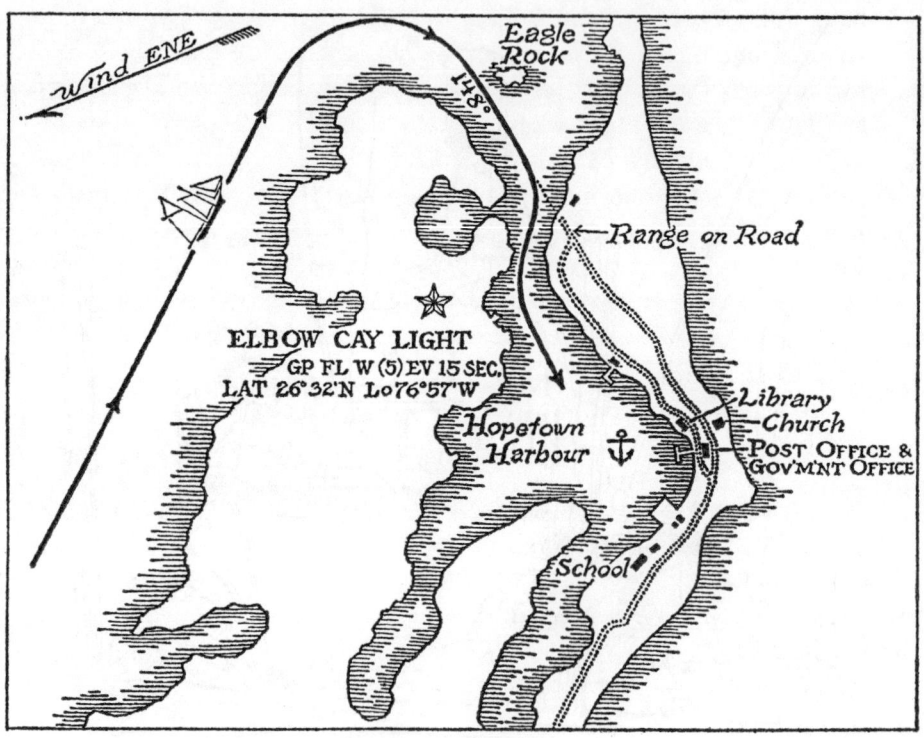

2. *Entrance to Hopetown, Elbow Cay, Bahamas.*

In a lifetime of boating you couldn't learn, or reinvent, all the possible tricks. You can learn some of them by watching other fellows handle their boats. The best teachers are probably single-handers. I don't mean the stubbly types who sail across the Atlantic or to Tahiti, but the usually clean-shaven, ordinary fellows who operate good-sized craft in your own waters regularly without crew. Out of necessity they have developed safe, backstopped maneuvers.

There is, I think, another way to become a better skipper. Try a game I've played for years.

It started when as a youngster I once complained to my father: "I'm bored." His reply, "Intelligent people are never bored," so scared me that I've not dared admit to being bored since. So I play this game. Waiting for a bus, or on a passage with nothing to do but watch the compass and steer a little, I give myself a problem and with or without pencil-and-paper try to solve it. In a barber chair I have undocked a sailboat without power against wind and current. In an airline terminal I once heroically rescued three castaways on a raft in water too shallow for my vessel. In a cafeteria line I've docked the late *Queen Mary* without assistance from tugs.

You can even make up a problem with steadily increasing complications. The all-time most horrible example must be this series of problems thrown at candidates for the Yacht Master's certificate, the British ticket for professional captains.

It starts, if I remember right, with the windward shroud of your sloop carrying away. The candidate immediately goes on the other tack to ease the strain on the mast.

"Too late," the examiner tells him. "The mast has just gone by the board."

The candidate orders the wreckage cut away to avoid damage to the hull.

"Sorry, the mast has just punched a hole at the waterline near the bow."

The future master manages to trim his craft by the stern, stanches the inrush of water, and has the bilge pumped almost dry. Before attempting to jury-rig a mast he orders the boat readied, just in case.

"The boat won't do you any good. You are upwind of sheer cliffs against which the surf breaks heavily."

"How far upwind, sir?"

"Oh, one thousand yards."

That lets out any jury rig. Rapidly running out of alternate plans, the candidate asks: "Have we got an engine?"

"Yes."

Relieved, he starts the kicker only to learn that it has backfired and set the engine compartment on fire. Of course the fire extinguishers are also hexed and the fire drives the crew from the pump.

Dismasted, sinking, on fire, and near a forbidding lee-shore he is asked what his next order will be. Here most candidates fail.

You pass if you have one more alternate plan and order: "All hands to prayer!"

2 Postgraduate Anchor Work

I have been very lucky. For several years I was able to arrange my life as one long cruise. I prefer swinging to the breeze over the unlimited ice supply of marinas. If I had to pay for anchoring and get docking free, I'd still anchor off most of the time. So in a few years I've raised more calluses from anchoring and up-anchoring than most day sailors, weekenders, and two-week vacation cruising men get in much longer sailing careers.

That's not to say that other people haven't had more experience in anchoring. But by one standard I certainly qualify as an expert. If you judge how seasoned a skipper is by the length of scope he pays out for a given depth of water over his anchor, I here want to enter my claim.

I had sailed along the south shore of Nova Scotia with the wind on the nose, day after day. Finally I'd get rid of head winds. After I'd round Cape Sable and enter the Bay of Fundy, the same SW breeze would become a beam wind. I didn't know what an important person I was, and that the wind gods would shift their bellows as soon as I had changed course. Not only that. They also darkened the sky. I already knew enough to trust the sky more than the marine forecast. It looked like a bad one. The coast pilot gave Stoddard Cove, entrance marked by a white light, as a place where vessels could find shelter. My schooner drew only four feet of water and so I carried to the north end of the cove to get a lee from the hills there. In inky darkness I dropped the hook. At first the rode didn't seem to want to run out, as if something had jammed. But then a gust quickly carried me away from the anchor. Snubbing all the way, I let out about a hundred feet. I took a sounding: ten feet. Everyone has heard of the large tides in the Bay of Fundy, so I checked my tide table: falling and I'd hit bottom. I let out more scope, took more soundings, and rechecked my figures. Still not enough. So I bent a spare rode to the first one. The night seemed long as I kept watch, shivering in three sweaters under foul-weather gear, ready to cut her adrift if the wind shifted. I'll make the story of that night short: At low water the schooner was hanging from almost one hundred fathoms of line with barely two feet of

3. *A world record?*

water under her keel. Long before low water I found out why at first the rode had seemed jammed. My anchor had dropped on a ledge just below the surface; there it was well wedged. How did I know? Just by looking up, at low tide ten feet up.

Was that a world record for ratio of scope to depth? Does the record still stand? You probably wouldn't care to break it. But you may be able to use some of the things I've learned in less hairy anchorings and from watching smart skippers handling their ground tackle.

First, let me admit that I'm partial to anchoring with chain. I know that's a minority view, but chain has several advantages over rope, not just natural fiber rope but even synthetic stuff.

Chain is chafe-proof at the bottom. Where a coral knob might cut fibers yarn by yarn, chain will grind away the rock. Chain lying on the bottom helps the anchor do its work. Anchors are designed for horizontal strain; the nearer to the vertical the pull, the closer to breaking out is the anchor. Rope is apt to foul the exposed fluke of an anchor; chain is more likely to sweep around it without hanging up. Chain, when enough of it has been paid out, will give your craft a pleasant ride in a seaway. Riding up on a wave your boat will pick chain off the bottom, but before the strain comes on anchor and fittings she'll be again on her way down into the trough. In the same way she'll pick up chain in gusts, but before all the chain has cleared the bottom, the gust will have passed.

Chain is practically self-stowing. On a boat adapted for its use, chain need never be on deck. It needs no coiling, just drops through a chute into its own locker. Unlike rope it's not subject to mildew and attack by borers. It outlasts rope, and that's the reason for its universal use in permanent moorings.

But its first cost is high. Chain chafes your rail and your topsides unless secured in a stemhead fitting or roller chock on bowsprit or pulpit. In strong gusts chain fetches up with teeth-jarring jerks that put hull and fittings under heavy strain. There are ways to ease these shocks. You can slide a weight—perhaps thirty to fifty pounds—down the chain to keep it on the bottom. The weight rides on a wide shackle to which a light line is bent that lets you lower it and haul it on board again. Such a rode-rider can be rigged to lessen shock load and make a smaller anchor do the work of a heavier one on any rode, not just chain. Another method for easing the load uses the spring action of nylon, which has made it the favorite material for anchoring. You bridge a bight in your chain with a piece of nylon secured by stopper knots on both ends. The line doesn't have to be as big in diameter as you'd use for anchoring in a blow. If it should part, the chain would take over.

The weight of chain is often considered a disadvantage. It isn't, except on very small craft, and on some special designs where every pound matters. Normally chain in its locker brings the weight deep down where it acts as ballast. At the same time being well forward it helps to counterbalance engine, tanks, and passengers near the stern.

As in much boating gear, the lowest price doesn't mean the best buy. Some chain, though galvanized, will rust abominably when used for anchoring. Buy chain made for anchoring, galvanized or wrought iron. For a little extra money both kinds can be bought pretested. Anchor chain is either short-link (also called close-

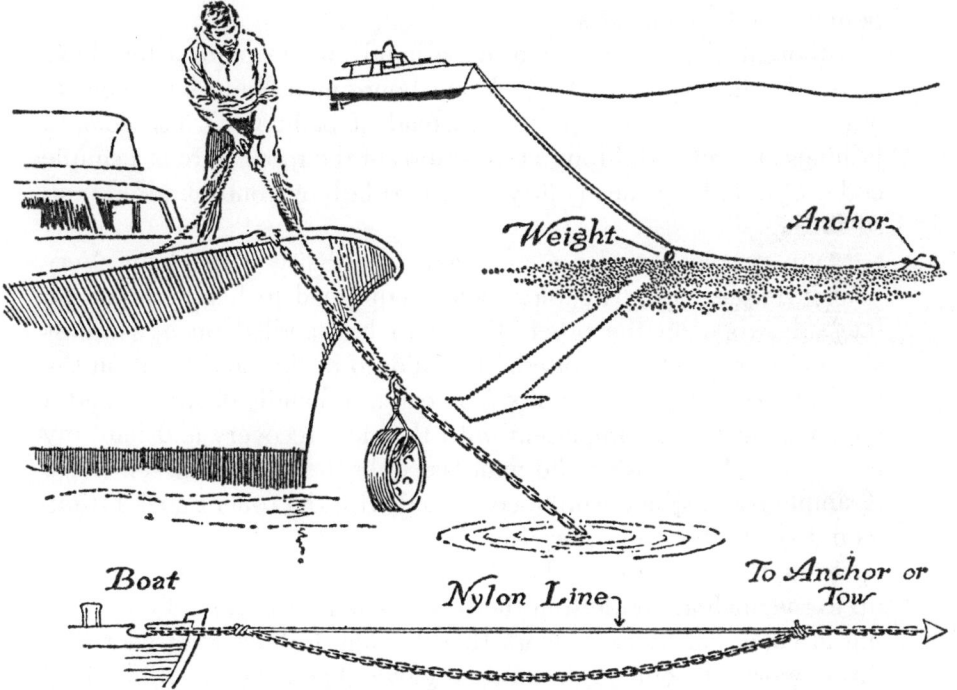

4. *A weight, riding on a shackle, lowered along the anchor rode reduces sudden shocks and increases the holding power of an anchor. So does a nylon line lashed into a bight of chain (bottom).*

link) or stud-link. The studs add to the weight—an advantage—but not to the strength of the chain. Their purpose is to keep the links from stretching. The stretch, unimportant in itself, would make the chain jam on the windlass.

Chain is sold in precut length, called shots, of fifteen fathoms. Fifteen fathoms of chain (90 feet) are often called a shackle of chain, although joining is done not with shackles, which would hang up on the winch and in the chock, but with special open links. Two shackles of chain (180 feet) should take care of pleasure boats in most cruising areas.

The size of chain—not surprisingly taken from the rod from which it has been made—should be chosen to suit the length, draft, and windage of your boat. By all means get expert advice on this point. Just to give a general idea: a 26-foot cabin cruiser with flying bridge, or a sailboat 34-foot over-all might both use $3/8''$ high-strength alloy chain, proof-testing at more than six tons and weighing about 250 pounds for two shackles.

Although it'll wear off soon, it's a good idea to paint a few links at regular intervals to let you know how much chain has been let out. That works with rope too. Instead of paint you'd use colored lashings around and through the strands of the rope. Here is a simple code: One lashing means fifty feet, two lashings one hundred, and so forth.

Many people consider a windlass a necessity with chain. Very neat little ones are available, usually equipped to handle chain on one side, rope on the other. Chain to be handled on a windlass should be ordered "calibrated." I would go farther and try it on the wildcat to see that it really fits. You can also handle chain without a winch. I usually get impatient with the slow recovery and haul my chain in by hand, using the windlass only to rest it between pulls. A simple pawl, which can be combined with the roller chock fitting, would serve the same purpose.

Using the standard tricks of anchor work—powering or sailing up to the anchor, and letting the boat break it out—you'll find bringing in chain hardly more work than horsing in fiber rope. Nor is it dirtier work. Of course you can wear gloves if you like; the rubberized kind worn by commercial fishermen or by stone masons will do nicely.

From the wildcat the chain drops through a spill pipe into the chain locker, which should have a grating at the bottom to let water drain into the bilge.

I had my first encounter with anchor chain many years ago when a desperate skipper asked me to crew for him. The other skippers always could pick up youngsters to work their craft, but not this fellow. Not that he mistreated his crew; it was just the dog he owned. Many boats are puppies in one way or another; his was a full-grown hound. "Barge" was the kindest name she'd be called around the club. Someone had called her a 20/20 motorsailer—she had 20 percent of the sail area and 20 percent of the horsepower she needed to move. The owner bragged how well she sailed downwind.

"So does a grand piano with the lid up," they told him.

Now he had entered her in an alongshore race. Everything that floated seemed to pass us, even the garbage we had thrown overboard. To wipe out the debacle at the buoy, the skipper decided on a grand entrance into the club anchorage. He'd drop anchor while running under full sail. All I had to do was to drop the anchor and stand clear.

I braced myself against the shock when our grand piano would fetch up against her anchor. The chain kept roaring out, then went quiet as the last link slipped overboard. The club launch hauled us out of the cow pasture and we grappled to retrieve chain and anchor.

What was I expected to do? Catch the last link with my teeth?

The rankest beginner would have had the bitter end of the chain belayed. It should be fastened to some structural member that can take the strain should the chain ever get away. But it should not be fastened at the bottom of the pile. Someday, caught on a lee shore or in some other predicament, you may want to slip your cable. If the bitter end is above the pile of chain you can start sailing away before all the chain has run out and before there is any strain on the fastening.

There is a device, called devil's claw, supposed to lock the chain to the deck. A nice salty-sounding rig, but don't trust it. A skipper I know almost lost his vessel when she dragged ashore in a small anchorage after the devil's claw carried away in a sudden gust of wind.

Though biased in favor of chain, I'll admit it's awkward to handle from a dinghy. For laying out a second anchor, kedging off, and the like, I'd certainly use my second anchor shackled to a nice fat nylon rope.

In basic boating you have learned to anchor. But nobody has taught you this: To anchor often, means to drag someday.

Aware of the possibility of dragging, and given a choice of likely spots, you can pick your lee shore. I'd rather drag toward a beach than onto rocks or cement piers. I'd rather find myself dragging out into the bay than toward the fleet anchored off the yacht club.

And when I see someone about to anchor directly upwind of me, I watch with fenders and boat hook mentally ready. If I see him throw, and I mean throw, a watchfob for an anchor, I'll find myself urgent business at some other anchorage.

Apart from failure of gear, there are three basic dragging situations.

First there is drag simple, usually soon after anchoring. It's caused by the elementary faults: anchor fouled in midair or by coils of rope thrown after it, too little scope, no strain taken before securing, etc. In every case the boat hasn't been anchored in the first place.

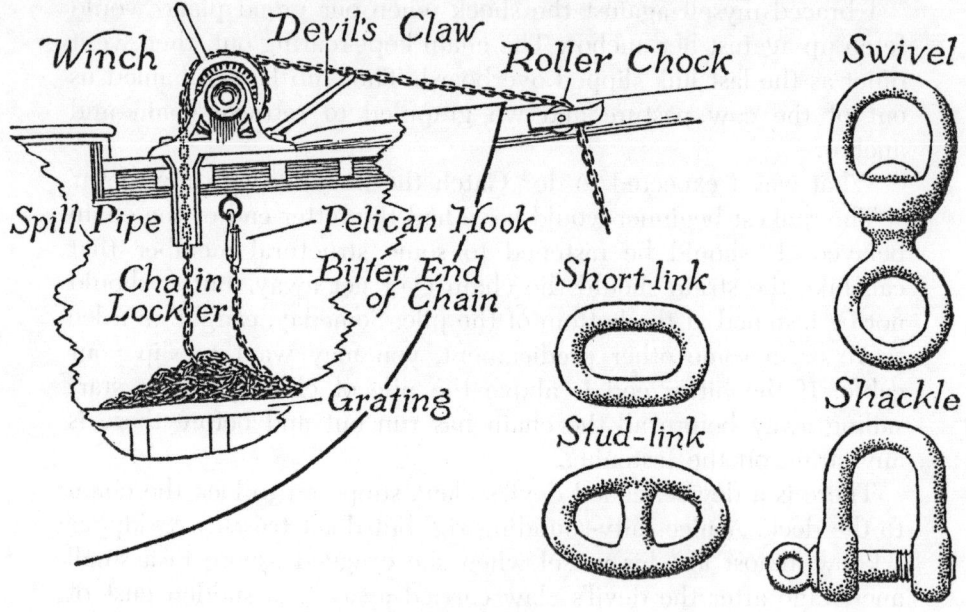

5. *Chain ground tackle—an efficient installation.*

That will never happen to you; you don't tolerate sloppiness on your little vessel. But listen to this. One day, after floundering in light airs, I finally sailed into the cove where I had planned to anchor. When it came to actually dropping the hook, I was too close to shore. So I let her drift while I furled sail, and stowed chart and binoculars. I went below for a long-delayed drink, when my crew asked politely: "Aren't we going to anchor today?"

Dragging after anchoring can go unnoticed if all hands go below to celebrate their safe arrival. Not so the second type of dragging:

the drag spectacular. You have been anchored for some time, and have held even in a pretty stiff breeze. Now a gust strikes your craft. She heels. Jumping on deck, you find yourself drifting rapidly, broadside to the wind.

The second anchor, ready on deck, may stop her faster than you can start the engine. Also you don't have to worry about the now useless anchor rode fouling your propeller. To bring the anchor that has failed you aboard, and get it over again might take too long. Also that anchor may be temporarily out of commission; perhaps a clump of underwater meadow stuck to a fluke or, wedged between the flukes of a patent anchor, has kept it from resetting itself.

Such freak gusts are mercifully rare. In Nassau Harbor I witnessed one strong enough to overturn planes at the airport. On deck in a second, I found my chain bar-taut, my anchor seeming to hold. But all around I saw so many craft—pleasure and commercial—tearing eastward that for a moment the shore seemed to move while the boats stood still.

A few of these boats may have been victims of the third variety of drag in my catalog: drag delayed.

You have been at anchor for days, swinging to the wind and perhaps a current. There may have been hours of calm and, in a tidal current, periods of slack water. Or perhaps at times wind and current were nudging your craft in opposite directions. Without any spectacular wind gust, you find yourself drifting—ahead or astern—true with wind or current, not broadside. In one of the calms, or during a reversal of current, your anchor rode has thrown a loop around some part of your anchor. Now tripped, it drags underfoot, acting merely as a weight, not as an anchor. You may quietly drag downstream or out of a harbor without knowing it.

It's probably against the possibility of such dragging that you are urged to find ranges ashore after you have anchored. Sounds good, but works only in the absence of current, with the wind blowing steadily from the same direction, and in a boat that doesn't yaw at anchor. Have you ever seen such a boat? Ranges would work if you could sight them from your anchor. But with one hundred feet of cable out, your foredeck sweeps out a circle with a two-hundred-foot diameter, your cockpit an even larger circle.

What then can we use for drag indicators?

A good one is the behavior of nearby boats. But a shallow-draft powerboat may lie at right angles to a deep-keel sailboat while both are perfectly secure. So use boats similar to yours as guides. Even that doesn't always work. In a cove an eddy can make two boats quite close to each other lie in opposite directions.

Boats nearby include your own dinghy if it's streaming astern. It may hit you in the transom, or bang your topside to report, "Cap'n, we are dragging." But you can't always believe these reports. The dinghy may ride to the wind, while your vessel with her deeper draft obeys a current.

Where there is no significant current you'll lie more or less into the wind. Your craft will yaw, of course, but as long as the midpoint of her swings is into the wind, you are probably all right.

In whatever direction you are heading, a buoy near your anchor —someone's mooring, for instance—will help you in locating your anchor. Or you could drop a buoy—a plastic bleach bottle with a weighted line attached perhaps—close to your anchor. Then you'd see if your anchor has moved. Sounds good, but I've never met a skipper who actually did that. A buoy tied to the anchor while sometimes helpful in breaking the anchor out, only shows where it is now, not where you've dropped it.

The best all-around drag alarm takes in the total situation.

At first you'll have to make a conscious effort, but soon the whole-picture method becomes almost automatic. When you have anchored you take a good look around, note other craft, landmarks ashore, buoys or moorings, and after a glance at the compass, wind direction and set of current if any. Whenever you go on deck, look again. Look again after dark when some landmarks have been swallowed by darkness, while others marked by lights have become prominent. When you next come on deck, after a glance at the compass and feeling the wind on your face, your mental computer will practically of itself report: "All Secure" or "Something Amiss."

When a sudden rainsquall obscures landmarks, other boats, even your own anchor buoy, and you suspect a slow dragging, put your lead on the bottom. If you allow for a sideways strain caused by yawing, you can tell when the bottom is moving under your keel.

Better than finding that you are dragging is preventing it.

Mooring with two anchors, angled widely apart, will often do it. It certainly will keep the rode, gone slack in a calm or current change, from looping around the exposed fluke of an anchor. At the same time such a moor greatly cuts down on the swinging room your craft needs. With an open moor your safety doesn't depend on an anchor turning and holding at the same time whenever the wind shifts or the current reverses.

It doesn't matter how you get the two anchors down. You can drop the first one while going ahead slowly, steering carefully away from the rode so it won't foul your prop. Give this anchor twice the needed scope or more, then drop the second anchor and falling back adjust the scope of both anchors so you'll lie halfway between them. You can do this under sail alone as the Bahamian smackboats

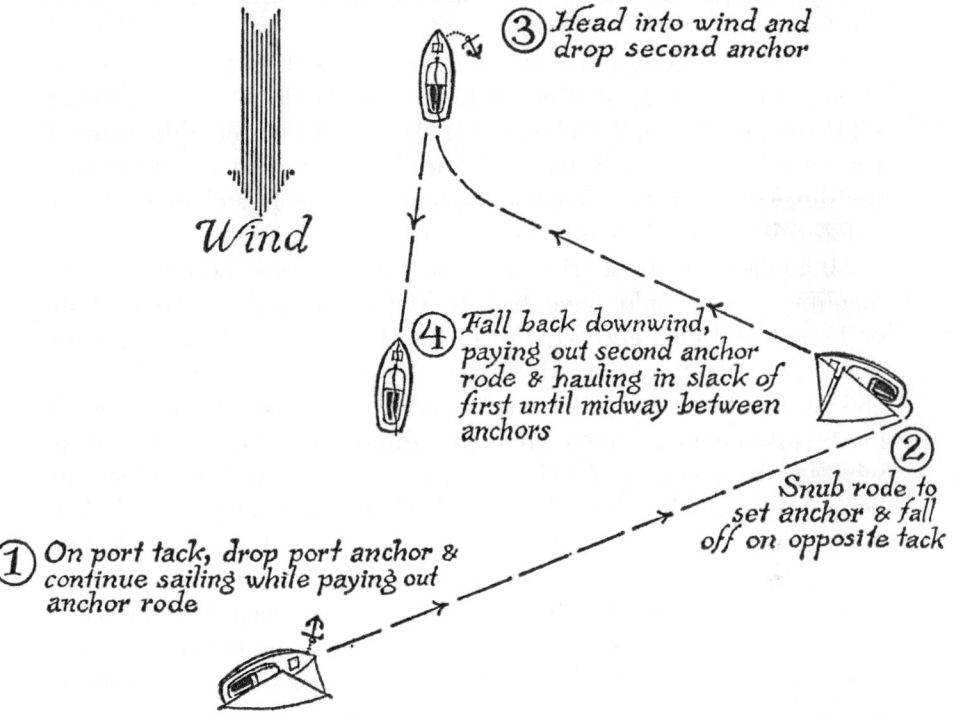

6. *Dropping two anchors under sail.*

do. When the rode of the first anchor nears its end, and the anchor is well set by the still-moving boat, they tack. Then after sailing part of a circle around the first anchor, they lower the second one, drop sail, and fall back to the midposition. If nothing goes wrong, you can execute this maneuver even single-handed. In all these running moors you are likely to rub off some bottom paint, and color your anchor rode red.

To avoid that, you can drop the first anchor in the usual manner, give it at least twice the normal scope, then lay out the second anchor from the dinghy. Backing and filling, you can also lay out both anchors from the deck under power, or even under sail when wind and current happen to co-operate.

By whatever method you have laid out the two anchors, their rodes will take turns around each other after changes of wind and tide. Don't let the turns pile up, but clear them or you may not be able to get either of the rodes aboard in a hurry. It's a nice chore for first thing in the morning. If one of your anchors is shackled to chain, simply pass the coil of the other anchor under and over it to undo the turns.

Sometimes a conspiracy of wind and current puts both anchors under strain, making getting under way difficult. In an emergency I'd buoy one and slip it to be picked up later. In normal departure, if you can't leave at slack water, I'd underrun one anchor rode with the dinghy and bring that anchor home at the last change of tide before my planned departure.

All anchors on the market must be good in some bottom or their manufacturers would have had to switch to making door knobs or breakfast food. Perhaps the claims for some light anchors are true only after they have dug in, and you can't expect a light anchor to dig in as a heavier one would. To find out what anchor is most suitable in a given area, ask questions. Don't just look at what's stowed on deck. A fluke count in a marina could be misleading. Some boats come with anchors all chocked and lashed on deck. The owners may leave them there and stow their favorite picks below. Don't ask the fellows who always tie up alongside even on a cruise. Wind-sailors often like to anchor off and are a good source of information, even if yours is a power cruiser. Commercial fishermen who depend on their anchors when caught out are also worth listening to.

In the Bahamas fishing smacks and interisland freighters rely on heavy five-pronged grapnels, wicked sharp-pointed things, awkward to handle and impossible to stow on a yacht. But there is an improved version available in Nassau: a folding grapnel. Small ones make good dinghy anchors, large ones—unfortunately they don't come heavy enough for really large yachts—make wonderful storm anchors for a pleasure boat. They stow flat, standing up or lying down, are inexpensive, and dig in in any reasonable bottom, sand and even grass. No anchor will hold you on a "hard bar," or tide-scoured cement bottom found in some places in the islands.

Two flukes of these anchors are always in contact with the bottom, leaving the other two exposed to foul your rode unless you prevent that by mooring with two anchors, standard practice in these islands. After a blow you may find three flukes dug in solid; after a really hard one I have seen all four flukes—and the shank—completely buried in the sand.

Have you noticed how on some boats anchoring resembles a Chinese fire drill, while on others everything goes smoothly without any shouted orders? The secret is simple: communication between bridge and foredeck. I don't say between captain and crew, because on many boats it's the skipper who handles the anchor (between attacks of lame back at least) while his lady steers, and works the clutch. On other boats, perhaps equipped with winches or with the anchor stowed on the bowsprit, no strength is required forward; the captain stays at his usual post. Either way he is in charge while anchoring or upanchoring, whatever the couple's arrangement ashore.

Wife forward or wife aft, the couples who successfully operate charterboats in the Bahamas and elsewhere have developed silent teamwork to a fine art. First they find urgent tasks for eager guests. When the anchor is ready to be put over the side the wife, if she handles the foredeck, turns aft and faces the skipper. A slow nod or a thumb down means let go. She pays out some scope slowly, then looks for another signal. A hand flip means more scope; a circling finger, belay it right there.

Coming to a mooring, she'll point to it with outstretched arm. Coming closer she may wave sideways, left hand for port, right hand for starboard. At the same time she gives an indication of the distance: scooping air with palm forward may mean forward a little more; palm down and still, dead slow; arm dropped rapidly, stop.

The same signals would do for steaming up to an anchor if you add the palm throwing air aft to mean reverse. You'll need another signal for rode-up-and-down, perhaps by vertical hand motion; anchor-broken-out could be shown by vertical hand motion. You'll probably see from the steering position when the anchor is clear of the topsides and you can pour on the horsepower.

You may not want to carry the signal system to the utmost perfection, but here is a fine seagoing tradition you may want to adopt: the anchor-down toast.

Here is a sample. A single-hander friend of ours pours himself

"Let go!" *"More scope"* *"Belay it"*

"Head starboard" *"Come ahead a little"* *"Dead slow"* *"Stop!"*

"Reverse" *"Rode up & down"* *"Anchor broken out"*

7. *Signals between helm and foredeck for anchoring and getting under way.*

a drink when the anchor is down, and proposes this toast: "Here's to another trip successfully concluded. No one fell overboard permanently. We are still afloat, and—as far as is known—have not sunk anyone else. And here's to this harbor we found, whatever its name may be."

3 Dinghy Management

If you always return to your dock or to your mooring within tooting distance of the well-bribed operator of the club launch, you'll have no dinghy problems. Especially if you don't have a dinghy.

It's different when you cruise. You anchor off in strange places, gunk-hole into uncharted creeks, hang up on sandbars, feel the urge to maroon a guest, or simply run out of beer. Then you have dinghy problems. Especially if you don't have a dinghy.

If you plan to sail around the world, you may get along without a dinghy. One of the famed single-handers did. He writes of jumping overboard in some Pacific Island lagoon and swimming ashore dressed only in a breechclout. By the way, on the beach he was greeted by the local chief, who perspired in black swallowtail coat and top hat.

Cruising one needs a dinghy. I found that out after losing my Nova Scotia-built dinghy in New Jersey. I decided not to replace it until I reached Florida. It'd just be in the way on the Inland Waterway stretches, and not needed on the outside passages. But several times before reaching Miami I wished I'd had a dink. John Alden, the famed yacht designer, asked what he considered the smallest practical size for a cruising boat, said, "A boat large enough to carry a dinghy on deck."

A dinghy lets you lay out a second anchor when it breezes up; sometimes the only way to get an anchor up again is from the dink. With a line rove under the thwarts and leading to bow and stern of the yacht it makes a painter's scaffold. It's survey ship, tug, and ferry boat. It's also lifeboat, rain catcher, laundry tub, bait bucket, fishing creel, and swimming ladder.

But what do you do with this useful companion when you are under way? Ask a dozen cruising men. They'll all tell you to carry the dink on deck. That's no problem on a yacht run on champagne. She has davits, winches, and a crew to bring the tender aboard, stow it in chocks, and lace on the canvas cover. But where do we

8. A dinghy has many uses.

stow a dinghy, we who run our boats on mere gasoline or puffs of wind?

Some boats have room for davits at the stern. With blocks and lines rigged as for raising and lowering a Venetian blind, Pete, who in his seventies single-handed the *Folly*, had no trouble hoisting his dinghy. On other sailboats the main boom and topping lift are used to hoist the dinghy suspended from a bridle of three short lines. These lines snap into rings at the bow and at the quarters, and form an eye directly above the dinghy's center of gravity.

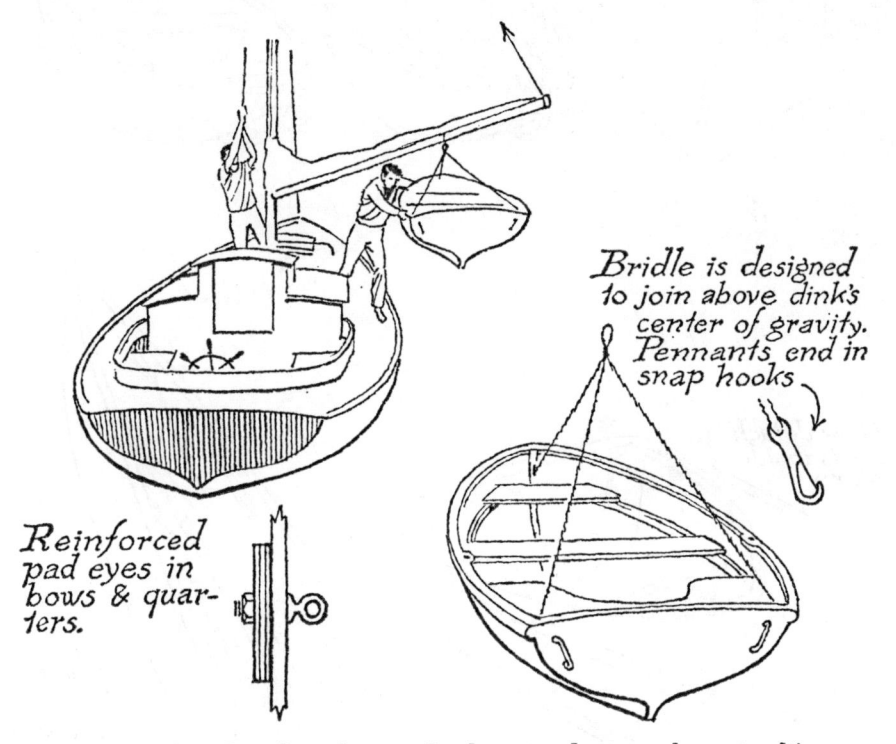

9. *Bringing aboard, or launching, a dinghy using boom and topping lift on a sailboat.*

Once on board the dinghy has to be lashed securely. Keel up is best. Right side up it'd collect more gear than a woman's purse. Worse, it might collect half a ton of seawater in an instant, and seriously upset the trim of your craft. But where do you lash it? On deck the dinghy is in everyone's way; on the cabintop it cuts the helmsman's vision; on the foredeck it interferes with anchor work and sail handling, and puts the forehatch out of commission; on the upper deck of a cruiser it becomes awkward—and even dangerous—to handle when you cruise short-handed.

It's a problem. So makeshift dinghies have been invented: dinghies

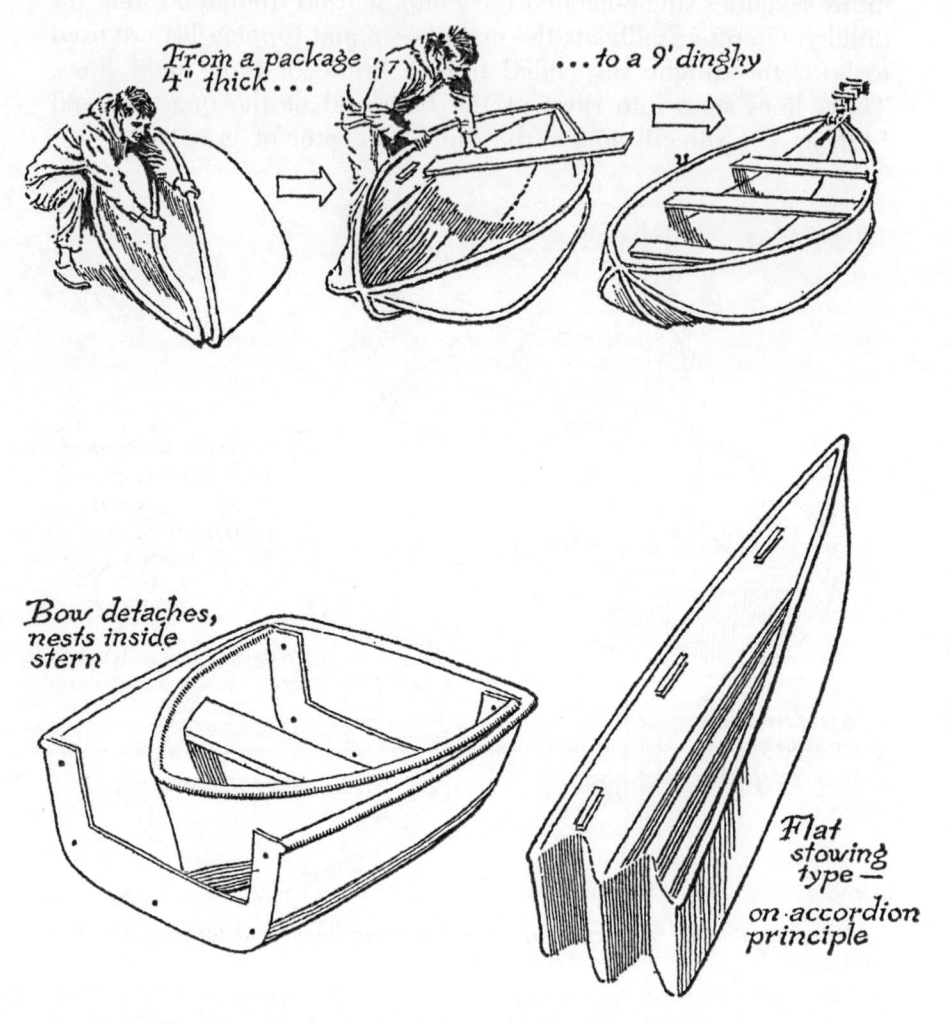

From a package 4" thick... ...to a 9' dinghy

Bow detaches, nests inside stern

Flat stowing type— on accordion principle

10. *Dinghies designed to solve the stowage problem.*

that inflate when needed, canvas jobs that stow in a flat bundle and are stretched into boat shape by battens and seats, dinghies sawed in half amidships so that the bow section can nest inside the stern section when stowed.

With all the ingenious methods for bringing the dinghy aboard and reducing its bulk when you are under way, the dinghy is still a nuisance on a small cruising boat. So the very cruising men who loudly advise you to stow your dinghy, tow theirs. In protected waters, in calm seas, you may get away with it many times.

But someday you'll regret it. The dinghy, a mere nuisance when stowed, can change into a sea monster when towed. It surfboards down the face of a wave until you think it's coming through the transom. At the last moment it changes its mind and aims for your head. When you straighten up again, it has sheared off and now runs ahead of you until—stopped by its leash—it comes to a halt that shivers your timbers.

A length of rope over the stern of the dinghy, as a miniature sea anchor, may slow these excursions. You may trail a single length of rope, or a bight fastened to her quarters. A rubber snubber in the tow rope will buffer the jerks. But only a stout rope—half-inch nylon is none too big—is up to this wild towing job. The rope has to be well belayed to a through-bolted cleat, and must be protected with split hose or canvas wrappings against chafe in the chock.

The other end of the tow rope also needs care. A well-tucked eyesplice over a pear-shaped thimble, shackled to the towing ring of the dinghy (the shackle pin secured with soft wire) is the proven gear that avoids rope-against-metal chafe.

Even that may not be good enough.

One evening in the Bahamas I had left my *Lucina* at anchor in the harbor at Allan's-Pensacola. The boys from the missile tracking station there had come out in their outboard and invited me ashore. A little later we were joined by the captain of an interisland freight-boat.

"What do you do with a dinghy you find adrift?" the captain asked me.

I was surprised at a professional's ignorance in such matters, but never one to withhold expert knowledge, I explained, "You'll have to take reasonable care of the boat, report it to the commissioner in the next place where there is one. If he has a matching description of a lost boat, he'll notify the owner; if not, he'll advertise . . ."

"Do you want to go through all this rigamarole, Steve?"

"What do you mean?"

"I mean, we picked up your dinghy as it drifted out the harbor."

A moment's inspection showed what had happened. Although

backed by a 2½-inch washer, the tow ring had pulled right through the fiber glass stem. Moral: Whittle a piece of hardwood into a false, inside stem and pass the ringbolt through the whole assembly.

A further moral: Have the name of your yacht and her hailing port permanently marked on the dinghy. Some yacht insurance policies —Lloyd's, for instance—make this a condition for insuring the dinghy. A screwed-on name plate or paint are not enough. A pirate might unscrew the plate or paint over your artwork. Burn or carve the information into some structural member.

But let's get back to towing that dinghy.

How long should the towline be? Sea conditions, your speed, and the personality of your dinghy will answer that question. Experiment! At times the dinghy will ride best one wave astern of the parent vessel; at other times the same dinghy may like to be dragged short, right under your transom. Most dinghies that have owned me towed best with some weight in the stern, and with the tow ring low on the stem, lower than most stock models have it.

Some dinghies tow dry hour after hour; others need constant watching. Once a dinghy starts to ship water, you have a problem. The water sloshing about will bring her down, now by the head, now by the stern. A few sloshes later she'll be full. Anything loose—oars, bailer, gas can, flip-flops—floats away. If you still have way on the parent vessel at this moment, the painter will probably part.

A dinghy adrift is harder to round up than a wild horse. You may come close to either, but how do you lasso a dinghy? One answer to this question has been worked out by crafty seamen: a short length of rope with an eye spliced to one end, the other end secured to the dinghy. It's called a "lazy" painter because normally it does no work, just lies in the dinghy; when you have to boathook a runaway dinghy it earns its keep. Don't try to hold on with the boat hook, though. Instead quickly pass a line through the eye while your crew tries to outguess the dinghy's next move with fenders. Don't let them use hands and feet for fending off. Arms and legs are no match for a waterlogged sea monster. Bail the dinghy with a bucket on a lanyard. Anyone who steps into a water-filled, or partly filled, dinghy is likely to wind up in the drink. And the dinghy may capsize.

Yes, even an unsinkable dinghy can capsize. Unsinkable means just that and no more, as I found out when my dinghy with flotation tanks in bow and stern filled. The water was warm, and rather than risk damage to my topsides I decided to bail her out from the water. Pushing a bucket ahead of me, I swam to her stern. Just resting one hand on her transom made her stern go under water. I next approached her from the bow. Down went the bow as soon as I touched it.

Some day a dinghy filling and parting its painter will do you a

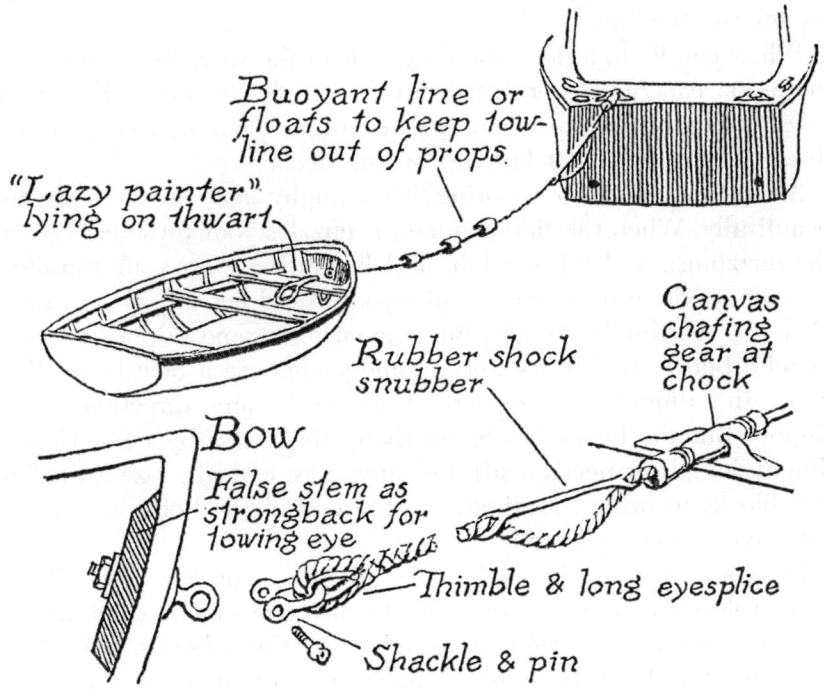

11. *Good dinghy towing rig (Shackle pin should be wired for safety).*

favor. It's the sort of favor a sail might do you by blowing out when it should have been taken in much earlier. There are other times when the seamanlike decision has to be: Cut the dinghy adrift. Caught outside, for instance, with a chance to return through an inlet close to breaking, sacrifice the dink rather than have it climb aboard.

But let's say you have cheated the sea gods once more and reach port still towing a dinghy. It's still a problem. As you slow down, stop, or reverse to make a dock or anchorage, the dinghy painter goes slack. A few idling turns of the propeller later, you'll have a bird nest around your prop. To avoid such mishaps, many skippers permanently detail one member of their crew to shorten the tow, keep the painter out of the water, and fend off the dinghy whenever they come to a dock or anchorage. But when you gently run on a sandbank that crew member will not have shortened up, and that's no time for a fouled prop. Floats along the towline are one remedy. Even better is rope that floats on the surface, such as polypropylene. This rope, size for size, is weaker than nylon, so use a larger diameter for the towline.

When you lie to a dock the dinghy is in the way. In a fourposter tieup you can run a sternfast from the dinghy to one of the outer piles, or you can hitch it bow and stern under one of your mooring lines. Better yet, lay it keel up on the dock.

At anchor, or at a mooring, the dinghy may at first stream beautifully. When the tide changes, it nuzzles your topsides. Ignore the nuzzlings, and it'll scratch, and finally bang on your topsides. It wants to lie into the wind while your vessel lies into the current. To make the dinghy lie also into the current some skippers recommend a bucket tied to its stern. Some yachts use a boat-boom that holds the dinghy off yet lets it swing in any direction. Very shippy! But the boom has to overhang the water by more than a dinghy length; it needs a lift and guys fore and aft, besides a line and blocks to bring the dinghy to the end of the boom and back. Effective but complicated.

So other skippers simply lash the dinghy alongside. The dinghy painter leads forward, a sternfast to any convenient cleat aft. A fender is needed between the dinghy and the topsides, and there —literally—is the rub. Every passing craft that throws a wake bounces the dinghy until fenders rigged from your rail end up *inside* the dinghy. A cylindrical fender lashed along the gunwale of the dinghy often works better.

In an uncrowded anchorage there is another method for discouraging a dinghy that seems to want to climb in your bunk with you. Tie a small anchor to the dinghy painter; tie a second line to the crown of this anchor. Then throw the anchor as far as you can, letting the line run out as it wants to. The dinghy will drift off and lie to her own anchor. Leave ample slack in the tripping line, then belay to a stern cleat. When you want the dinghy, you haul it in by that line. That's the theory. In practice the anchor may foul this line in midthrow or later during a change of wind or current. No matter: The dinghy and the anchor are still solidly tied to the parent yacht.

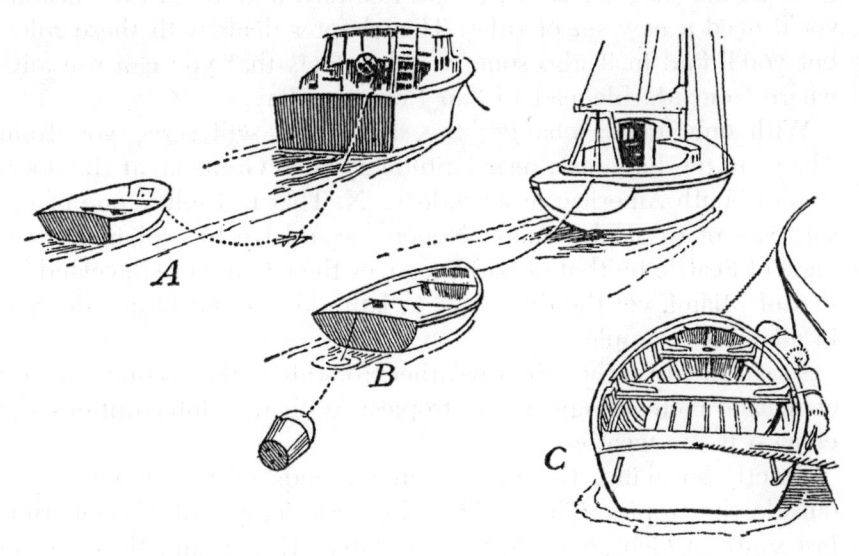

12. *Curbing the dinghy in an anchorage* (A) *anchored off* (B) *with bucket astern* (C) *lashed alongside.*

Anyone who has done some cruising understands why sailors apply the pronoun "she" to dinghies. You can't live without them, and sometimes you can't live with them.

4 Advanced Weather Lore

Weather for the small-boat skipper is well covered in basic boating books. If you want to know more, you have a choice of weather books on every level: from old sayings to differential equations. Also, where you do your boating you have learned to read the signs in the sky, perhaps since childhood. Even when you move to a different part of the country, you only need to add a little here, change a little there, and your earlier knowledge will serve you in your new area of operation.

Not so when you get into southern waters. From the Bahamas, through the Virgin Islands, to the Leeward and Windward Islands you'll need a new set of rules. This chapter deals with these rules, but you'll find in it also some weather facts that you can use anywhere from Marblehead to San Francisco Bay.

With only minor changes the same rules will serve you from Abaco, in the Bahamas, near latitude 27°N to Grenada, at the doorstep of South America, in latitude 12°N. That in itself is one of the surprises of tropical climate. Nobody would try to explain the climate of Seattle by that of San Diego, or the climate of Cleveland by that of Miami, yet the difference in latitude is about fifteen degrees in all three examples.

I say climate rather than weather, for this is the second surprise of marine meteorology in the tropics: With rare interruptions the climate *is* the weather.

Strictly speaking, the most visited islands of the Bahamas are outside the tropics. The dividing line, the Tropic of Cancer, runs just south of George Town through Great Exuma and through the north end of Long Island. But the climate doesn't change suddenly at latitude 23°27′ N, so tropical weather patterns also cover the northern Bahamas and the Florida Keys.

For brevity, let's call the area covered by these patterns the Islands. They'll include—from N and W to the S and E—the Florida Keys, the Bahamas, the Virgin Islands, and the Leeward and Windward Islands. Where figures are useful Nassau can serve as example for all the Bahamas and the Florida Keys, St. Thomas for the Virgin and Leeward Islands, and Grenada for the Windward group.

Ever since fourth grade you have known that it gets warmer as you move southward. You know you could enjoy boating in southern Florida the year round, while in your area the boats get hauled out perhaps after Labor Day, and get back in commission only after Memorial Day. But that warming, so noticeable between Boston and Fort Lauderdale, ceases in the Islands. The annual mean temperature is 77°F in Nassau, 80° in St. Thomas, and 78° in Grenada.

Most people who live in the temperate zone with its sharply defined seasons, think of weather on tropical islands as the same the year round. Not so. In the Islands you'll find two definite weather patterns: summer and winter. One is more likely to fall to dreaming about a southern cruise to escape northern winter, so let's look first at the winter weather throughout the Islands.

The first Norther, in October or November, starts the winter in the Bahamas. These outbreaks of cold continental air will interrupt the normal easterly maritime surface air flow for the next six months. Before the arrival of a Norther the wind typically veers into the south or perhaps SW. When the cold front arrives, the wind suddenly shifts to NW, then gradually to N, to blow itself out after it has veered to NE. In midwinter this merry-go-round may take several days; in spring it's often around the clock in one day.

Northers give little local warning of their impending arrival. The low which commonly precedes a high in northern areas, is, more often than not, absent here. So the barometer is steady until the wind is upon you, and then rises rapidly.

In my first year in the Bahamas I was anchored in an open roadstead having just crossed the Great Bahama Bank, when my schooner was joined by a whole fleet of crawfishing boats seeking shelter. I hadn't seen any warning signs in the sky, so I asked one of the captains how he could tell a blow was on its way.

"Just listen to your radio, man."

That's still the best advice. Nassau and Miami are the obvious stations. You may get earlier warnings by listening to upwind stations, say in Georgia. When the weather turns cold there and in northern Florida, you can expect to get it in the northwestern out-islands. When West End, Green Turtle Cay, and Hopetown report high barometer readings, cool temperatures, and wind speeds above twelve knots, look for it in Nassau, Eleuthera, and the northern Exumas within a few hours.

Northers come in all strengths. Sometimes the front makes a spectacular entrance with thunder and lightning and cold rain. A quarter of Nassau's annual rainfull comes from such squalls.

About thirty Northers reach Florida during the six winter months. December to February are the most active months; in March Northers are less common but often nastier; in April they become rare and are usually light. Not all of Florida's thirty Northers reach the Bahamas. Some stall right in Florida, others over the Gulf Stream. By the time they reach the central Bahamas you wouldn't recognize them as the cold Canadian air that has dumped inches of snow over the Middle West. It's dry air, but the more water it has crossed the warmer it gets. The mean air temperature for the coldest month in Nassau is 77°F by day, 65°F by night, but a Norther will cause a drop of perhaps ten degrees below these figures; the all-time low recorded in Nassau was 47°.

In a mild Norther the usual 5–15-knot winds merely become 8–18-knot winds, the lower figure more typical of sheltered areas and the land, the higher of open stretches of water. A severe norther will have you weatherbound for two or three days. But that's a relative term: a twenty-four-foot cruiser had better stay in port, even while the mailboats keep running on schedule.

Windspeeds above thirty-four knots are not to be expected in winter. But every few years an anchor-rattling duster strikes. It may arrive as a line squall with first gust of hurricane force. It soon moderates to the tempo of a brisk Norther. These blows seem to be hard to forecast. The ones I experienced all came without warning from the radio, and for what it may be worth had this in common: a front that had become stationary, and a dead calm just before hell broke loose.

Northers are felt throughout the Gulf of Mexico and reach into the Caribbean, sometimes as far as Panama. But they don't stretch to the Leeward and Windward Islands, and hardly ever to the Virgin Islands. In fact, many Northers that were quite dusty in Abaco and Nassau die out before they reach even the southern Exumas, a hundred miles SSE of Nassau.

Winter winds in the Virgin Islands and from there south can be boisterous. You can expect force five winds (17–21 knots) about a quarter of the time. Twenty-five-knot winds are common, especially between Christmas and February, but you won't encounter gales (speeds over thirty-four knots). The winter winds in the southern islands, known as the reinforced trades, blow from the East 40–60 percent of the time depending on the island; almost all the rest of the time they come from NE or SE.

Why? You remember all about the trade winds. The books say they are caused by air flowing from belts of high pressure toward the equatorial low pressure area, from N to S, but then are deflected toward the west by the rotating earth. Therefore the trade winds in the Northern Hemisphere blow from the NE. All the Islands are in the Northern Hemisphere, of course, but the winds don't seem to have been told to blow from the NE. How else can you explain the prevalence of winds from the E, or how do you explain SE winds anywhere in this area, especially such regular SE winds as

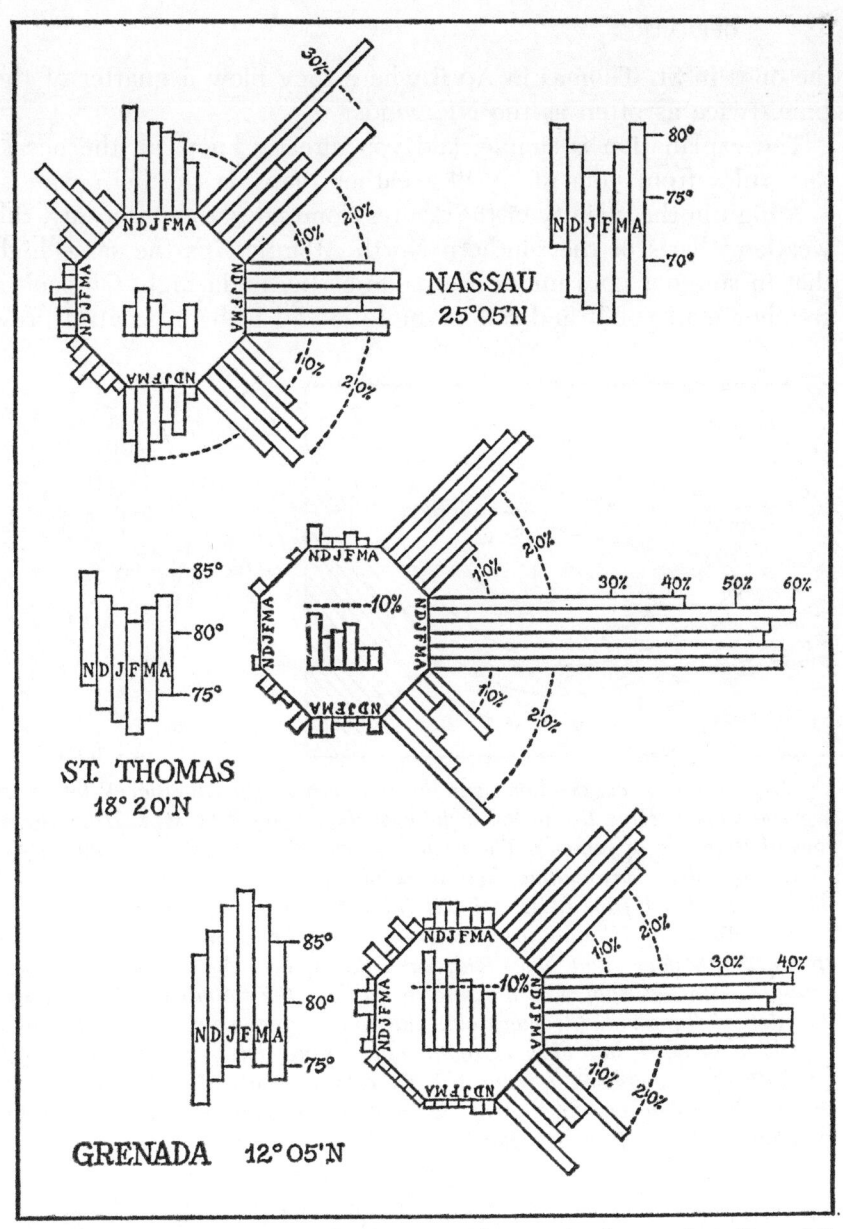

13. *Winter weather in the Islands—November to April, month indicated by first letter. Windroses show how much of the time (in percent) the wind blows from a given direction. (For example, at Nassau, in November, the wind is out of the East in a little more than 20% of all observations.) Calms are shown in the center of the windroses. (For example, at Grenada, in March, no wind is recorded about 10% of the time.)*

Bars show average daily maximum and minimum air temperatures for the month. (For example, at St. Thomas, in November, the average daily maximum is 85°F, the minimum 76°F.)

34 OPERATION

the ones in St. Thomas in April where they blow a quarter of the time, twice as often as the NE winds?

The explanation is simple, and you already know all the necessary rules from your study of weather maps in northern waters.

A high in the vicinity of the Azores dominates, day after day, the weather charts of the southern North Atlantic. It's the same high that in summer goes under the name of Bermuda high. On such a weather map you'll find one or more closed isobars (central pres-

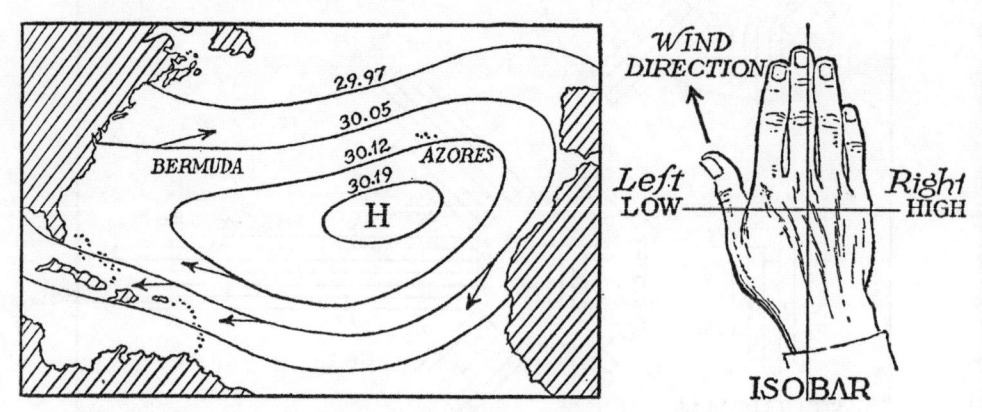

14. *Left: Pressure distribution over the southern North Atlantic (Winter). A semi-permanent High lies in the vicinity of the Azores. The same High moves toward Bermuda in summer. The islands lie in the Southwest quadrant of the elongated isobars surrounding these areas of high pressure. Arrows show wind direction predicted from RULE OF THUMB at right.*

Right: Rule of Thumb for predicting wind direction in northern hemisphere. With your right hand laid, palm down, over an isobar so the high pressure is to the right, low pressure to the left, the thumb will indicate the direction of the wind. (Memory aid: RIGHT-HIGH, LEFT-LOW.) *This rule works anywhere in north latitudes; in south latitudes use left hand. You can work wind direction problems in reverse. Let the thumb lie with the wind and get direction of isobar, and location of high and low pressures—the center of a hurricane for instance—from your hand.*

sure above 30.20 inches) surrounded by several more lens-shaped isobars spanning the entire Atlantic. The 30.00-inch isobar usually crosses the Windward or Leeward Islands. As the high-pressure center changes position and varies in intensity from day to day and month to month, the satellite isobars shift and curl a little.

As you know, winds blow clockwise around highs, and outward, forming a small angle with the isobars. When these lines of equal pressure tend about ESE to WNW, as they do most of the winter in this area, the wind will be in the east. It's as simple as that.

Pressure patterns, wind direction and force, temperatures . . . all are interesting to the boatman, but they don't give a very poetic, or even clear picture of a winter day in the Islands.

One way to describe such a day is: The picture postcards here don't lie. Cottonball clouds really float in a deep-blue sky almost every day. These trade wind cumulus clouds often have flat bases as though sliced off straight. They are formed locally by warm moist air rising and encountering lower temperatures the higher they get, much as you find it getting cooler as you drive up a mountain, say $3\frac{1}{2}$ degrees cooler for every thousand feet of climb. Near the two thousand-foot level the air is at the temperature of the dewpoint. It can hold no more moisture; water droplets in the rising air condense and become visible as clouds.

When you fly over the Islands you'll often find the cloud tops, though rounded, all at the same level, perhaps between five thousand and eight thousand feet. Here is the explanation for this phenomenon: At that level the rising air runs into a temperature inversion. In plain English: The warm rising air that has encountered lower and lower temperatures on the way up (that's what kept it rising), bumps into a warm layer. There it is suddenly heavier than the surrounding air and stops rising. By the way, the air above the inversion layer is drier than the surface air, which also stops further cloud formation. The inversion is a fixture of normal weather, the year round, in the Islands.

Seen from high above, say by the camera of a weather satellite, not just around the Islands but everywhere in the trade wind belts of the world, one-third of the ocean surface is hidden by these fluffy cumulus clouds, their flat bases at the dewpoint level, their heads scraping the inversion layer.

Seen from the surface, the cloud cover is between four-tenths and six-tenths. You might get a similar monthly mean elsewhere. In the Pacific Northwest the sun might shine all day about half of one month, while during the other half the sky is covered by dripping stratus clouds. Not here: The cumulus clouds are scattered over the sky almost every day. Overcast days in the Islands in winter are rare, and cloudless days even rarer, except in the Bahamas in the later stages of a Norther when the air is too dry for cloud forming.

Hours of bright sunshine tell the story even better. In Nassau, for example, the six winter months average eight hours of bright sunshine daily out of the eleven hours the sun is above the horizon. Even when the sun hides behind one of these puff balls, it usually still casts a shadow, and glitters on the water less than a mile from you.

You'd expect air over the ocean to be near saturation. Actually the humidity is pleasant throughout the area. In figures, the relative humidity varies (in no set geographic or seasonal pattern) between 64 percent and 79 percent. Some experts consider 70 percent ideal for comfort. Relative humidity may be a good indicator for the efficiency of air conditioning in your office, but it doesn't really tell the story. In the delightfully cool first hour of the morning it's probably near 100 percent after depositing some dew on your deck. As the sun gets higher, the air warms and the relative humidity drops to, say, 75 percent. When a large cloud hides the sun at midday and gives a quite welcome drop of a few degrees, it shoots up to 90 percent again.

Perhaps the spread between air temperature and the point at which the air would be saturated with moisture, the dewpoint, gives a better idea of what to expect in the Islands.

Over several years and in many places I have whirled my slingpsychrometer and found the difference between the readings of the dry bulb thermometer and the one with the wetted wick monotonously between six and eight degrees, morning, noon, and evening, even a few minutes after a shower. So the almost constant breeze, which corresponds to the whirling of the thermometers, has a good chance to cool your skin (or your shirt, if you wear a shirt) by evaporation.

Rain here is not likely to spoil a winter vacation for you. Although there is much local variation in frequency and amount of rainfall, winter throughout the Islands is the dry season. That doesn't mean it never rains, but what little rain falls comes in sudden showers. They are often so localized that you may have to bail out your dinghy, while the weather station a few miles away records no rain or perhaps a trace.

Fog, that nightmare of skippers in some areas, is so rare here that you'd have a hard time explaining it to a native. I have met an old man who one day, fishing by himself, hurriedly sailed home to see the local nurse because his eyes were suddenly going bad on him. "Everything turned milky, all around." But that was in the northern Bahamas, not far from Florida where fogs are not unheard of. Once, in Nassau Harbor, I saw fog an hour or so before sunrise; none of the later risers believed me.

A haze formed of salt particles suspended in the air sometimes keeps hidden an island that should be visible, until you wonder how you could have missed your landfall.

In a heavy shower you may not be able to see your bow from the cockpit. That's something to keep in mind before attempting to run a narrow channel ahead of a shower about to let go.

What about seas and swells? The nastiest water on a cruise to the Bahamas is before you get there, in the Gulf Stream that kicks up fiercely when a northerly wind blows against the northgoing current. Once you are across that hazard, in the Bahamas, seas are much quieter. Many of the passages are in the lee of land or over the Banks. These underwater plateaus—typically under two fathoms of water—and their fringing reefs break up the larger waves and swells that work in from the open ocean. Also they don't seem to produce the nasty shallow-water chop that makes boating on some large, shallow lakes often uncomfortable.

Perhaps once each winter the Bahamas get a "rage"—high swells, outrunners of some storm far off in the Atlantic. During a rage even the Nassau bar, twenty-eight feet deep, breaks all the way across. The Virgin Islands get their "rollers" that have been seen to break in nine fathoms of water between Tortola and Guana Island. Lesser ground swells regularly work around the ends of the islands in the Leeward and Windward group, making many of the roadsteads uncomfortable.

Occasionally white squalls—sudden blasts of wind under an unchanged sky—rush down the leeward valleys of these islands and churn the sea into white froth for several miles from shore. Dominica is notorious for these squalls.

But most interisland passages in the Lesser Antilles are a sequence of smooth ghosting in the lee of high land, followed by a brisk sail across an opening, before another serene sail in calm water under the wind shadow of the next island. In these open passages, in winter, seas will be less than three feet about half the time, three to five feet a third of the time, and five to eight feet the remaining one-sixth of the time.

Around the larger islands you'll meet regular land-and-sea

breezes. After sunup, when the air over land warms and rises, air to replace it flows toward the land. In the evening the direction is reversed. On the windward side of the islands this shows up merely as an increase or decrease in the force of the regular breezes. But on the leeward side the land breeze for several miles from shore may seem to blow against the normal easterly air flow.

People who think of the Islands as only a winter cruising ground miss the best season. From April on there are no more Northers in the Bahamas; they, like the rest of the area, are entirely under the influence of easterly surface flow. Temperatures are only a few degrees higher in summer than in winter. Nassau and St. Thomas have registered extreme highs of 95°F, but daily maximums are more typically around 85°, with nighttime minimums of about 75°. Grenada once recorded 100°F, and that was in May. Grenada's extreme low in almost half a century was 65°, of all months in July!

Summer winds are less boisterous everywhere, typically Force 3 or 4 (7–16 knots). In many places after a first gustlet at sunrise there is a light breeze that increases until midafternoon to a gentle to moderate breeze, then diminishes and sometimes drops off altogether—near land at least—during the night. Calms during the day, most unusual over water in winter, are not uncommon in summer.

Unless you consider a calm a hazard to a sailboat, thunderstorms are the only weather to bother the yachtsman during settled periods.

Heat-caused updrafts over land or shallow water make some of the normal cumulus clouds go wild. They grow in height, and several may join until they form a sky-darkening, many-domed thunderhead. Their heights are impressive: thirty thousand feet is common, fifty thousand feet—almost two Mount Everests—not unusual. Lightning near the top of such a cloud in the Bahamas could be seen in Florida, even from the west coast of Florida.

The greatest danger to a small boat in a thunderstorm is the first gust. That is normally the stiffest in any storm. Sixteen knots faster than the prevailing wind is the measured average of many such first gusts. The direction of the first gust can be a hazard to a sailboat. In a frontal passage you are used to seeing the wind shift suddenly by perhaps ninety degrees. In a thunderstorm, when it lets go and the first cold downdrafts hit the water, the wind fans out in all directions and may jump halfway around the compass. Em-

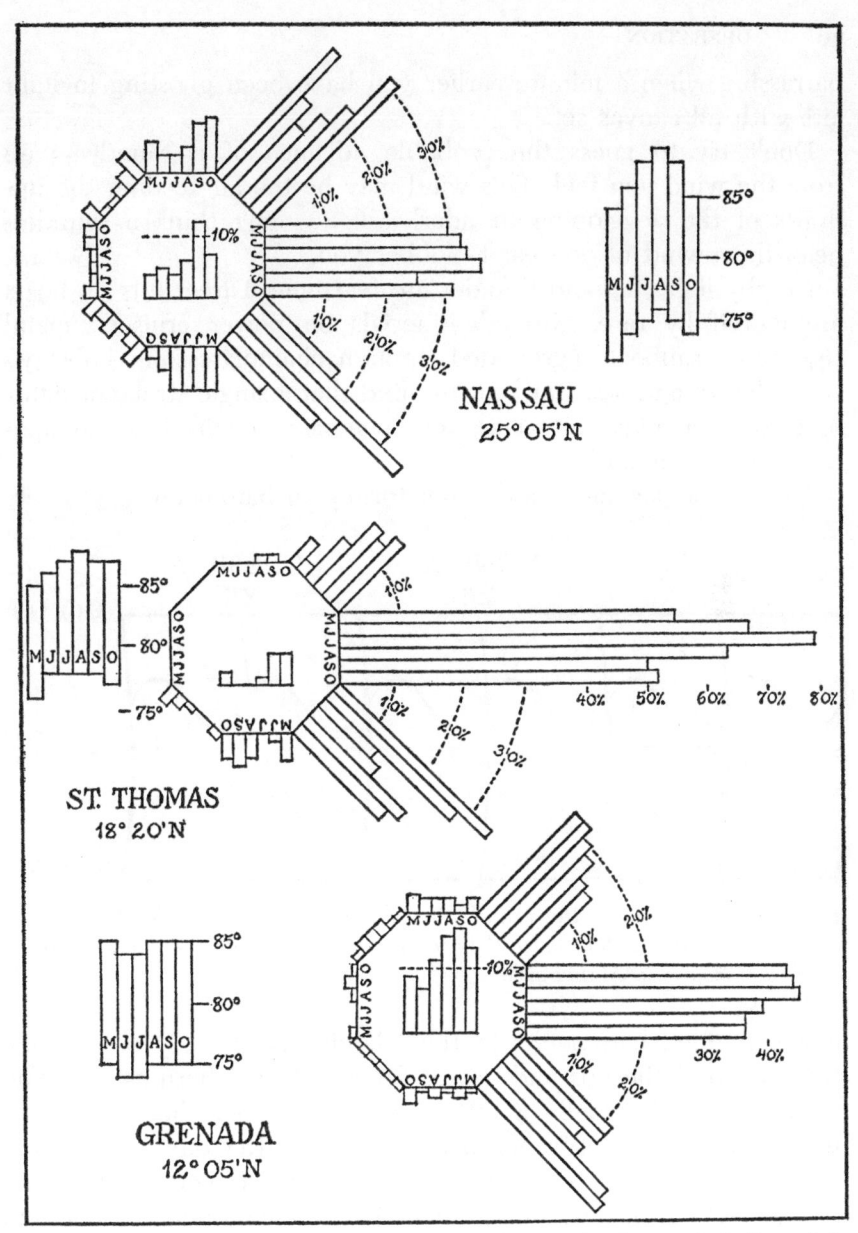

15. *Summer weather in the Islands—November to April, month indicated by first letter. Windroses show how much of the time (in percent) the wind blows from a given direction. (For example, at Nassau, in October, the wind is out of the East in 30% of all observations.) Calms are shown in the center of the windroses. (For example, at Grenada, in May, it is calm a little less than 10% of the time.)*

Bars show average daily maximum and minimum air temperatures for the month. (For example, at St. Thomas, in May, the average daily maximum is 85°F, the minimum 76°F.)

40   OPERATION

barrassing when a minute earlier you have been ghosting in light airs with all canvas set.

Don't try to guess the probable advance of a thundersquall from the wind you feel. This wind may be the air feeding the updrafts of the developing thunderhead. So don't think a thunderhead downwind of you can't clobber you.

Nearby lightning and thunder are fearsome. Direct hits on boats are mercifully rare. Grounded aerials on power cruisers, metal rigging on sailboats (grounded through chainplates and bobstay) act as lightning rods. But bear in mind that a single stroke of lightning, even a miss, can make your compass lose its head, temporarily or permanently.

During the passage of a thunderstorm your barometer may barely

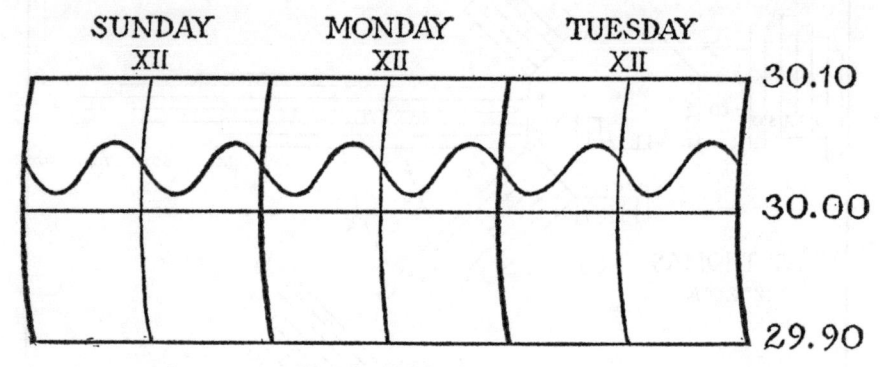

16. *Barograph trace: In the Islands the barometer indicates little change from day to day, but registers twice-daily atmospheric tides, always high at 10AM and 10PM, low at 4AM and 4PM.*

move. In fact, barometers in the Islands take it very easy. They show none of the ups and downs familiar to northern sailors. The reading, though usually a little lower in summer than in winter, remains at almost the same mean level day after day. But it does show a very distinct twice-daily tide of about .06 inch, a little more in winter, a little less in summer. These atmospheric tides—high every day at 10 A.M. and 10 P.M. and low at 4 A.M. and 4 P.M.—seem to continue through most Northers in the Bahamas and even through more severe summer disturbances. To find out whether the glass is rising or falling, tapping it is not enough here. Before you draw any conclusions from the jump of the needle you have to ask yourself: Should it be falling at this time of day, or rising?

The pleasant summer weather pattern—cumulus-flecked sky, low humidity, steady, gentle winds, spoiled only by local thundershowers—the flatness of the daily weather map if you like, sometimes gets interrupted.

The trades, these paragons of constancy in strength and direction, may back, become fickle, and even die. The glass drops. Humidity increases. In place of isolated thunderheads you see rows of them, sometimes with cirrus and even stratus clouds between them. Showers are frequent and not of the quick-over kind; it may drizzle or rain between heavier showers. The wind may be gusty and pipe up to winter strength.

The underlying cause for all these changes was found only in 1946 by G. E. Dunn, who later became director of the National Hurricane Center at Miami. He called it an easterly wave. It's a trough of low pressure running across the easterly air flow south of the Bermuda-Azores high. Such a trough, up to a thousand miles long, often lies in a SSW to NNE direction and drifts westward at 8–10 knots.

Unlike the familiar fronts in northern areas, and the winter Northers in the Bahamas, an easterly wave brings no change in air masses. The air ahead of, in, and behind the wave is of the same temperature.

As may be expected, all easterly waves don't behave alike. The worst weather may precede the arrival of the trough; it may come when the glass is lowest right in the trough, or after the barometer has started its climb back to normal. The intensity of easterly waves varies from slightly increased shower activity, through a couple of days of intermittent rain, to conditions much like those at the fringe of a full-blown tropical storm.

From June to September the weather map is seldom without such a wave somewhere in the Caribbean area. During these months such waves—usually of the mild kind—may pass a stationary observer once or twice a week. In May, and in October and November these waves are less frequent.

Much of the annual rainfall in the Islands comes from these waves. On the higher islands the windward side, where the trade winds—forced to rise—jettison moisture, gets far more rain than the leeward side. There are great differences in amount of rain between islands, but not much more than in the amounts the same island receives in different years. Nassau, for example, records an average of fifty inches yearly; it got half that in the driest year, twice that in the wettest.

Through observation at land stations, reports from ships and planes, and photographs taken by weather satellites the weather bureau keeps close watch over easterly waves. Harmless in themselves, they sometimes develop a "closed circulation." How a trough of low pressure becomes a more or less circular low is not at all clear yet.

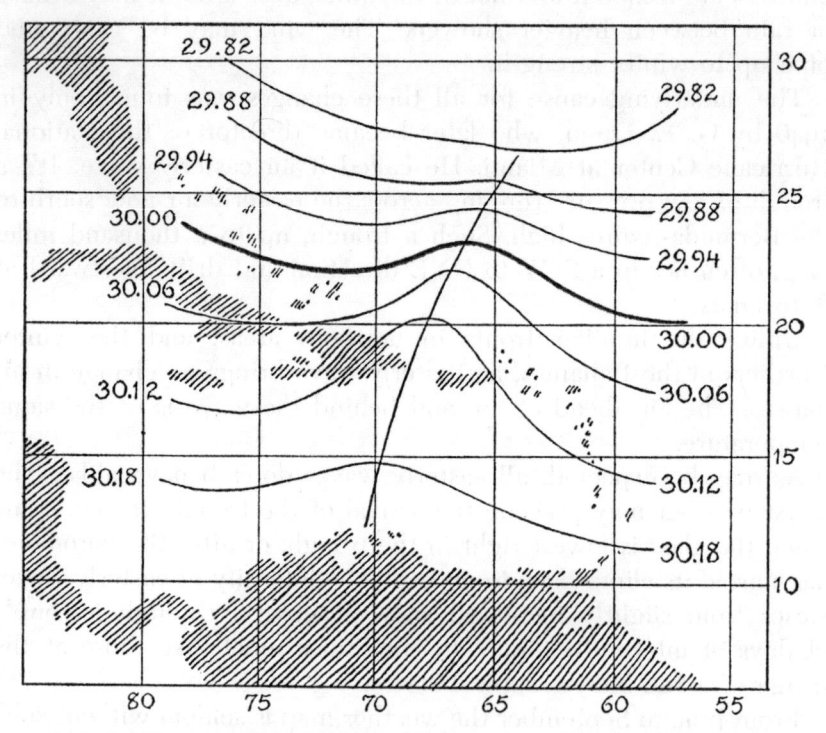

17. *Easterly Wave over the Islands: The trough of low pressure, which typically tends SSW to NNE, shown west of Puerto Rico will drift slowly westward.*

I have seen it happen. With a couple of other yachts I was lying in an anchorage off one of the small cays in the Abacos. A typical easterly wave sat on top of us. For two days band after band of showers filled our dinghies. When I bailed between showers, it drizzled. For a time the wind was strong, gusty, and out of the north, where wind has no business in June. Most of the time it was too nasty for rowing ashore or for visiting between yachts. Neither

Miami nor Nassau radio had anything beyond "winds locally higher near showers." On the third day the weather bureau had found a tropical depression centered above my masts. It later became the first tropical storm of the season.

Now a tropical depression is described as having a weak closed circulation. It's weak if you call 28–33-knot winds weak. Usually it takes a tropical depression several days to intensify and to get organized into a tropical storm. Most depressions never make it but dissipate in rags of showers. One authority believes that a tropical depression has to be just the right size to develop further: too small it doesn't get enough energy from the outside to maintain circulation; too large it cannot keep the merry-go-round going.

When the winds increase above thirty-four knots, but stay below sixty-three knots (Force 7–11), it's a tropical storm. Above sixty-four-knot maximum sustained winds (Force 12 and up), it's official: It's a hurricane.

Tropical depressions, tropical storms, and hurricanes all are cyclones in the sense that the winds blow around them counter-clockwise, as they do in the Northern Hemisphere around all lows with closed isobars. But the term "tropical cyclone" is not used by the weather bureau at this time. You'll find it in many books where statistics are given for tropical cyclones, including hurricanes. Translate that to tropical storms and hurricanes.

Over the entire North Atlantic, during the last eighty years, an average of eight storms a year has been recorded, of which five or six developed past the magic sixty-three-knot wind speed. But averages are misleading. One year had twenty-one storms, two years a single storm; for two years the table gives eleven full-blown hurricanes; for another two years, none. In September 1950 three separate, though somewhat related hurricanes showed on the weather map at the same time. Also, in 1967, three hurricanes traveled at the same time.

Not all storms and hurricanes of the North Atlantic brush the Islands. Some starting near the African side, drift across the ocean and dissipate or turn north before reaching the Islands. Others form to the west of that area and move into the Caribbean or the Gulf of Mexico.

The long-term statistical chance for a storm or hurricane in any one group of islands is from one to two per year. It is the lowest

(0.9) in the Windward group of islands, higher (1.5) in the Leeward, Virgin, and Bahama Islands south of Nassau, and highest (2.0) in the Bahamas north of Nassau. That difference in probabilities is readily explained. In the low latitudes of the Windward group only storms that travel westward are to be considered. These storms cannot form near the equator, where the force that provides the spinning movement is zero. The northwestern Bahamas, on the other hand, gets storms that have visited the more southerly islands, and also some that have already recurved toward the NW.

Officially the hurricane season runs from June 1 to November 30. In other months tropical storms are very rare. In the Bahamas as a whole, August, September, and October are about equally storm-prone, with September having slightly more storms than the other two months. June is quite safe as a rule. In July and November storms are only a third as likely to strike than in any of the three peak months. In the Virgin Islands and the Lesser Antilles, June and November are considered practically safe. August and September account for three-fourths of all storms; October has brought half as many storms as these months, but twice as many as July.

Although storms sometimes develop rapidly, in these latitudes they move rather slowly, perhaps 5–10 knots. So normally you'll have several days' warning of anything nasty making up or traveling. The charter captains in this area used to stop booking guests from June to November, but then they went cruising themselves. Keeping a close radio watch, you too can enjoy extended cruising between harbors that provide hurricane shelter.

Cruising even in the statistically most threatened area, the northern Bahamas, as I have done for several seasons, you'll only get one or two alarms, official or self-forecast. And that's for a storm that may affect an entire area. For any given point the chance of dangerous winds is even less.

What do you do when you get warning from the weather bureau or decide from your own plot of a storm track that it might be heading your way? Make for the nearest accessible hurricane hole or harbor. "Accessible" here is a key word.

On a cruise I made for the purpose I located a half dozen or more hurricane refuges, not all generally known, and each only a few hours' sail from the next. But sailing might be out of the question long before a storm arrives. The wind might be all wrong in direction, too strong, or even totally absent for once. Even under power some safe anchorage may not be accessible. Seas or swells might make an entrance, normally just deep enough for your craft, impossible to navigate. Also just when you need it, the tide may be low and you wouldn't want to lie off for several hours waiting for high water as you would in settled weather.

The remedy is obvious: Head for shelter long before you need it.

There are harbors, known to every skipper in the area, that serve as refuges from storms. There might be a hurricane chain stretched there between huge anchors. You deliberately drag your anchor until you snag that chain. Better yet, dive and tie or shackle directly into one of its links. The best tieup of all is a mangrove creek, which isn't a freshwater creek but an arm of the sea, natural or man-made, lined on both sides by mangroves, the taller the better. Tie to as many mangroves as possible, as low down as feasible. Then settle down and wait. Of course you'll plot the progress of the storm but don't try to outguess the boys at the weather bureau. They have information that you don't have: pictures from satellites, hurricane hunter plane observations, long-range radar, and upper air soundings that indicate steering currents. And they are experts.

Of course storms sometimes don't listen to their forecasts. You can expect that at two points of a storm's progress: when it stalls, indicating that pressure differences and steering currents are weak, and when it begins to recurve, changing course from, say, NW to NE.

So while sweating it out in the mangroves I have made it a rule to consider any favorable storm movement, however confidently read by the radio announcer, as merely an educated guess. And I have always, mentally at least, drawn a band on both sides of the track, rather than only the path of the center. Call that the band of uncertainty of movement, or the strip of devastation, but think of the path of the storm as a strip rather than a line.

Everyone has heard of the calm near the eye and the winds that may hit you from almost the opposite direction when the eye has passed. But even after the winds have subsided, stay in the mangroves a while. Even if they stain your deck, even if the sandflies get through your screens, stay. The storm may hook, hairpin, even double back. Stay until it has done its worst somewhere far away from you or has become totally disorganized. You are in no hurry: seas are likely to be rough to very rough for several days anyhow.

Perhaps you think I've just had good luck, the luck of the dumb. You are right, of course. After I left the Hopetown area where I had sweated out several hurricane scares, that settlement and much of Abaco was clobbered by a storm that had already passed clear and was off the Georgia coast, then returned on very short notice.

Perhaps I'm all wrong in giving the impression that with reasonable precautions you will not be exposed to much more than

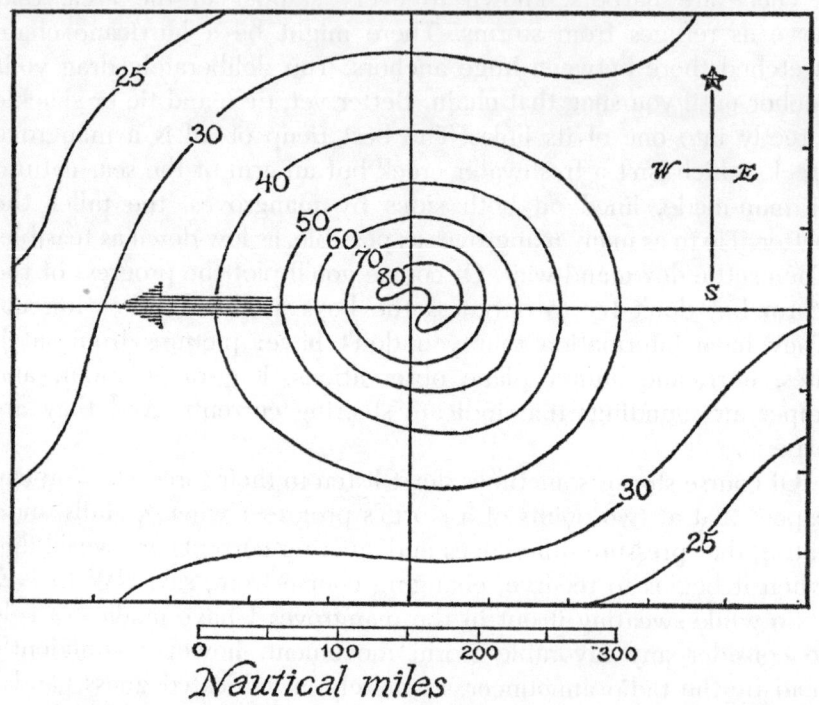

18. *Wind strength (in knots) around a hurricane moving westward in the latitudes of the Islands. Winds, above 80 knots near the center, drop off rapidly away from the eye of the storm, are typically less than 40 knots one hundred-and-fifty miles from center.*

discomfort and, at most, gale force winds. I'm not just milking statistics. Nor do I base my statements on a few hurricane seasons I survived without damage, sometimes wondering how a storm could be raging not far away while I lay so snug in the mangroves. No, I can show you old trees on any island and ramshackle buildings that couldn't have withstood a single storm. And I'll invite you to guess the average age of native boats that must have survived quite a few hurricane seasons.

5 Sailing for Powerboat Skippers

You own a powerboat.

You can understand youngsters borrowing mother's washtub, rigging a pole, and with a bedsheet for a sail, having fun on a pond. (That, Cap'n, shows your age. Mothers have no more wooden washtubs. Youngsters con the old man into buying them a molded saucer with aluminum mast and dacron sail.)

But why would grown-up men play with rags (sometimes affectionately called kites, never sheets) and strings (perversely called sheets) to get absolutely nowhere compared to the progress of the slowest outboard rig?

Perhaps you are broad-minded and reserve for wind sailors the same tolerance you accord habitual yogurt eaters. You may have the it-takes-all-kinds attitude that bowlers have toward surfing, or Ping-Pong players toward chess. Perhaps you have a nagging feeling, fostered by the secret language of the kite-and-string boys, that theirs is the true sport while you are merely a waterborne bus driver. That's what makes some people buy motor-sailers even if later they let the sails rot under their covers. You are entitled to any of these attitudes and others besides. You own a powerboat. Sailboats don't concern you.

But they do.

For one, there is the law. The International Rules of the Road are most specific. Under Rule 20(a), when a power-driven vessel and a sailing vessel are proceeding in such directions as to involve risk of collision, the *power-driven vessel shall keep out of the way of the sailing vessel*. Article 20 of the Inland Rules says the same thing in practically the same words.

The few exceptions to these rules are not likely to affect the skipper of a motor-driven pleasure craft. One covers the unlikely case of a vessel under sail overtaking you; as usual the overtaking vessel then has to keep clear. Another exception charges the sailing boat (like all other boats "not engaged in fishing") to keep out of the way of vessels engaged in fishing. But the fishing isn't your kind and mine; it means fishing with nets, trawls, etc., and does not include trolling.

The only exception that possibly can apply to your craft has been written into the International Rules in the revision that came into force in international and coastal waters in September 1965 as Rule 20(b): "The above rule [20(a)] shall not give to a sailing vessel the right to hamper, in a narrow channel, the safe passage of a power-driven vessel which can navigate only inside such channel." That's to keep kids of all ages from playing chicken under the bow of an ocean liner. Don't count on that rule, even in waters where it applies, to give you the right of way. Sailboats draw much more water than powerboats of the same over-all length. A thirty-footer might draw five or six feet; so she may be the one that can navigate only in the channel, while you could safely skim over the spoilbank or stay in the undredged part of a coastal waterway.

The law protects sailboats, just as it protects children and idiots, because they are somewhat helpless. To understand fully the difficulties in operating sailboats, compared with the ease of handling power-driven craft, you should know a little about sailing. You don't have to know all the fine points, nor all the salty terms with which wind sailors bewilder their more efficiently propelled friends.

Sailing is really very simple: There is the wind and here is a sail, or several sails, that make the boat move in one direction or another. You can readily see what makes a square-rigger move before the wind. With the wind not directly astern, but somewhere aft of her beam, the explanation is still fairly obvious. The wind tries to push the vessel downwind, sideways through the water. But she's been designed to go forward; her underwater shape including keel and rudder resists sideways motion, so part of the wind force will be used to make her go forward. Some of the force of the wind is wasted in making her heel, some more in making her course sag to leeward of the direction in which she points, but even without bathtub and model you can see how it works.

And you can see how the action is very similar on a modern fore-and-aft-rigged sailboat as long as the wind is, say, four points aft of her beam. Let's skip her action when the wind is nearly abeam and look at her "on the wind"—that's when the wind is four points or so from her bow. Square riggers couldn't get that close on the wind and keep moving. Modern sailboats get even closer to the wind because the wind gods favor the sailor. They provide not only the pressure on the windward side of the sails to push the boat, but also cause a partial vacuum on the other side of the sail to pull her forward. That's not just a marginal effect; on an efficient, modern sailing rig it can amount to three-fourths of the propelling force.

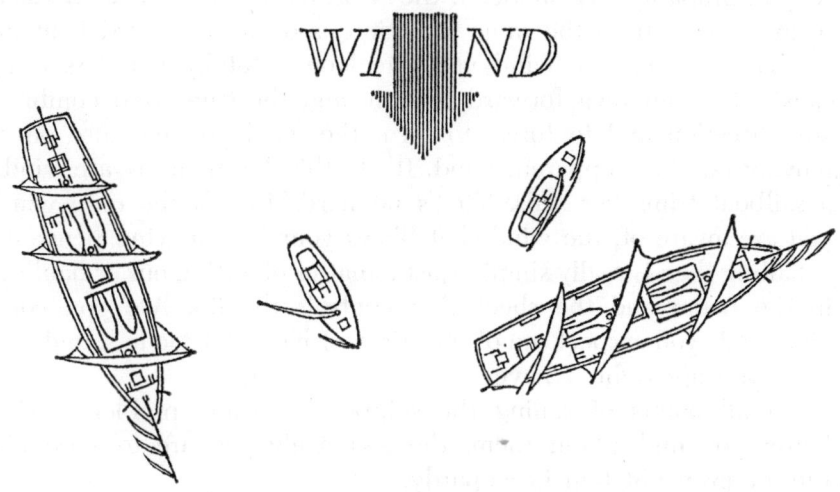

19. *Wind and sails*— Obviously the wind will push the square-rigger at left downwind. The modern fore-and-aft-rigged sailboat, though less efficient before the wind, is propelled in the same manner. The square-rigger at right will move forward because its hull and keel resist sideways motion through the water. The modern sloop will sail closer to the wind than a square-rigger; suction on the lee side of her sails helps her.

Let's look closer at the various points of sailing, that is, courses in relation to the direction of the wind. As an example we'll use a sloop, a single-masted craft that normally wears a large sail (the main), and forward a smaller sail (the jib). You change the trim of the main through the sheet attached to the boom, the trim of the jib by the jib-sheet.

You'll see that, basically, sailing on all points—before the wind, off the wind, and on the wind—is the same. You just change the angle the boom makes with the center line of the boat, and trim the jib to match the main.

From a course where the sloop resembles the square-rigger most, the sloop can go "up," closer to the wind. Haul in the main-sheet and the jib-sheet going through a broad reach, to a beam reach when the wind is abeam. Haul in some more on the sheets and you'll sail on a close reach. If you haul in until the boom is almost amidships, you are close-hauled, on the wind.

From the broad reach you could have brought the wind farther aft by simply letting out more of the main-sheet.

Before someone jumps on me, I should mention one minor point. As you probably have noticed, the wind on a moving boat doesn't seem to blow from the same direction as on an anchored boat in the same place. The wind you'd feel on a totally windless day, caused by your own forward motion, and the true wind combine —in direction and in force—to form the wind you measure on a moving boat, the apparent wind. It's to this, her own private wind, a sailboat trims her sails. That's no hardship; it's the only wind you are aware of, the wind that blows your flag or wind pennant.

Sailing then is really simple—just a matter of letting out or hauling in the boom and the sheet that controls the jib. Are you convinced? If you suspect me of cheating, of having it made sound too easy, you are right. I have.

On all points of sailing the skipper has some problems. The better you understand them, the less likely you are to spoil his fun, or even put him in jeopardy.

ON THE WIND, close-hauled, beating, whatever you hear it called, is the most exciting point of sailing. It is also the wettest. It tests helmsman and boat; more races are won and lost on the windward leg than on any other. One author estimates that sailboats spend more than half their time going to windward. Cruising men don't share the racing skippers' enthusiasm for thrashing to windward, and have been known to go elsewhere rather than work to windward by the hour. The fellows who make long passages pore over pilot charts and pick their seasons to avoid beating. If they have done their homework well, and if the wind gods co-operate, they can sail around the world without ever having to thrash to windward.

The skipper's basic problem in beating is summed up in the old order to the helmsman: Full-and-by, meaning, keep the sails full, and steer a course as close by the wind as you can.

However steady the wind, it shifts somewhat so the helmsman here is not expected to steer a straight line. The wind also changes in strength. To keep the boat moving in a lull, the helmsman has to bear away; to make good a course as close on

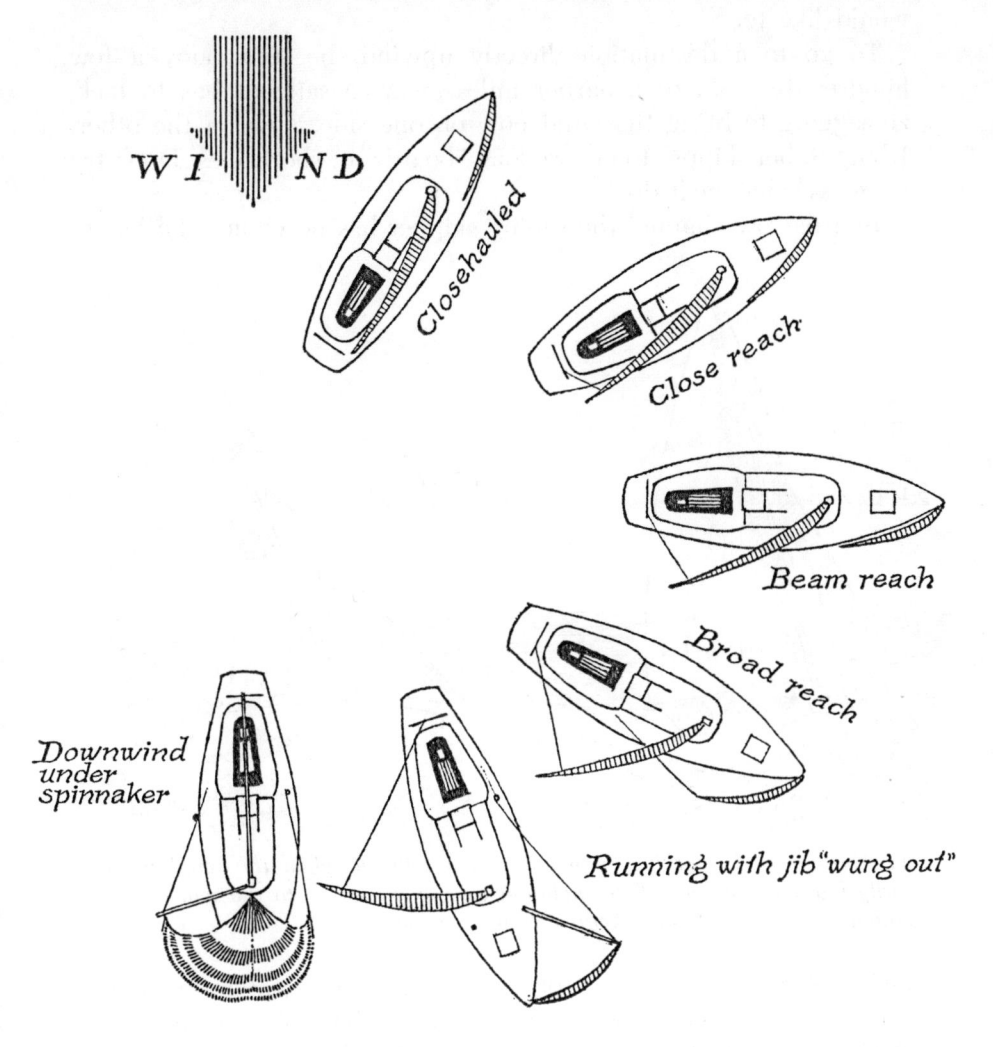

20. *Points of sailing. From a broad reach a modern sailboat can go up, that is closer to the wind, by bringing main sail and jib nearer to the centerline of the boat. To make her more efficient going downwind, she can hold the jib out on the side opposite the main, or set a baggy jib, a spinnaker.*

the wind as possible, he'll point her up in a puff. So don't expect a sailboat close-hauled to keep to a compass course. She can't.

No sailboat can sail into the eye of the wind. So, on the wind, the helmsman can't change course if it means coming closer on the wind. Neither can he cut your wake at right angles as he would like to.

To go to a destination directly upwind, be it a buoy a few hundred feet off, or a harbor miles away, a sailboat has to tack, zigzagging to bring the wind now on one side, now on the other. It's up to her skipper to choose long "boards" or short ones. Don't try to guess what he'll do.

In a narrow channel the sailing skipper has no choice; he has to

21. *Close-hauled, working to windward, a sailboat when the wind momentarily lightens will fall off to maintain way, come closer to the wind when it stiffens. Don't expect her to keep a straight course.*

tack before he runs out of water. In open waters, watching through binoculars, you may sometimes be able to tell when she'll go about. Someone may be getting busy at the jib-sheet that up to now has been peacefully cleated; also she may sail a bit farther off the wind just before tacking. That's not to be compared to the farmer's driving over the centerline before turning into his corn patch. The sailboat may need the extra momentum to bring her into the wind, through the wind, and over on the new tack.

Sailing for Powerboat Skippers 53

However smart the crew, however weatherly the boat, it takes time from sailing smartly on one tack to filling away on the other. During that time a sailboat is most vulnerable. The wash from a powerboat, even the wake of a water skier can put her back on her old tack, or make her miss stays. Missing stays, she's in irons: her sails slat uselessly, she doesn't answer the helm, and can steer

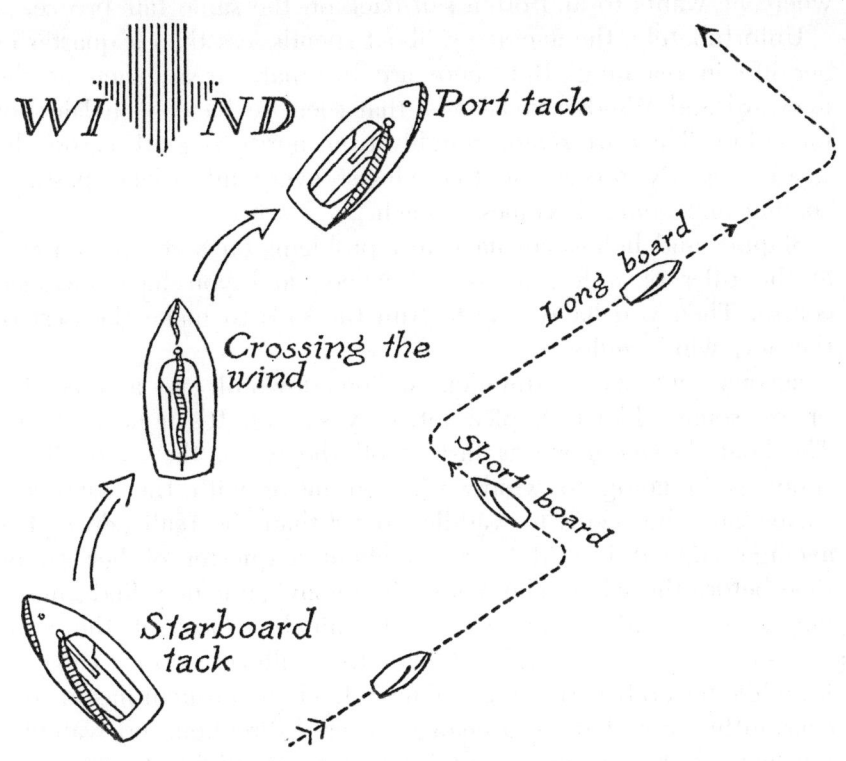

22. *Tacking— To make good a course to windward, a sailboat follows a zig-zag course bringing the wind first on one side, then the other. With the wind coming over the starboard bow she is said to be on the starboard tack, with the wind over her port bow on the port tack.*

neither to one side nor the other. This can be embarrassing, infuriating, and—lacking sea room—downright catastrophic.

But you never hear of crews starving to death in irons. There are ways of getting out of this hangup. You may see someone sprint forward to hold the jib to weather, catching the wind to bring her bow around. Or the skipper, given maneuvering room, may calmly wait until, drifting astern, he gets steerageway again.

Then there is the crash method: start the engine. But before the engine takes hold, the boat may drift aground or crash, stern-first, into the seawall.

OFF THE WIND, reaching, with the sheet started, is comfortable sailing. The boat makes her best speed, and can be kept on a steady course. It's a cruising man's delight: He can go directly where he wants to and often sail back on the same fair breeze.

Unfortunately, the average sailboat spends less than a quarter of her life in reaching. But there are fortunate areas, such as the Leeward and Windward Islands, that seem to have been laid out for sailors. They are strung roughly from north to south across the steady easterly breezes so that almost every interisland passage, coming and going, becomes a reach.

Skipper and helmsman have few problems on a reach. A touch at the tiller or a few spokes of wheel, and you have changed course. Then you have time to trim the sails to make the best of the new wind angle.

BEFORE THE WIND, running, sailing downhill in a following breeze sounds like fast, pleasant, easy sailing. It's none of these. The boat doesn't move as fast as off the wind, there's no flying spray as in going to windward. You move with the wind and waves, and she seems to waddle slower than she really does. The average sailboat is said to spend about a quarter of her sailing time before the wind. The world circumnavigator may find himself before it day after day, rolling abominably most of the time.

Even when the rolling isn't bad, the sailboat skipper can't relax while his craft is running downwind. The helmsman has to steer constantly, ever alert for a change in wind direction and watching the water not only ahead but also astern. A slight steering error can bring the wind on the wrong side of the sail; then the boom lifts, half the sail stays on one side, and the other flies over in a messy sail-threatening debacle called a goosewing jibe.

A wave hitting the stern unexpectedly can roll her until the tip of the boom hits the water. The corner of the sail scoops up water and acts like an anchor around which the boat will pivot, disobeying her rudder. A small boat may capsize.

Some boats, tripping over a sea, may want to broach to, suddenly coming up toward the wind with the boom still broad off.

A slight wind shift, an unseen wave, sloppy steering all can cause that horror: a jibe all standing. From broad off on one side the boom slams across to broad off on the other. Heads, including the helmsman's, get bashed, guests get knocked overboard. The sail may tear, the sheet part, the boom break. Worse, the boom may take out a stay that supports the mast, and mast and all the rest of the rigging may go by the board.

Can the sailor provide against this catalog of catastrophes? He can and does. He'll avoid sailing directly before the wind. He may tack downwind, sailing a wavy course to bring the wind first on one quarter, then the other. While wearing ship—going through the wind that blows from astern—he'll carefully nurse the sheet to keep the boom from slamming across.

Perhaps he temporarily imitates a squarerigger, which is happier before the wind than a fore-and-aft-rigged sailing craft. He may rig a pole to hold the jib out on the side opposite to the main. In this wing-and-wing position the jib does some useful work instead of flogging in the wind shadow of the main. On racing craft you'll see the crew setting a spinnaker, a parachute-like sail that takes a boat downwind more efficiently than her regular canvas.

Why do I bring in all this technical stuff in a chapter addressed to skippers of powerboats? Just to alert them to the rather precarious balance of a sailboat that's running, the more exactly before the wind, the more precariously. The wave that makes her jibe or broach to, the roll that makes her dip her boom into the water, could be your wake. The wind catching her sail from the wrong side could be caused by your passing her too closely.

At this point of sailing the helmsman can't quickly change course to high-step over your wake. Even when no preventer is set, wearing ship is a slow maneuver that involves rudder, main-sheet, and jib-sheet. To move a spinnaker from one side to the other takes the synchronized action of three hands. So please watch your wake and give the poor handicapped wind sailors sea room.

Sometimes you'll see a sailboat driven by sails *and* engine. Some call it motor sailing. It's a good way to take a shortcut to windward, sometimes the only way around a shoal. It may be just a short-time expedient to get through the lee of a headland.

Whatever the reason, the sailboat propelled by power forfeits all her special rights under the rules of the road. The strange thing is this: Her skipper knows she's under power, but how are you to know it? Her little engine probably can't be heard over the purring of your own power plant. You may see her exhaust, especially the steam caused by some of the cooling water being discharged through the tailpipe. But even when you see that cloud of steam, she may not be power-driven. The engine may be idling for later instant use, charging her battery, or cooling her refrigerator. If she's stepping right along, directly into the wind with sails shaking, you can be sure she's under power.

Now here is a dividend for the patient powerboat skipper who has read this far. Someday you may be sailing yourself. I don't mean buy a sailboat, but your engine may have let you down. An improvised riding sail rigged in the stern and sheeted in flat amidships will keep your disabled boat out of the trough and headed more or less into the wind. That'll stop the rolling which makes even a minor engine repair a feat of acrobatics.

If you've broken down offshore or in the middle of a lake, a sail may get you close to home, or to some other shelter. Don't expect to sail to windward or make a respectable speed. But any jury-rigged sail patterned on a squaresail rig, or even a spinnaker, will get you downwind even against a current that otherwise might set you on a shoal. Without your engine, your rudder will probably not control her. Improvise a sweep; even a board over the stern may do the trick.

Probably you won't have to sail far with this emergency rig. A bunk sheet hoisted as a squaresail, or ballooning as a spinnaker ahead of a powerboat makes a wonderfully effective distress signal, although through your own ingenuity you are really in no distress at all.

P.S. to wind sailors who happen to come to this page: Please be kind to powerboats, in distress or otherwise. Many of them have only one engine; when it quits they are in trouble. Even with two engines a powerboat has problems of synchronization, cavitation, and what-have-you. With one engine of a pair out of commission some powerboats become hard to handle. So be kind to powerboats. Don't force them out of a channel. Don't, whatever the situation, pass them unnecessarily close; your wake may disturb the baby in his crib.

Seriously, now: Don't tack in narrow channels that carry a lot of traffic; start your engine instead. If you have no engine, arrange for someone to come for you to get you in before dark; don't expect strangers, or even members of your own club, to haul you in *every* weekend.

Even though you have the right of way, look aft before you come about. Luff a little to waste time if a power-driven craft, however small, is about to pass you. Sure he's supposed to keep clear, but how can he if you tack in front of him?

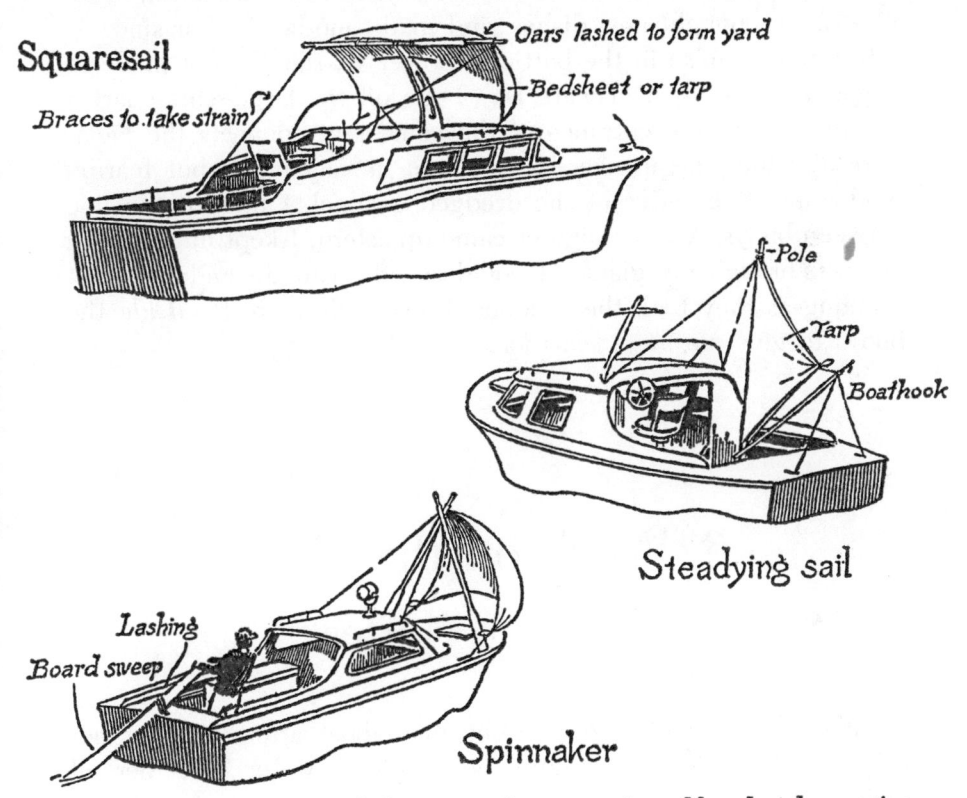

Squaresail
Oars lashed to form yard
Bedsheet or tarp
Braces to take strain

Pole
Tarp
Boathook
Steadying sail

Lashing
Board sweep
Spinnaker

23. *Jury sailing rigs may help a powerboat out of trouble when her engine breaks down. Plan yours now and keep needed gear aboard.*

If your boat steers herself on some points of sailing—many boats do very well by themselves when close-hauled—congratulations, sir. But keep a lookout anyway. Figure it out for yourself: Your little sloop may travel five hundred feet in one minute.

In channels where big ships operate, check the chart to see if you can't stay out of the fairway altogether.

I have had water splashed all over me and my chart by passing water skiers in Georgia. I've been washed into the bulrushes by a powerboat that after taking close-up photographs of my little schooner put both engines full ahead in North Carolina. The only dishes ever broken aboard, under way, fell victims to an outboard in Connecticut. My sails have been taken aback by the slipstream of a helicopter in Virginia. I've been faked out from the entrance to a harbor by a power cruiser in New Jersey. But I've dried out, come afloat again, bought new dishes, and made another harbor since.

But one skirmish in the battle of power vs. sail I'm not likely to forget. Heading up Delaware Bay I ran off the large-scale chart a few miles from the entrance of the canal that connects the Delaware and the Chesapeake. No problem in navigation, but fearing spoilbanks at the edge of the dredged channel, I hugged the line between buoys. A fast freighter came up astern. I kept hugging my buoys. Through my glasses I could see the captain and the pilot grinning as they took the steamer drawing thirty feet *outside* the buoys to give me more sea room.

6 Work on the Hull Between Tides

A lot of useful work can be done on a boat after standing her ashore at high tide and before the next high water floats her off again.

Don't let the lack of tides in your home waters keep you from reading on. Even a thousand miles inland, many jobs on the hull—above, at, and below the waterline—can be done, or done more easily, when the boat is on the hard. Any boat too large to be hauled out by hand or on a trailer can use some of the tricks seamen have used before the days of marine railways and traveling hoists.

Perhaps work of any kind scares you. Perhaps you are rich enough to let the yard do all the work. But someday knowledge of ways of beaching a boat may keep all the stuff aboard from getting soaked, and may even save the boat from sinking.

It's not just a way for cheating a yard of a hauling fee. Sometimes there's no yard handy; the railway may be tied up with a boat in the cradle; you may not have the time to wait for your turn on the waiting list; or perhaps you just feel silly to haul for a job that'll take only a few minutes. You may also find the nearby yard unable to handle your sailboat without unstepping her masts, often a major operation.

The list of jobs you can do, or do better when the boat isn't afloat, is long. It ranges from trivial to serious, from cosmetics to essentials. You can clean and repaint a boot top that grows grass and gets to look ratty at midseason, or varnish a transom without danger of a drop of water clouding your work. Anybody can fill, sand, and patch topsides from a dinghy, but have you tried lettering or cutting in a waterline on a boat afloat? You may have hit some floating object, or brushed a rock. What's the damage? Insurance policies often provide for the cost of hauling for inspection; but collect under this clause a few times and you may have to find another company when the policy comes up for renewal. Perhaps you find only a little bottom paint scraped off. Only! In saltwater that's what the teredos have been waiting for; leave it unpainted and the worms'll eat into your little ship.

At another time you may have a pesky leak. Nothing serious while you lie to the dock, but perhaps not safe to leave the boat unattended between weekends. Not safe to go out in her next weekend either. She may open up when she hits a chop. On the other hand it may be just a single fastening. Until you haul her, or partly haul her, you can't tell. Perhaps you have to tighten up on an outside stuffing box, an easy job out of the water. There you can also repack a stuffing box, change a bearing, change a prop, or pull a shaft.

Even such well-above-water jobs as replacing a rub rail are easier on the hard than when you're hanging from the deck, or working from a dinghy that wants to slide out from under you whenever you use your screwdriver.

Where there are suitable tides, all these jobs and many others can be done between high tides. The underwater shape of your hull will decide whether it's wise to be your own marine railway.

In one part of England, where the water gets thin at low tide, all craft—from work boats to yachts—have twin keels to keep them upright when they run out of water. The usual centerboard or keel sailboat takes to the bottom well, the longer and wider the straight part of the keel, the better. I wouldn't attempt to beach a racing-type hull with cutaway forefoot. In such a hull we once ran aground on a sandbar on the French side of the English Channel. Tidal range there is about fifteen feet, and the tide was falling. We didn't quite dry out, and the lead keel was probably well bedded in the sand, but for wretched hours until the tide came back, nobody moved or dared to sneeze.

Powerboats with shallow-vee bottoms usually rest comfortably and almost upright on keel and chine. But an exposed propeller may get in the way. You wouldn't want to beach a boat that comes to rest on a propeller blade, just to fix a scratch in the topsides. The propeller shop probably gets enough business from you already. If she'd sprung a massive leak, I'd beach her, and later gladly pay to have her prop straightened.

You can predict how your boat will lie by laying a straightedge across keel and chine at different stations on the plan. If you don't have her plans, sight along a straight batten, from astern, the next time she's on the railway.

Even if this inspection shows that she won't lie happily, don't give up the idea of working on her between tides. Much will depend on the height of tide where you plan to work. For a long job—such as painting the entire bottom—the difference between high and low water should be the same, or a little more, than the draft of your boat. In areas where usually the range of tide isn't quite enough, you may still get a complete dry-out by working at spring tides, usually one to three days after full and new moon. The tide tables will tell. Looking up the nearest station you'll find the difference in heights and times for some reference station for which daily predictions are published for every year.

If it's a close race between the range and your draft, go one step farther. Compare the tide level at the very spot where you'll be working with the data in the tide table. A couple of miles up the bay you may have several inches less range than at the entrance. Gauge the heights on any suitable dock piling or seawall. Look for highest and lowest levels and don't be misled by the change of current. In most places that's not at the time of high and low water.

While you are at it, make sure the next high water is at least as high as the one on which you plan to beach. During part of each month the morning tides are higher, during the rest of the month the evening tides. If you guess and guess wrong, you could be stuck overnight, and theoretically for two weeks, four weeks, six months, a year, and if you hit the very highest tide of a cycle, for almost nineteen years.

In areas where successive tides are of very different heights, as on the western coasts of the United States and Canada, you may have to plan on getting off twenty-five hours later, rather than roughly twelve hours later.

The time-honored method of working on a hull is by careening. You lay the vessel more or less parallel to the shore at high tide and make her lean toward the shore. This method, used by the Phoenicians, by Columbus and Cook, is still practiced by many workboats. You can watch it in Malcolm Park in Nassau. A halyard to the seawall gives the vessel a list toward shore; an oil drum and an old tire serve for blocking under the bilge. Next day at high tide the crew will turn her end for end, and work on the other side. Careening lets you work on a vessel that draws more water than the range of your tides. In Nassau even at springs the range is only four feet or so, while the larger smackboats draw five and six feet.

Yachtsmen don't like to see their boats lie on their bilges, and dislike securing everything in place. If your draft doesn't exceed the range of tide, or when it doesn't matter whether she dries out completely—teredos don't get into iron or lead keels—there is another good way, one that leaves the vessel practically upright. Find yourself a quiet dock or seawall that juts out into the water. At low tide inspect the bottom, remove rocks, broken conch shells, and other debris. At high water you go alongside with fenders out, take a line ashore, and haul her in until she gently grounds. Then you give her a list toward the dock, using a halyard from the masthead, or by shifting some weights. A couple of storm anchors on the side deck may do it. If you have found a spot with the proper slope, she'll lie on an even keel, down neither by the head nor by the stern.

After the tide has dropped part way, put in some blocking on the off-side as a precaution. I'd support the bilge, or the entire hull rather than putting props under the rail, however solid it may look.

The dock should be, as I've said, quiet. I don't mean free of old salts who may offer advice. I mean undisturbed by surge and wakes that would make your boat pound when she's just about floating. Pick your weather. Of course you don't want a wet day for painting; but also avoid days with chance of high winds.

The last time my schooner had been hauled professionally was in Chesapeake Bay. After that I maintained her for several years and painted bottom and topsides in the Out Islands of the Bahamas. There at springs the high tides fall at most convenient times, about 8 A.M. and 8 P.M. Most often I'd use a seawall along which the bottom sloped to the west. I'd do the port side with the schooner leaning against the north wall one day, float off in the evening,

24. *Careening, ancient method for laying a boat over for work on her hull, is still practiced in the Islands.*

spend the night at anchor in the harbor, and the next day do the starboard side, having the schooner lean against the south wall.

I either dropped an anchor astern when I went in, or I took it out in the dinghy later while waiting for the tide to drop. Either way, docking and undocking was a one-man operation. When on the evening of the second day I was afloat again, the schooner's hull all painted, the brushes soaking, and everything smelling of kerosene, I'd lie back and calculate how many bottles of the best I'd saved by doing the work myself.

Sometimes that work would not have passed the critical eye of the foreman in a high-class boat yard, but at least I knew that the important underwater work hadn't been done by some clown who doesn't care whether you float or sink.

In some places the bottom will be so soft that your keel would sink in. In a place you plan to use again and again, your own dock,

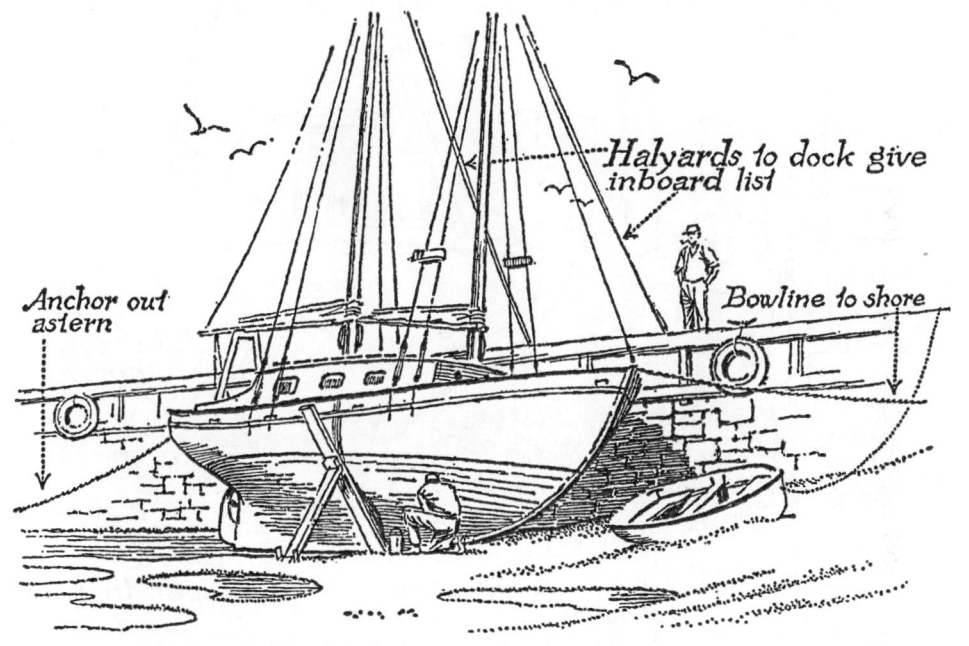

25. Drydocking against seawall—boat protected by fenders leans against wall; some blocking is a wise precaution.

for instance, you can build your own grid inexpensively. I have used one originally built for a heavy forty-five-foot cruiser. The dock was of open construction, so you could work on both sides of the hull in one docking. You could even paint the underside of the keel, all except where it rested on the sleepers.

But I needed two working days on the hard anyhow, so on the second day I'd simply move her ahead a foot or so and catch the places I had missed the day before. And that's more than most yards will do.

Sometimes the time between tides gets a little short for the work to be done. But when you have to, you'll find shortcuts. You can, for instance, cut in the waterline and paint perhaps six inches above it, leaving the rest of the topsides to be done from the dinghy. In filling gouges and many other minor jobs I found powdered plastic glue a great time-saver. Being mixed with water, it will stick to a wet plank and will set in time to be painted over a few hours later. I've used the same glue where a plank feathered, raising

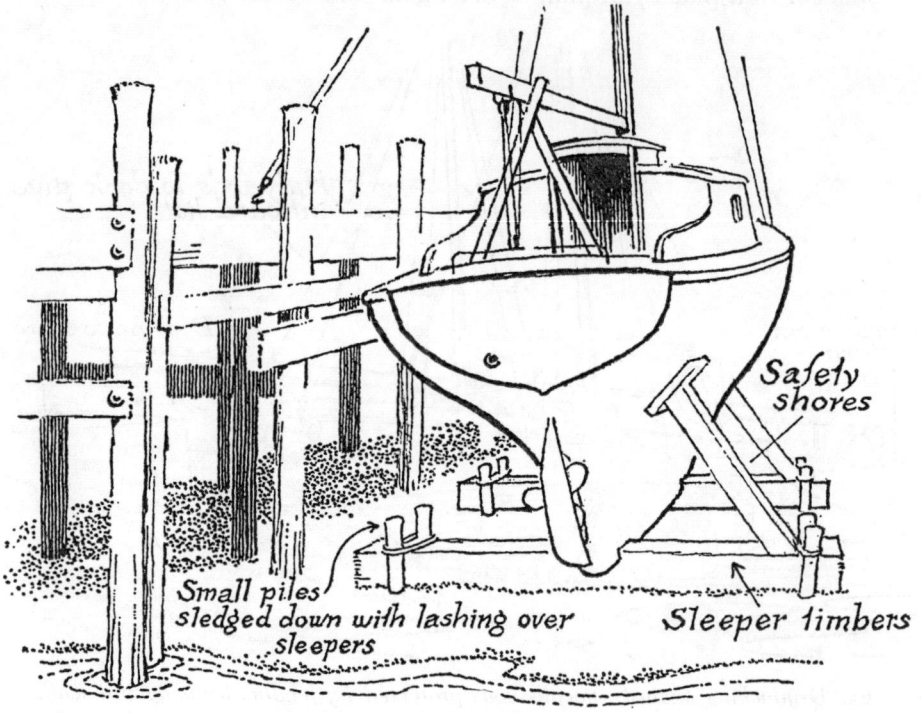

26. *Poor man's marine railway, recommended where bottom is soft. Sleepers placed at low-water preceding docking, can be left in place for future use.*

little stubbles of grain that get worse as you sand them. I applied the glue with a brush; when it had dried you could sand the plank yacht-smooth.

Don't let the thought of the returning tide stampede you. If you have drawn the bungs to drain the bilge, don't forget to replace them. When you've tackled a job below the waterline and see you can't finish it, don't panic. Say you had planned to put in a short plank and the only suitable piece of wood aboard splits, or you cut

Work on the Hull Between Tides 65

it too short. Cover the opening with sheet-lead, or plywood and canvas. There'll be another tide tomorrow. If the hole is near the waterline, perhaps you can ballast your vessel so she'll keep that plank (or lack of it) out of the water.

Giving the boat a list is a useful trick where there are no tides, or where the rise and fall is not enough for your draft. I have used it for jobs ranging from painting the waterline amidships to installing through-hull fittings for a head. On a sailboat there's an easy way to give her a list. Swing out the boom and rig it as if you'd want to hoist the dinghy aboard. Use chafing gear around the sail and rig guys fore and aft to keep the boom broad off. Then fill or partly fill the dinghy and hoist away. The dinghy won't come, the mother vessel will list.

You can also change the fore-and-aft trim to bring head or stern out of the water. (Better plug the exhaust in the transom if you bring her down by the stern.) You could do it by shifting weights, but you'll find that you'll have to move a lot of heavy gear to change her trim. Again the dinghy can help. Chock it temporarily athwartships in bow or stern, whichever you want to bring down. Then fill it with water. When you have finished your job, pull the plug and let the dinghy drain.

You can use this trick to check the inrush of water, say after a collision. In nontidal waters it can be used for partial beaching.

For a complete haulout where there are neither yards nor tides, there is the brute force method. Fishermen on rocky coasts the world over use it. It works best on flat, wet rocks. Oxen, horses, a truck or Jeep, or the village men haul the boat out. No fitting on the average yacht can stand that treatment. So you'll have to harness her with a stout rope all around the hull to distribute the strain as widely as possible. You'll find more about that in the chapter on towing.

Rollers, just round pieces of wood of approximately the same diameter, will ease the strain considerably. Only three or four are needed and a couple of boys to pick them up astern and quickly place them in front of her as she gets dragged ashore.

To get back into the water once you are high and dry is a bit of a problem, but at least this time gravity is on your side. A heavy workboat can pull you down, the villagers can push; best perhaps is a boat anchored as close as she'll dare go, winching you back into the water with long, steady pulls rather than jerks.

Such a haulout will never replace a marine railway for a paint job, but it's good to know that it can be done in an emergency. Under full power you may be able to ride up some rocks clear of the water. Even if you bust something, it's better than sinking in the middle of the lake.

Given a choice of places to beach in an emergency, I'd pick first the foot of a marine railway. Even if it's closed for Sunday. There

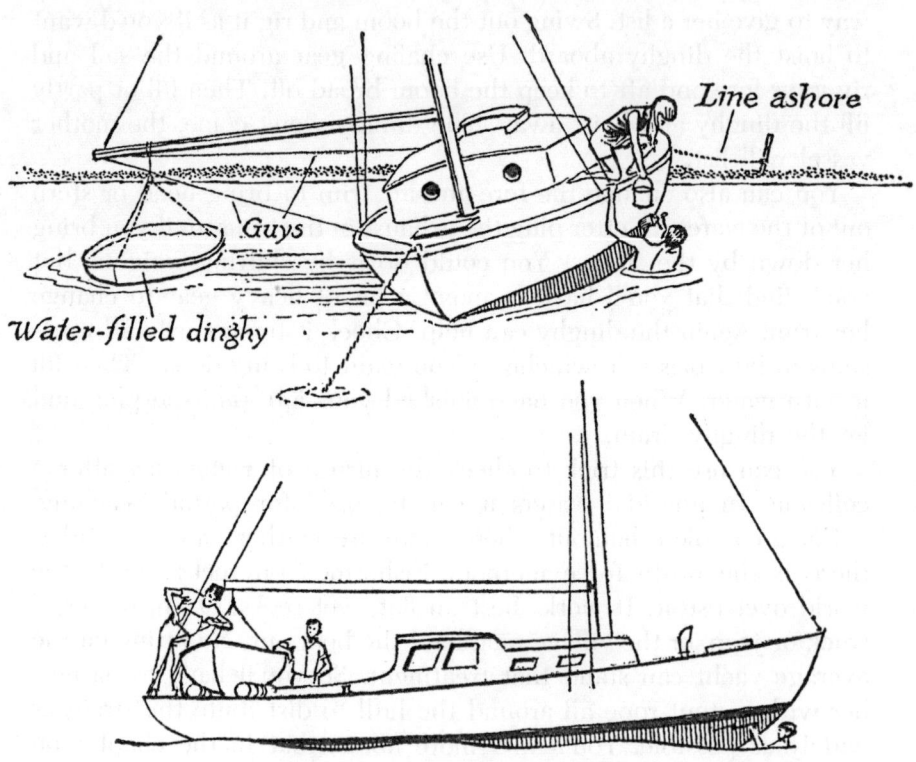

27. *Trimming vessel with water-filled dinghy for work on hull below the waterline.*

they are equipped to haul you out, and perhaps even to put you back in. Most likely they also have a pump big enough to handle any leak short of a missing plank.

Next choice would be a sandy cove. If there are houses nearby, I'd count on finding planks, rollers, and perhaps a truck that could haul her out. I'd avoid sucking mud bottom. And steep-to shores scare me, even when I'm not in any distress.

7 Skin Diving for Boat Work

Everybody knows of skin diving as a sport, but have you thought of it as part of boat work?

I don't mean diving with SCUBA gear. The tanks and regulator that make up the Self-Contained Underwater Breathing Apparatus are expensive. The technique has to be learned from an expert, and you are dependent on tanks that have to be refilled ashore.

The diving I have in mind is the simple kind that uses only a face mask. Almost everyone, lean or stout, floats in seawater. Even in fresh water the vast majority of people float. Unfortunately, without swimming motions one floats with only the bald spot of the head above water. You don't see well under water, even if you can keep your eyes open, something many people find difficult. And you can't breathe through the top of your head.

Put on a face mask, and you'll see as well below water as above. Add a snorkel—a short tube held in your mouth—and you can breathe while your face is under water. Don't let the diving part of skin diving scare you. As you'll see, for most of the work around the boat you'll stay just below the surface.

How about the skin part of skin diving? In southern waters you can stay perhaps an hour in the water before your teeth start rattling. In the waters around New England or in the Pacific Northwest, even in summer, you may get uncomfortable after one minute in your bare skin. So skin divers have invented the wet suit. Unlike the dry suit of helmet divers, which relies on woolen underwear and a waterproof outer covering, the wet suit is made of a spongelike material worn directly against the skin. The rubber-like material and its built-in air bubbles insulate you against the cold of the surrounding water, and keep your body from trying to warm the sea around you.

In really cold waters skin divers wear hooded suits that leave only the face exposed. In less chilly waters they do away with the hood. In even warmer waters, or for short immersion, they wear a shortie model. It has long sleeves, covers the torso, and buttons in the crotch. Any local expert will gladly tell you what suit you'll need. You can buy it ready-made, or better, assemble it in one evening from material and patterns sold at divers' supply shops. No sewing is needed; it's all done with tape and gunk.

By the way, a wet suit with its entrapped air bubbles will make you float better than any life jacket. Unlike a dry suit, which feels like the inside of a rubber boot, a wet suit, even when wet, feels warm and comfortable.

In warmish or warm water all you'll need is a face mask. There are many models to choose from. Avoid the ones that cover the mouth and have built-in snorkels. They are likely to fill your nose and eyes with water, the very thing you try to get away from by wearing a mask. Some of the snorkels have valves supposed to prevent flooding when they get under water. They can be downright dangerous. You come up gasping for air; the valve happens to be closed. The harder you fight for breath, the tighter you seat the valve. Panicking slightly, but still pretty bright, you try to tear off the mask. You'll find it stuck tightly to your face, held by the vacuum created by your struggle for air. At this moment you'll probably cough, and the mask will come off easily, saving you from drowning with your head above water.

I'd avoid chrome-trimmed and white masks. A shark or barracuda might misread the bright flashes for the SOS of an injured fish, or mistake it for a tasty fishing lure. Comfortable fit is the most important requirement. Test the mask by holding it lightly against your face and inhaling through your nose. The mask should stick to your face. In use you'll moisten the edges of the mask and get an even better seal. Among equally comfortable masks I'd pick the one with the widest field of vision. If you have to wear glasses, talk to your optician. He can rig you a pair with wire temples to wear under the mask. He can even cement prescription lenses right to the face plate; but the farther the lenses are from your eyes, the narrower your angle of vision. Contact lenses are fine; many professional skin divers wear them.

My personal favorite is a mask that, unlike most, has a molded nose under a goggle-shaped face plate. It holds a minimum volume of air, makes equalizing pressure easy, and the glass being close to the eyes gives a wide field of vision. The cost of this fancy piece including snorkel is about the price of a fifth of grog.

You can manage without a snorkel. But this J-shaped tube lets you breathe with your face under water. Pick a snorkel with soft rubber forming the bend to act as shock absorber. Sooner or later you'll come right up under your own boat or dinghy, and feel foolish enough without spitting teeth. Stick the upper part of the

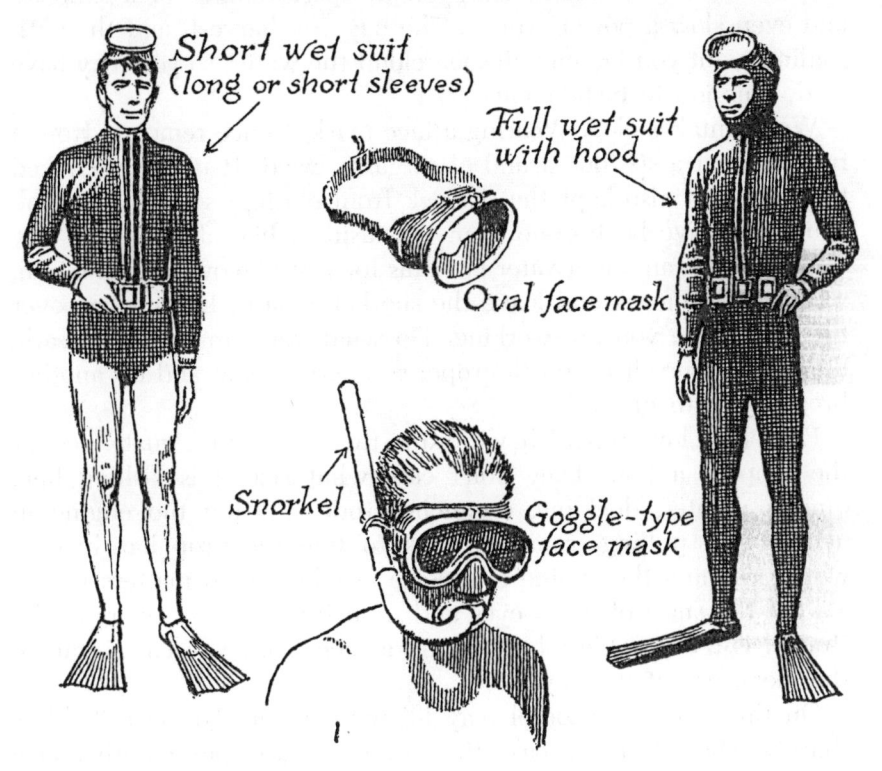

28. *Skin-diving gear.*

snorkel under the strap that holds the face mask, or better fasten it with a wide rubber band to the strap.

Even if you can't swim more than three strokes at one go, with a face mask and snorkel you can do many jobs around the boat. (Single-handers wear life line.)

The waterline or boot top scummy or getting green? Go for a swim, one stroke at a time, never more than a foot from the safety of your little ship. Start at the stern while your craft lies in a weak current.

A little rubbing with a plastic dish scrubber will remove scum and grass, and the current will carry them away as you work toward the bow.

If you use a snorkel on this job, you may take a few drops of spray. Most experts would simply swallow it. A little seawater won't harm you.

In warm waters the bottom of your craft will quickly grow spinach that in a few weeks will spoil the performance of a sailboat, and even slow a power cruiser. The hay you harvest, and the antifouling paint you loosen will soon cloud the water, so you may have to do this job in installments.

Water intakes clog. Wearing a face mask, I once removed from a friend's boat a six-foot strand of sargasso weed. It not only choked the pipe, but also kept the seacock from closing; so that little job could not have been done from the inside while afloat.

When such an underwater job calls for work below snorkel depth, wear just the mask and leave the snorkel aboard. Drop a line over the rail where you are working. Do what you can on one breath, then haul yourself up on the rope; submerge again and do another breath's worth of work.

Propellers love rope. They'll drape themselves in a goat's nest at the drop of a line. They don't care what size it is—fishing line, dinghy painter, dockline, or anchor rode. Putting the engine in neutral and pulling from the deck to free the prop hardly ever works; running the engine in reverse usually makes matters worse. To get the snarl off with eyes and nose full of water, working by Braille, is a miserable job. Wearing a face mask you can untangle the mess, or cut it away.

On this job your snorkel may fill with water. To clear it, blow sharply when its top breaks the surface. With your mouth above water you can also remove the mouthpiece, straighten the rubber tube, and let the snorkel drain.

Outside stuffing boxes develop leaks that keep the crew at the pump or drain your battery if you have an automatic bilge pump. Exercise between meals may be good for the crew, but with a mask you can easily stop this and other minor leaks. If you are working with the boat in deep water, secure your tools; they won't float. Use lanyards from the rail for heavy tools such as the stuffing-box wrench; tie lighter tools to your belt or sling them from your wrists.

Even a damaged propeller can be changed afloat. You'll find the job easiest when the boat is in shallow water where you can stand or squat on the bottom to get a better purchase.

Things have a habit of falling overboard. Never useless things, always favorite fish-cleaning knives, special wrenches, and needle valves for the outboard motor. You'll spot them more easily by swimming with a face mask than by staring down from the deck. Even without diving, a swimmer has the advantage over the man on deck. Without refraction, ripples, and reflections, you can dangle a magnet on a string, wield a net, or grapple with a shark hook, seeing exactly how you are doing.

Your face mask also lets you check damage to hull or propeller. In cold, murky waters you'd have to haul for inspection—a nuisance even when the insurance pays for it. In southern waters you swim once around the vessel, and know what, if any, damage she has suffered from a coral head you brushed, or from an accidental grounding.

When you have run aground—in some areas only liars never touched the bottom—follow this one-two routine. One: stop the forward motion by putting the engine in neutral or spilling the wind from her sails. Two: go over the side with your face mask and see what's holding her. (Once having gently touched while ghosting in a directional calm, I found nothing more serious than a king-sized conch under my keel.) A one-minute inspection will often also show the best way to get off.

Perhaps you'll never run aground, but in the palm belt you'll anchor far more often than in marina-studded northern waters. And the face mask is also useful in anchor work. Careful skippers swim down over their anchors every time the hook is down. Is it really dug in, or merely resting on the bottom? Is a fluke merely caught behind a tuft of grass, ready to drag at the first gust? In clear water you can tell after a glance through the face mask. Of course, if you are opposed to getting wet, you can row out in the dinghy, and sight the anchor through a glass-bottom bucket.

If you learn to dive with a face mask you can do a lot more than merely inspect the lay of an anchor. Shallow diving isn't difficult. Your problem at first will be getting down to the bottom. Swimming down furiously, you'll have used up all the air in your lungs when you get to the bottom and will have to come up again for another breath. That at least is what you'll think. Actually the little voice that tells you to turn around is wrong. It figures on your using more air for coming up, while most people pop back up like corks. Try it. You can also give up smoking. If you have smoked heavily, cigarettes especially, you'll find your breath lasting twice as long a few days after you've given up the habit.

Even if you won't quit smoking, you can stretch your diving time by a diver's trick called hyperventilation. The pearl divers in the Pacific have practiced it for centuries. Just before going down they take long, deep breaths for perhaps two minutes. That is said to store extra oxygen in the blood. The explanation may be all wrong, but the technique works. Only one warning: some people, even perfectly healthy ones, pass out while hyperventilating. Have someone stand by ready to catch you. Single-handers lie down.

You can make reaching the bottom easier by counteracting the buoyancy of a wet suit, if you wear one. Don't improvise, though; use only the standard skin diver's belt that has a quick-release buckle. Try the weights at some spot where you can't get into trouble, and ballast yourself so that you'll still float to the surface without swimming.

Without a suit don't wear a weight belt. For work around the boat you can try another diver's trick, a disposable weight. Let the weight—your sounding lead, for instance—carry you down, doing your work; then ditch the weight. A thin line, such as your sounding line, lets you retrieve the weight.

Don't use too heavy a weight. A few feet down, your ears will hurt, and you'll want to stop at that level. The pain is caused by unequal pressure on the two sides of your eardrums; blow some air into the mask to increase the inside pressure, and the pain will stop. With the mask I use, I pinch my nose and blow air directly into the ears. If you can't clear your ears—because of a cold or plugged sinuses—don't risk ear damage—come up and let someone else dive.

A little diving lets you retrieve gear dropped overboard. But its real payoff comes in anchor work. You can drag an anchor from a hard spot to a sandy one and set it by hand. If there's no sand nearby, you can wedge the anchor firmly in a cleft in the bottom rock. If you use chain—highly recommended in coral waters—you can loop it or shackle it to a coral head. Then, of course, you'll have to go down again when you want to leave. But you may have to anyway: Anchors sometimes find their own cracks in rocks, foul old moorings, or lasso a coral knob all by themselves.

Experts use flippers to get to the bottom quickly. The real purpose

29. Skin diving is useful around a boat.

of swim fins is for distance swimming; they're not needed for work around the boat. And you'll need some practice before fins help you; at first they'll tire leg muscles you never knew you had, and may even start painful cramps—just what you don't need in the water.

If you want to try flippers, let an expert show you the proper technique. If you can't find a teacher, imagine yourself on a bike, and pedal. That's not an elegant stroke, nor the most efficient, but it'll get you there. A teacher will also show you a quick way for getting down. You porpoise out of the water, then jackknife, and let the momentum carry you down.

Fins are habit-forming. So, by the way, are face masks. I feel naked in a pool swimming without a mask, though I have been known to forget about trunks. People who have used fins for some time forget how to swim without them. Once hooked on the habit, you may be in trouble if you lose a fin. So, if you buy fins, buy the kind that float. Flippers should fit snugly but comfortably, and have full heels rather than straps. The rubber heels raise fewer blisters and are some protection for your own heels.

Don't bother with a knife. It won't scare sea monsters but may cut your own skin. By the way, underwater cuts are surprisingly painless. Often the first sign that you have been hurt is a blob of blood in the water. At the merest trace of blood, get out and get everyone else out too. You may not see a shark in several weeks of cruising, but blood—from man or fish—calls them to dinner.

Yachting, fortunately, isn't all work. The same face mask and snorkel that are so useful around the boat also help you and all hands in play by opening the underwater world. Seeing only the surface sights in the Florida Keys or the Islands is like going to Switzerland without looking at the Alps.

You can let the scenery drift by under you as a gentle current carries you over the bottom; or, almost motionless, you can study the variety of life around a single coral stack. The colors will range from garish to pastel. Mounds of brain coral, forests of elkhorn, patches of leaf coral await you. Seafans, purple and yellow, will wave you a welcome.

You'll see little fishes that look carelessly torn out of black tissue paper, blue-and-yellow-striped grunts, yellow-and-black-banded sergeant majors, yellow fishes dipped head first in bright blue paint, seemingly four-eyed butterfly fish, young blue tangs that are golden,

Skin Diving for Boat Work 75

electric-blue neon gobies, and—if you are lucky—a jewel box, its polka dots sparkling as if lit from the inside.

An angelfish glides by with a heavy list, parrot fish graze on the rocks, and a well-camouflaged loose-lipped grouper rests on the bottom. A pink squirrel fish with a trollop's black eye makeup pretends to ignore you, and a school of almost transparent spade fish practices close-order drill.

The red-and-white flowers that grow on the bottom are really feather worms and vanish when disturbed by your shadow. Sea urchins lazily wave their long black spines, a red starfish plays dead, and a velvet-upholstered sea cucumber inches along the bottom. A dark, rubbery loggerhead sponge is unpaid landlord to a horde of tiny shrimp whose chirping fills your ears as soon as you submerge.

Contrary to the impression you get on television, the underwater world is not crawling with sea monsters and enemy agents, all bent on doing you in. Your worst enemy is the sea urchin. There are stingers and biters also just below the sand, so wear thick-soled sneakers or don't put your feet down. Stings and bites also wait in the niches of the coral wall, and the fire coral, which disguises itself in three very different forms and isn't really a coral, gives painful burns.

So don't touch the display, unless you wear heavy rubber gloves.

Enjoy the spectacle, but catch only what you need, take few souvenirs, and leave nothing behind but your air bubbles.

PART TWO / NAVIGATION

8 Tools for Pilotage and Navigation

We all think we know the difference between pilotage and navigation. But try to give a definition of pilotage, and some nasty sea lawyer will make a monkey out of you.

Use shallow water in the definition, and he'll invite you to show your methods for piloting on the Bahama Banks, where in two to three fathoms of water you can be out of sight of land and without lighthouses or buoys for fifty miles or more. Use the term "out of sight of land" in a definition of navigation, and he'll trip you again. He'll put you in the Erie Canal in fog, fog so tarnal thick you couldn't spy the land. Then you hear a dog bark on shore, and change course. That is navigation?

Pilotage or navigation, their purpose is to get your little ship from the place you've been to the place you want to be—or at least some other pleasant place—keeping water under her keel all the time.

From basic pilotage—learned from a book or a course you've taken—you know about the three L's of pilotage: Lead, Log, and Lookout. Perhaps we can add a little to that.

Whoever made the phrase "swinging the lead" mean to loaf, had never swung a lead. It's stinking hard work, skilled work, right under the eyes of the mate, while the old man anxiously waits for results. The deep-sea lead ("deep-sea" pronounced to rhyme with "gypsy") weighs anywhere between thirty and one hundred pounds. You have to heave it far enough ahead so that it has time to sink to the bottom before the moving ship brings the line up and down. Much too hard for yachtsmen. We use 7–14 pound leads to measure the depth of water in an anchorage, perhaps as a shot line in skin diving, or as a drag indicator. On the rare occasions when you use the lead as a navigational tool, you might as well slow down, stop the engines, or heave to. For normal navigation the echo depth finder has taken over.

To feel your way into a sandy cove, there is a simpler tool: the sounding pole. A bamboo pole, perhaps twelve feet long, is popular. You can make your work easier by drilling a hole in the business end of the pole, filling the cavity with shot, and plugging the hole. That'll make the pole seek the bottom. Then mark the depth in feet by wrapping the pole with tape. If you draw four feet, make the first wrap at four feet. A pole is not only easier to use than the lead, it also saves the sing-song between foredeck and bridge; the skipper at the wheel can read the depth while someone in the bows works the pole. If you don't find it convenient to carry this bamboo pole, which on a sailboat can hang from a shroud when not in use, you can mark your boat hook to make it into a sounding pole.

Log, as a navigational tool, means as you know a device to measure speed, not the book that records your trips. The old chip log, dear to all writers on nautical lore, is a bit obsolete. The most interesting part of the device is that it has given us the worldwide measure of speed through the water, one knot meaning one nautical mile per hour. To get to this measure the knots in the chip log line were spaced 47 feet 3 inches apart, with five smaller knots in between for two-tenths of a knot. The number of knots that ran out while the sandglass emptied—28 seconds—gave directly the speed of the vessel in knots. Why $47\frac{1}{4}$ feet (or similar length), why 28 seconds? Why $437\frac{1}{2}$ grains to the ounce avoirdupois?

The taffrail log—a spinner towed astern that drives a counter and measures the distance run through the water—was a great improvement and is still a useful tool for the small-boat sailor on a long overwater hop. It has a few drawbacks. It sometimes catches floating weed and then stops or slows down enough to make its reading useless. To guard against being misled by such false readings, you can mount the register right in sight of the helmsman, where supposedly he'd notice when it acts up. Have him read the register every half hour, on the dot, and write the figure read in the margin of the chart. When the reading suddenly drops, he'll notice, and clear the weed from the spinner. You can later allow for the underrecorded distance by using an estimated half-hour run.

Tools for Pilotage and Navigation 79

When a sailboat gets becalmed, the spinner she tows sinks to the bottom where it may anchor the boat. When she starts sailing again, the line may part. To save the register, the most expensive part of the rig, secure it with a lashing much heavier than the log line. And, of course, carry a spare spinner, line, sinker, and hook.

Sharks are supposed to be attracted to the whirligig, and some skippers paint theirs black, dull black. I've towed one over hundreds of miles—it lets a single-hander get some sleep without losing track of his dead reckoning—in waters where sharks must have lurked (where don't they?), but never lost a spinner that way.

But once I almost lost my boat to the log line. I gently ran aground under power; the line wrapped itself around the propeller and stopped the engine. Before I could throw out an anchor, a wicked surf bore us ashore.

Even with all these shortcomings a patent log is a very useful gadget, especially on a sailboat. It lets you calibrate your senses for speed. After you have measured runs at a few typical speeds on different points of sailing, you can guess your speed to a few tenths of a knot from the feel of the tiller, the angle of heel, the gurgling at the bow, and the fuss she makes in the water.

Under power, engine revolutions, adjusted for sea conditions, give a good indication of a boat's speed, as long as her bottom is clean. Ideally rpm's times propeller pitch (converted to feet) gives the boat's advance through the water in one minute (in feet), from which you can calculate speed or distance run. But there is always slip.

On a freighter, over breakfast one morning, the chief engineer announced that, as far as his department was concerned, we had arrived at New York. "And where are you fellows?" he asked with a stern look at the watch-keeping officers who placed her only three-fourths across the Atlantic.

Knowing the percentage of slip under various conditions of sea and foulness of bottom, you can estimate your speed very accurately. Even without tachometer or revolution counter, you can gauge it pretty well by throttle setting.

An interisland freightboat skipper let me in on his personal speed-indicator secret. He opened the throttle one notch above its cruising setting. Soon you could feel the whole vessel vibrating. "See, one notch back from that, we make exactly nine knots."

"What about bad weather?"

"In bad weather, one notch past. The vibration stops and we still make our nine knots."

Then there are the magic wands you hold over the side, and speedometers and odometers that show speed, or distance run, right in the cockpit. We have come a long way since the chip and the sandglass. But a knot is still a nautical mile per hour, and when your chrome-plated gadget reads in statute miles, you must not forget to deduct about fifteen percent to convert to nautical miles, or from miles per hour to knots.

The third "L" stands for Lookout. Most of the time the helmsman on a yacht will also be the lookout, and perhaps he'll also be the navigator. And you'll be all three. So make life easy for yourself—get a pair of binoculars. Other authors seem bashful about recommending sizes. I'm not. I find glasses of more than 7-power difficult to hold still on a moving boat. So I'd get 7× glasses.

The second number on binoculars indicates the diameter of the far lenses in millimeters. Never mind about millimeters, but the greater the number, the better you'll see at night. A 35mm glass will show no more than you can see without glasses. A 50mm glass will bring out unlighted buoys and daymarks you can't see with the naked eye. Even if you don't plan to run at night, ever, someday you may come in late; then you'll be glad you got 7×50's. All good glasses now are coated to cut down reflections and improve night vision. You'll see that coating as a colored film when you look at the lenses sideways.

You have a choice of center-focus or individual-focus binoculars. The word focus is misleading: you don't have to focus for distance, unless you want to watch the girl on the boat in the next slip. You focus to adjust for your own eyes. In center-focus glasses you adjust until the image for the left eye is sharpest for you, then you adjust the right eyepiece to make up for any difference in power between your two eyes.

In individual-focus glasses you adjust each eyepiece separately. If you always sail alone, it doesn't matter much whether you get CF or IF binoculars. But if your crew and guests occasionally use the glasses, by all means get the individually focused kind. Shipboard etiquette requires that you reset the glasses to how you found them. But only you can adjust CF glasses for the captain's setting. On individually focused glasses resetting is simple: You just have to remember the original setting—and yours, so you can adjust them quickly the next time.

When I want to look through my glasses I want them right away. So I put triangular bits of tape where they adjust for me. Even if some clown has screwed them all up, I can set them for myself in seconds, even in the dark.

Individual-focus glasses, having no sliding tubes, also happen to keep spray out of the works. They are simpler to make, and so are usually less expensive than center-focus glasses of the same quality and make.

So I strongly recommend 7×50 IF's. Make sure everyone who uses

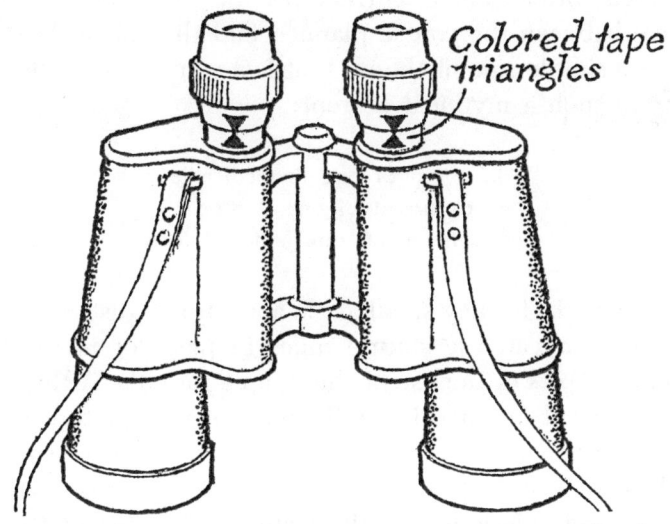

30. *Binoculars of the individual focus type are quickly reset by aligning tape markers. One can do it by touch in the dark.*

them also uses the neck strap. Even so, you may lose a pair overboard someday. That's why I'd get Japanese glasses. A good pair will cost about thirty dollars. A few small bubbles in the lenses don't matter, but make sure that looking through them is comfortable. One pair I once tried, after a few minutes made my eyes feel as if they wanted to come out of their sockets, sideways.

Back to lookouts, including yourself. Naturally a lookout looks forward; if he has been drilled in the Rules of the Road, he concentrates his watchfulness in the right quadrant where a vessel approaching from starboard has the right of way over his own vessel. Of course he also looks forward to port. But that is not enough. An overtaking craft has to keep clear of you. But if some fast big craft barrels down on you from astern, unseen and unheard over the noise of your own power plant, you might unthinkingly put the wheel hard over when you first become aware of her, and get right in the way. Even escaping that, you'd like to have taken evasive action before her wake hits you. How can you, if you never look aft and don't know what's on your tail?

There is another reason for the helmsman to look aft frequently. Wind, current, compass deviation, and helmsman's error all combine to set you off course. The compass gives no indication of these effects, often called "current" as the universal alibi for any difference between the course planned and the course made good.

Here is a simple rule of thumb that lets you evaluate the amount of set from such a mythical current:

**In a run of one nautical mile
a current of one degree
will set you off one hundred feet.**

This rule works for any small angle and for any distance. Without much error you can use statute miles in place of nautical miles. Here are examples of the use of this simple formula. A three-degree error, in a run of one nautical mile, will set you off three hundred feet. Or, on a five-mile run, a one-degree error will set you off five hundred feet.

That last example is just to illustrate the working of the rule; I know that yachts with their usual compasses can hardly be steered to one degree close.

This rule also lets you estimate how accurately you'll have to navigate. On a run from sea buoy to sea buoy along shore in deep water for ten miles, a three-degree error will probably not get you into trouble in clear weather. You'll be three thousand feet, about half a mile, from the buoy at the end of the run; but you'll see the buoy in ample time to correct your course.

On the other hand, if you are starting in the middle of a two-hundred-foot-wide dredged channel, the same three-degree error will have you on the spoil bank in one-third of a mile. That's probably the cause of many of the groundings of shallow-draft pleasure boats in the Inland Waterway, where tugs with much deeper draft don't even stir up the mud.

How does the tugboat skipper do it? He knows that merely pointing the bow toward the next marker, or steering by compass, isn't enough. He looks over the stern. If the last marker he passed stays dead astern while he aims for the next one, he knows he'll stay in the channel. If the mark astern drifts off to one side, he knows he's being set toward the bank. If he can, the skipper will try to line up the mark astern with some object ashore, a tree perhaps, to give him

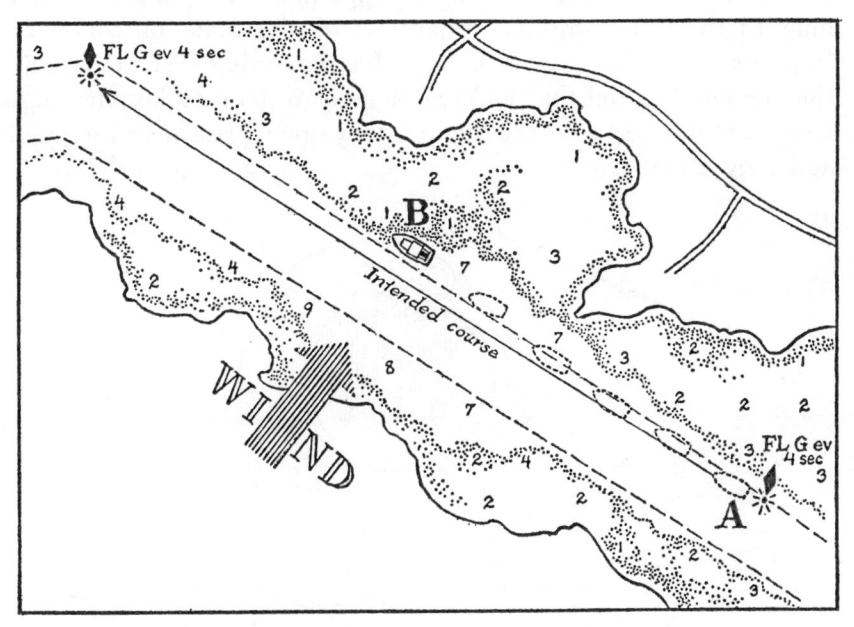

31. *Leeway—the boat that started from "A," although steering correct course, and pointing straight at the next marker, will run aground at "B".*

a range astern. As long as marker and tree stay in line, he is on course; when the range opens, he'll correct to bring the marker and tree again into transit. That method is equally useful when leaving port for a long dash across a sound or across a lake. Teach it to your helmsman-lookout, and you'll make better landfalls.

We have strayed from basic tools of navigation and pilotage. Some of them need little discussion. Obviously you'll need pencils; equally obviously the hexagonal kind doesn't roll off the chart table as easily as the round kind. Don't hesitate to do your chart work on the chart. It's printed on paper meant to be written and drawn on with soft pencil—HB or No. 2—and to be erased later. An art eraser works well. If around your home port the chart gets a bit smeared after a season, all the better; you should get an up-to-date chart next year anyway.

For measuring distances, a piece of paper, transparent or other, will do. Small-craft charts have scales printed on them to which you can transfer your marks made at the edge of your paper. On *all* charts one minute of latitude (on left and right margins, unless the chart is tilted with north not being uppermost) equals one nautical mile (1.15 statute miles), regardless of the scale of the chart. Dividers are perhaps more elegant for measuring distances. I like the one-hand model that looks as though Admiral Columbus might have used it; press near the top and they open, press near the points and they close.

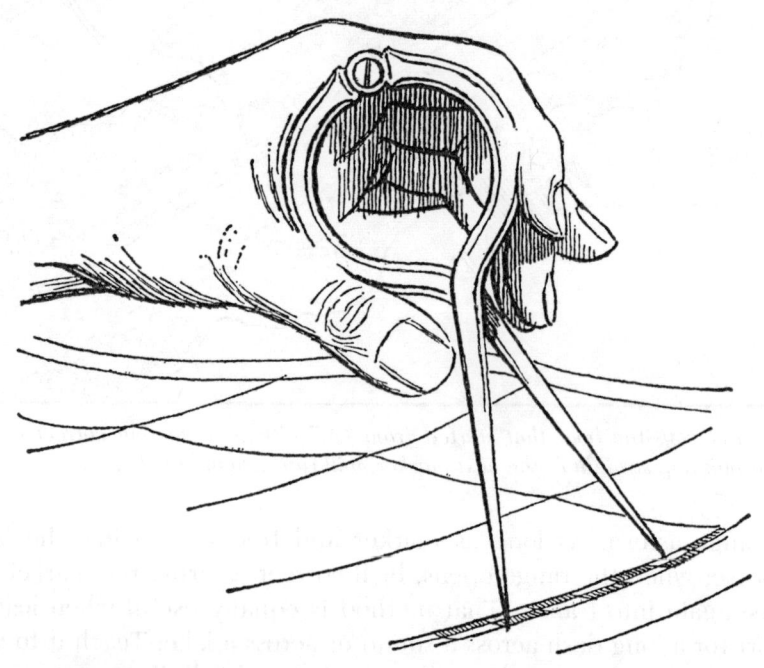

32. *Single-handed dividers.*

I also prefer dividers to calculators in speed problems. The trick is simply to open the dividers to some convenient setting. Say you steam at twelve knots. How long will it take to cover seven nautical miles? I'd open the dividers to two miles, the distance made good in ten minutes (about two inches on 1:80,000-scale charts), and step off the dividers along the course, counting ten, twenty, thirty, and coming to thirty-five minutes.

Next, one needs some way for picking up a compass course from the chart. Some *Coast Pilots* and lake and river charts give courses to follow. Most charts don't. And sometimes at the meeting of two channels you'll encounter too many buoys. Which ones lead to where you want to go? The chart will tell.

When I first came to the Bahamas native skippers in the Out Islands were always surprised how I'd found their harbor. "Who gave you the course?" An old man who used to go to sea would offer to give me the course to the next destination. He and other skippers had memorized the courses for everywhere. If they ever had to go to a strange place, they'd go ashore and from some second cousin by marriage get the next course.

About the same time, *Sailing Directions for the West Indies* dropped the warning to ship masters not to follow native craft into harbor. These craft, so earlier editions stated, were likely to mislead the unwary skipper and plunder his wreck as soon as she'd piled up on the hidden reef.

Even where the wreckers have found other steady sources of revenue, don't navigate by proxy. It's so easy to get your own course from the compass roses printed on your charts. If your compass has been adjusted—we'll talk about that later—you can use the inner rose on the chart without any arithmetic.

All you need is some mechanical device to transfer a line (say from one buoy to the next one) to the nearest compass rose on the chart. Here you can let yourself go. If you have a proper chart table you can use parallel rules, sliding rules, a hexagonal pencil, a pair of triangles, any of several types of course protractors (with or without movable arm), and if you have room for it, a drafting-machine-type plotter.

For on-the-lap navigation as practiced in the cockpit of a sailboat, a courser—a piece of plastic with parallel lines drawn on it—is about as simple and reliable as you can get. You can improvise this gadget in a few minutes on a sheet of tracing paper.

Whatever gadget you use to transfer courses (and plot bearings), try not to become too attached to it. Or secure it firmly. I once dropped my favorite, an English number called Douglas, behind

86   NAVIGATION

the ceiling and into the bilge where I couldn't retrieve it without removing a whole mess of iron ballast. Yes, you're right: I removed the ballast and restowed it . . . all to get back a square 360-degree protractor that had cost me all of fifty cents.

For cockpit and by-the-wheel navigation I like a protractor that lines up with the meridians of the chart. Then I convert this true course into a magnetic one by laying a straightedge from the outer rose to the center and then reading the course on the inner rose, in degrees. If you prefer to steer by points and quarter-points, you'll find those by the same method on the innermost compass rose on the chart.

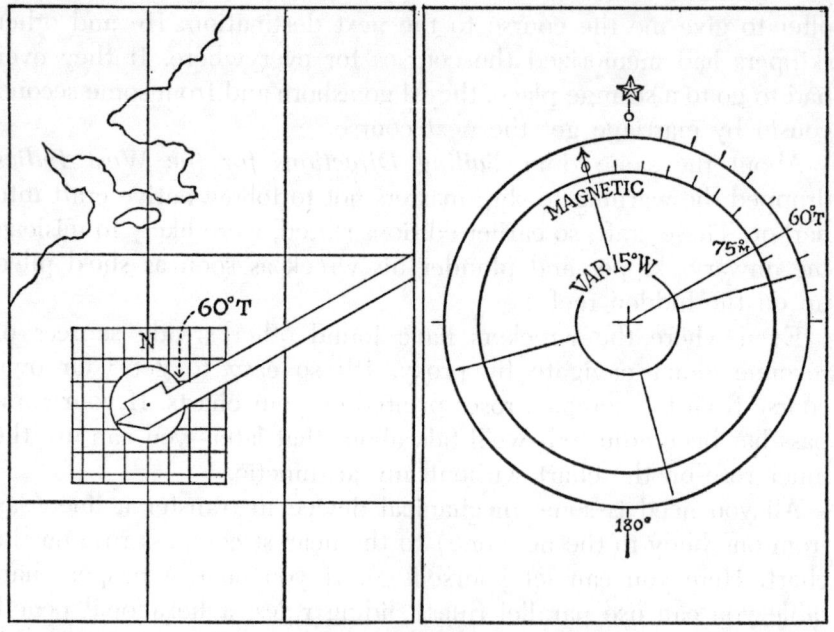

33. *Finding magnetic course—proceed in two steps: ONE: Move arm of protractor over intended course, say from one buoy to the next; align protractor grid with grid of chart, then read off the TRUE course on scale of protractor (e.g. 60°T.). TWO: Draw a line from True course (e.g. 60°) on outer scale of nearest compass rose on chart toward its center; read off MAGNETIC course on inner compass rose (e.g. 75°M.).*

After chart weights have dropped a few times on your bare toes, or made dents in your deck sole, you'll consider replacing them by shock cord over the chart table to hold the chart flat and more or less in place.

There is one navigation tool I would like to carry, but I've not found the right one yet. Perhaps one is made, but I've not come across it. The gadget I want is a rangefinder. How often have we all steered wide around a headland, fighting current and popple, when we could have shortened the misery by knowing exactly how far off we were? How many times haven't we bucked a midstream current not trusting our own distance estimate enough to run close to shore? How often does a sailboat go off the winning tack too soon rather than stand on, with nothing but the skipper's eyes to guide her around some hidden hazard?

I know how to take a vertical sextant angle on an object of known height, I know how to calculate the height of tide at any time, and I can find Tables 9 and 22 in Bowditch as well as the next guy. But often I don't know which hill to measure. I also know how refraction makes all angles near the horizon extremely doubtful. And it's far too much trouble all around. And who'd carry a sextant just for distance finding? So please design me a rangefinder, or let me know if you have found one that's reliable and that every small craft skipper can afford.

Although I like to do most of my chart work right on the chart, I always keep a clipboard with a spray-proof cover handy. On that I scribble fuel aboard, and taken on; time of departure, of starting and stopping engine (to keep oil changes and other maintenance chores scientific), of sail or wind changes; readings of the log, estimates of speed, and other figures that often don't belong on the chart but are soon forgotten unless one jots them down somewhere.

Unless I ran a very hungry ship, I wouldn't want to be without a hand bearing-compass. It lets you take bearings accurate to one degree, all around the horizon, by day and by night, something that most yacht compasses won't do. Squinting over the steering compass is all right for deciding whether to take this channel or that. But on most yachts the main compass won't let you take bearings in all directions. How about yours? Can you take a bearing dead astern on the last marker to check your leeway? Can you take a bearing on a star with your compass? Can you without leaving the wheel tell when you are exactly abeam of a lighthouse?

I use my bearing compass not just for taking bearings, but for adjusting the main compass, and seeing that it's still in adjustment. But that belongs in another chapter.

9 Lines of Position

Whether you learned navigation by watching an expert, from a book, or in a course of lectures, you have been told—more than once, no doubt—to keep a plot, and know your position at all times.

This teaching takes with some skippers. They'd rather plot courses than fish or watch the seagulls. I saw a friend of mine making three entries in his log between the gas dock and his mooring, half a mile distant and in plain sight; but then he was a retired rear admiral.

More likely you have fallen into the opposite extreme, doing a minimum of figure and chart work, and keeping what little you do in your head rather than on the chart. That's bad too. Not so long as everything goes smoothly. But when things go wrong, you'll be in a pickle. What if sudden fog or rain wipes out all visible marks? How can you take a guest who cuts his jugular on a beer can to the nearest doctor, when you don't know what harbor is nearest?

The real distress comes when you, the navigator, get knocked out. You see your feeble-minded helmsman about to jibe. You rush to the cockpit. Too late; the boom catches you, and you are mackereled on deck. If you have carried all the figures in your head; right now your head is no help in getting the boat in. You don't let idiots steer, you say. You don't rush on deck. You don't get clobbered by jibing booms, because you have a sensible, boomless cruiser. But are you immune to food poisoning, the vapors, and all other disabling ills?

Just for self-preservation, I'd keep some sort of running plot and teach my lady, my kids, fishing pal, or whoever goes out with me often, the art of fixing position. I'd call it an art. That'll raise their hackles and they'll be out to show *you* how simple it really is.

I'd teach them the navigators' code, the four-figure way of writing time, the three figures for course in degrees, and

    C for Course
    D for Distance
    S for Speed
    T for True
    M for Magnetic

Then I'd show them the compass roses on the chart, the outer one always giving true directions, the inner one magnetic ones, and I'd show them how to convert one into the other. I'd show them how to measure distance, and here I'd probably get involved in explaining the difference between nautical and statute miles.

You could explain the difference between dead reckoning (DR), estimated position (EP), and fix (FIX).

Then, in a distress, the pupil will be ready to report your position to the Coast Guard. Perhaps you'll give them a drill in that.

The simplest way is reporting your dead reckoning position. It can be as simple as: "We are on our way from Homeport to Picnic Harbor, three-quarters of an hour out, cruising at twelve knots." When the course has not been a direct one, the report will be a bit more complicated. So you'll have to explain how, after you've reached the first buoy, or other mark, your first reckoning is finished, and how a new one starts at the buoy.

That automatically teaches them another good way to report your position: "About two miles SE of Nasty Shoal buoy." Here you'll have to explain about reciprocal bearings. I wouldn't use that frightening word. Anyone will understand that when Nasty Shoal buoy bears west, distant one mile, you are one mile east of it, and so on around the compass. So rather than letting my students add or subtract 180 degrees, I'd have them draw a straight line through the center of the nearest compass rose and get the right bearing that way.

There is, of course, a more elegant method for fixing position—by the grid on the chart. That one I'd teach only to my honor students. I'd drill into them that the horizontal lines represent latitude, the vertical lines longitude. That's on standard charts that have north uppermost. Some inland charts are tilted to save space, and so the pupil has to read east-west lines for parallels of latitude, north-south lines for meridians of longitude. You'll have to teach the purely arbitrary convention of always naming latitude first. It doesn't too much matter whether the pupil forgets the "north" after the latitude, the "west" after the longitude. There'll seldom be the slightest doubt. What is important is that the pupil remember that where these letters are used—everywhere in the Northern Hemisphere and west of Greenwich—the figures run opposite to writing: latitude upward, longitude toward the left. Failure to make this second nature is the cause of uncountable mistakes in reporting and plotting co-ordinates.

Here would be a good place to repeat the lesson that distance is measured in minutes of latitude (not longitude); that is on the left and right margins of a chart that has north on top; that one minute of latitude equals one nautical mile, and that one knot means a speed of one nautical mile per hour (about 1.15 or 1⅐ statute miles per hour).

For yourself, you'll use latitude and longitude mainly for correcting charts, and plotting hurricanes. Hurricane co-ordinates, by the way, are not given in degrees and minutes, but rather in degrees and tenths of a degree. Don't you think the weather bureau is doing pretty well to locate the center of a moving, distorted spiral to the nearest six minutes of latitude (six miles) and longitude?

But someday you may hear a MAYDAY, close enough to help, if only you can translate the co-ordinates into the more familiar "so far in such direction from what's-its-name light."

There is yet one more way to locate yourself, but it hurts some sailors' ears so much that I wouldn't mention it, except as a horrible example of lubberliness. You'd never think of it, but your lady may report for you while you are unconscious, "Right on the 'I' in Long Island Sound."

Back comes the Coast Guard: "On what chart? Over."

"Oh, 1212. Over."

Ignoring the last horrible method, we then have position by DR, from the bearing of a charted object, and by latitude and longitude. Have you ever thought of all these as lines of position? If you have, you have just proved yourself to be an expert navigator.

Let others think of DR, EPs, fixes, bearings, cross bearings, three-point bearings, bow-and-beam bearings, danger bearings, vertical danger angles . . . to you they are all lines of position. The fellows who spout all those other terms may not even know what a position line is. If they press you for a definition, try this: Imaginary lines in nature, or lines drawn on a chart along which your vessel very likely is, was, or will be.

They still don't know. Then give them an example. You pass a spot where Fumble Shoal buoy and Moot Point light line up. Obviously at that moment you crossed a line (in nature) that connects the two. If you can find them on a chart, you can draw a line through the point and the buoy and know you have just been on the outboard extension of that line, the line of position. How simple can things be?

Lines of Position 91

If you decided to steer toward Fumble Shoal buoy, keeping it covering Moot Point, you obviously are somewhere on the line just drawn on the chart. Unless you can somehow measure your distance from the light or the buoy, you know you are on that line, but not how far from the buoy.

While running toward the buoy (still keeping it in line with the

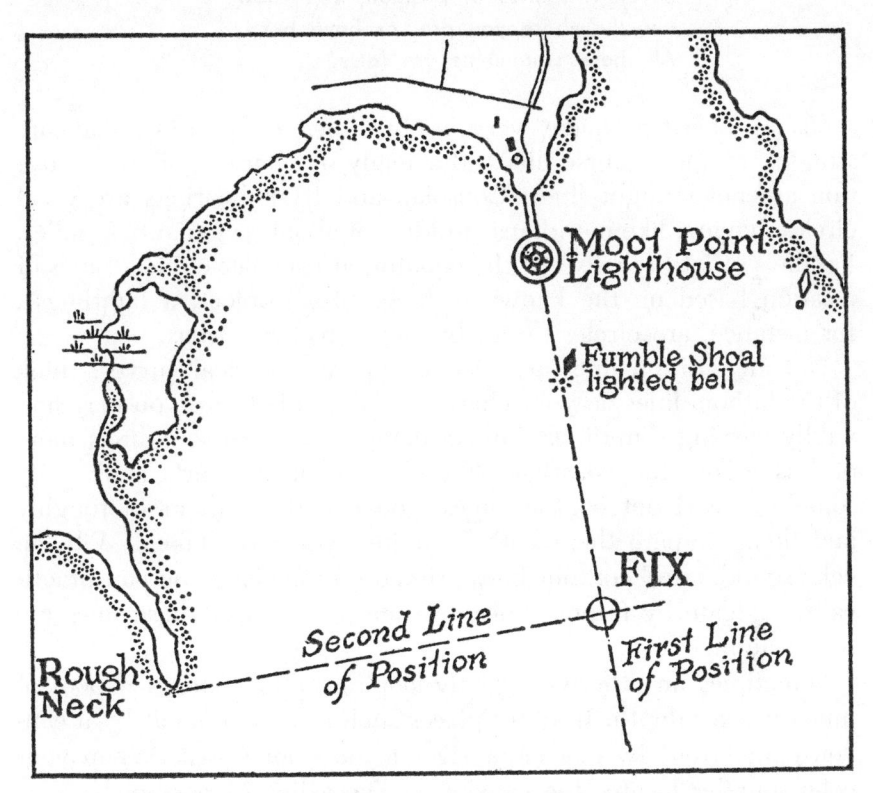

34. *Lines of position—* When lighthouse and bell line up for you, your boat must be somewhere on the first line of position. When steaming for the buoy keeping buoy and light in line, you bring Rough Neck abeam—that is at right angles to your course—and you are on the second line of position. Being on both lines at once, you must be at their intersection, the point marked FIX.

point) you get to a spot where Rough Neck is exactly abeam. Now you can lay down on your chart another line of position, this one at right angles to the first. Being on both lines of position (in nature) at once, you are where the two lines cross on the chart. You've got a fix.

From that example your friend may draw the following conclusions:

> Lines of position are bearings
> Lines of position are straight lines
> One line of position is not much use, but
> Given two lines of position, you know
> exactly where you are, or have been.
> All these statements are *false*.

Visual bearings make very useful lines of position and are straight, or short-course, lines. But many other useful lines of position are not straight lines. Consolan and RDF bearings are great circles, having, like meridians, a radius of about 3440 nautical miles. Parallels of latitude, except the equator, are smaller circles. Lines of position based on the known distance of an object, a lighthouse, for instance, are circles; loran bearings are hyperbolas.

Not all position lines are nice smooth geometrical curves; think of the fathom lines on your chart. On uneven bottoms you may find wildly varying soundings, but on many shores the soundings more or less follow the coastline. Even where older charts show only soundings and not contour lines, you can draw them in roughly and then compare them with soundings you have taken. With an echo sounder and contour lines printed on the chart you can practically navigate by fathom lines on some coasts. But these lines are not straight.

Sometimes an otherwise gently sloping bottom shows a pool of much greater depth. In other places such a bottom is cut by a canyon gouged out by glacier or river in days long past. When your echo sounder locates the canyon, you've a line of position.

That contradicts the statement that one position line is of little use. The canyon shows you the way home; you simply follow it toward shoaling depth. The deep pool—an oval or perhaps dumbbell-shaped line of position—gives you a fix.

Do you want a list of other odd but useful position lines? How about the castaway who sees birds that he knows always roost on land flying in a certain direction in the evening. Or, more practical for most of us, a jet plane, which habitually roosts on land; after you have steered various courses during a day's fishing out of sight of land, it might show you the way to the airport. In the Islands an up-to-date airline schedule can be as useful as tide tables and light lists. In the Bahamas the clear water lets you see the bottom, and you'll find lines of position much used by native skippers. Here's an example: Over the bank headed east for Nassau, aiming for Northwest Channel, you'll find the bottom generally grassy north of the proper course, while south of it it's bare and brown. Handy?

The oddest single line of position I've come across was in British Columbia during World War II. I was crew on a sailboat. Somewhere at the mouth of Burrard Inlet the wind dropped and we were carried by the tide toward Vancouver. The chart showed no hazards to navigation west of Lion's Gate Bridge. It showed, however, a purple circle prohibiting navigation within one mile of the "secret" gun emplacement in Stanley Park. Although we had an engine, we weren't supposed to have any gasoline for pleasure boating. So we drifted, and drifted. Suddenly a shell swooshed into the water close enough to spatter the chart. The skipper pointed to the purple circle. "At least we know exactly where we are," he said, and started the engine.

Don't wait for fire from a shore battery, a submarine canyon, a jet plane, or a flight of birds to give you position lines. Look for them all the time. In two directions a single line of position is most useful: parallel to your course, and at right angles (more or less) to it.

> Directly ahead or astern, or parallel to your
> course, a line of position shows that you are
> on course, or how far off it, and in what direction.
> On either beam a line of position shows how far
> you have come along your course.

To illustrate: If you are sailing south along the New Jersey coast, a few soundings will reassure you that you are keeping the proper distance from the shore; a positively identified landmark abeam will give you the distance made good along your track.

Looking for, and using all lines of position you can find you'll be navigating by the total situation, taking advantage of all the tools of the pilot, not just the compass, depth-finder, or what-have-you. It's one of the things that separate the savvy skipper from the basic navigator.

But it's not enough. The beginner considers a line a line. Perhaps he has forgotten that in geometry a line has no width, but he acts as if it hadn't. And lines of position have widths. Sometimes they taper, form bands—straight or curving—even doughnuts. Even the hairline fathom lines have widths. The soundings may have changed since the chart survey was made, the tide is probably not at datum level right now, your depth finder's calibration could be a few feet off.

All these uncertainties spread out the width of the line of position formed by the curve of soundings. Now compare this rather slim width with that of the projected track of a hurricane. First you have the movement of the center, itself a vague point; then you have to allow for a slight shift from the forecast direction; last but certainly

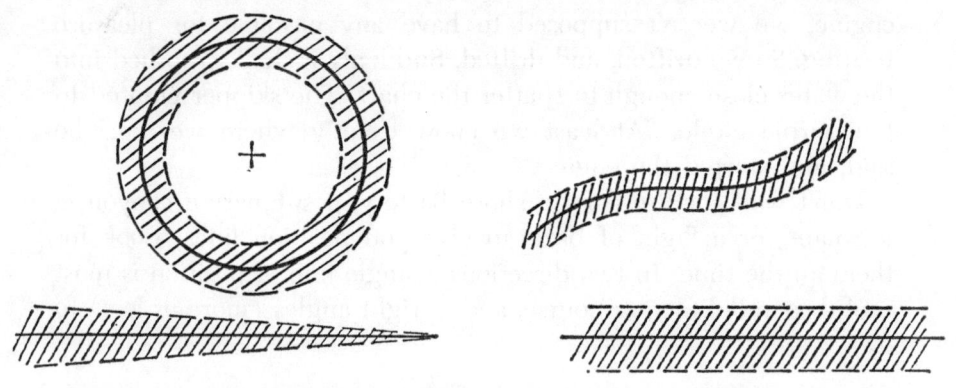

35. *Lines of Position can be straight, curved, circular. . . . The areas of uncertainty around them may be straight or curved bands, sectors, doughnuts. . . .*

not least, the area of devastating winds may extend over dozens, even hundreds, of miles. A pretty broad band to stay clear of!

Most lines of position will fall between these extremes, wider than the error of a contour line but not a couple of hundred miles wide either. Assign, at least mentally, a width—a probability of error—to every line of position you lay down on the chart.

When you think of a single line of position having width, sometimes considerable width, you won't fall into the error of fixing your little ship where two thin pencil lines cross on your chart.

You can also readily see why you have been told in basic pilotage to use lines of position that intersect more or less at right angles, and to mistrust small-angle cuts.

You are familiar with the "cocked hat," the small triangle formed

Lines of Position

where *three* lines of position—bearings or star sights—intersect. When you are aware of the width of these lines, you won't expect your craft to be in the center of the little triangle; you won't be surprised when you find yourself *outside,* even when the lines seemed to cut nicely.

Let's look at just one more related problem, one we are all familiar with: our own dead reckoning. Suppose a sailboat tacks through

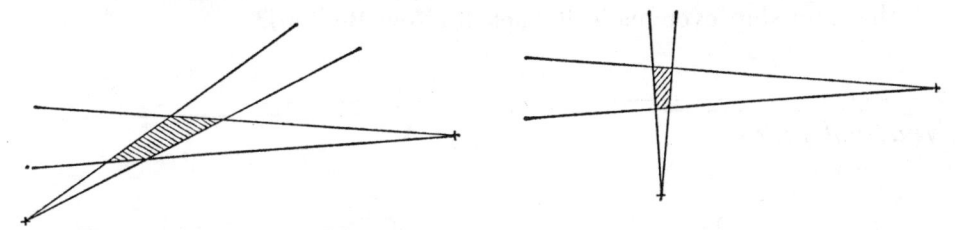

36. *The area of uncertainty at the intersection of* two *lines of position is smallest when these lines cross at 90-degree angles.*

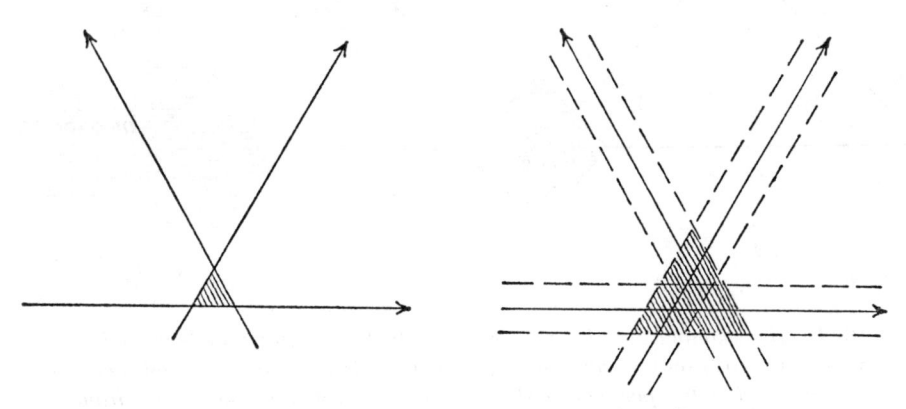

37. *The area of uncertainty at the intersection of* three *lines of position is smallest when these lines cross at 120- or 60-degree angles.*

ninety degrees and, trying to make good a course of 90° true, makes four boards at an estimated speed of five knots. She'll steer alternately 45° and 135° but may actually make good a course over the bottom 5° above or below these courses. She should in an hour cover five nautical miles, but that could easily be 10 percent more or less. A power boat fishing might make a similar track. Now let's see what happens.

At the end of the first hour she might be anywhere within the shaded area around the position marked DR 0100. Depending on where in that quadrilateral she changed course, she'll be in the DR 0200 area after two hours and so on. At the end of four hours, dead reckoning puts her fourteen nautical miles, on a course of 90° from home. Actually she could be anywhere from eleven to seventeen miles from her point of departure and have made good any course between 79° and 101°. That's after only four hours. Isn't it a marvel that any ship ever made it back to New Bedford?

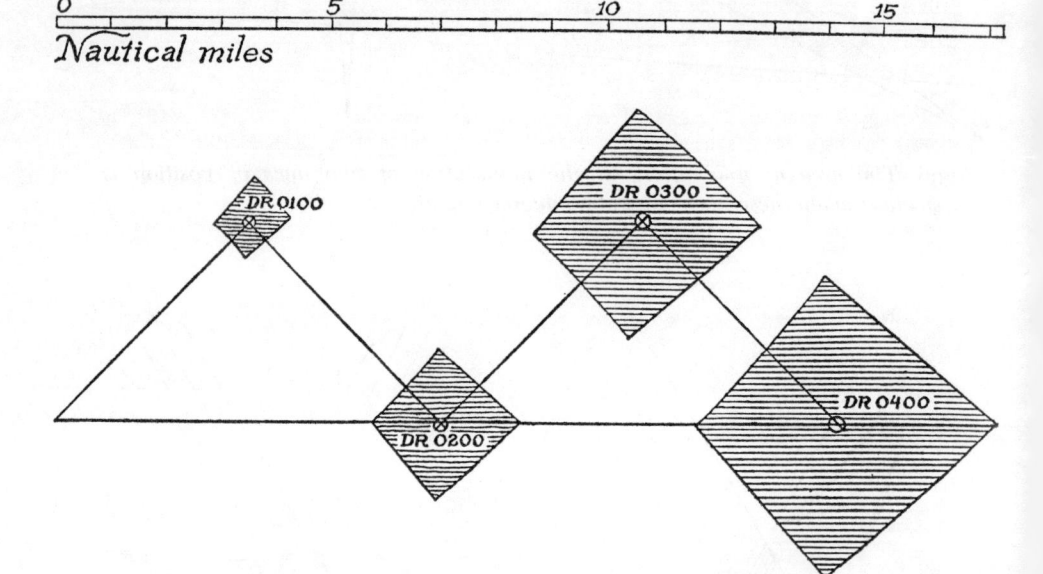

38. *Dead reckoning deteriorates rapidly with time. After four hours sailing at 5 knots (±10%) on four tacks on 45° and 135° (±5°) courses, dead reckoning puts a vessel at the position marked DR 0400, 14 nautical miles 90° from her point of departure. Actually she could be anywhere within the shaded area surrounding that position.*

Familiarity with the concept of lines of position, awareness of the usefulness of a single such line, and knowledge of the width of all such lines and of the areas of their intersection will make anyone a better pilot and navigator.

There is a bonus: If you decide to take up celestial navigation, you already know the most difficult part. All any sextant sight gives you is a line of position, as we'll see in a later chapter.

10 Fine Points of Pilotage

The beginning pilot has never heard of geographic range of visibility of lights. Then he discovers the charted range of lighthouses. If he uses them, he may stand into trouble. If he doesn't, he passes up lines of position valuable even to a skipper who has never heard of lines of position.

Later he discovers Distance of Visibility tables on the back endpaper of *Coast Pilots,* or perhaps Table 8 in Bowditch, and works them for position lines and for predicting times of landfalls. When the atmospheric refraction is not normal (that is, most of the time at some places), he is all wrong.

The tables are habit-forming. Once used to them a skipper without them may feel as if he had left his pipe at home.

All quite unnecessary: All visibility problems (How far off course will I still see the next buoy? From how far away can I hope to spot my lost dinghy? When will I make a certain light?) are one and the same problem. All can be solved without tables, in your head or on the margin of a chart.

And then there is a puzzle I hope some reader can solve for me.

The basic visibility problem is this: Given a point so many feet above water level, how far can I see before the curvature of the earth cuts my line of sight? Answer: The horizon. The question then becomes: For a given height above the water, how far away is the horizon?

The geometry of the problem is simple. Pythagoras could have solved this plane right triangle. But his solution would have been wrong; he left out the effect of refraction. Everyone has seen the apparent bending of an oar where it leaves the thin air and enters the denser medium, water. The atmosphere shows no such sudden changes of density, but as we all know it is denser at sea level than at the top of a mountain. That gradual change in densities causes slanted light rays to bend into a curve, and extends the distance to your horizon. So an object that according to Pythagoras should be a little below the horizon, will actually appear above it.

98 NAVIGATION

For example: When the lower limb of the rising sun just seems to leave the sea, the whole disk of the sun is still below the geometrical horizon.

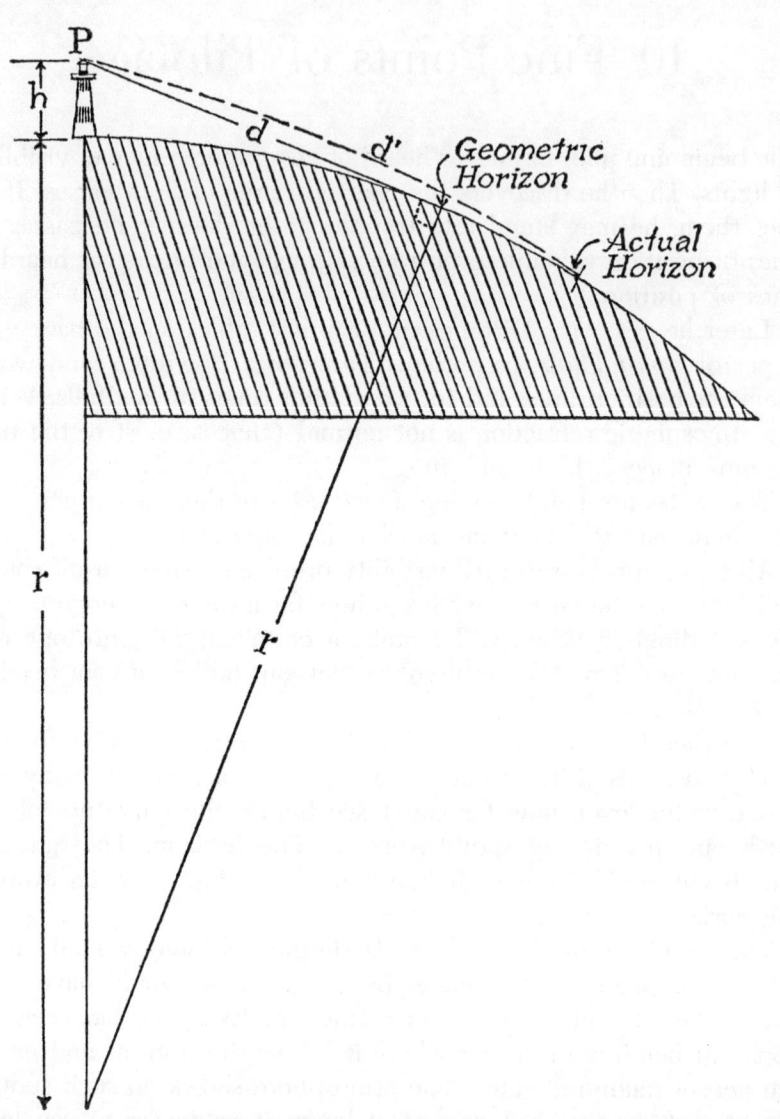

39. *Geometry of visibility problems*— *The geometrical limit of visibility (d) from a point (P) at a given height (h) above the sea, is at the horizon where light rays from P are intercepted by the curvature of the Earth, whose radius is r. But the atmosphere bends light rays and so extends the distance from P to the horizon to d'.*

Fine Points of Pilotage 99

The tables and the charted range of lights are corrected for the effect of normal refraction, that is, refraction at a certain temperature and barometric pressure, etc. The navigator who reasons, "I can't see this fifteen-mile light yet, so I'm more than fifteen miles off" could be quite wrong. Nor can he be sure that he is fifteen miles off when he first makes the light.

He has forgotten, or never learned, that ranges of lights are charted for a height of eye of fifteen feet. If he sits in the cockpit of a sailboat, or stands by the wheel of a cabin cruiser, his eyes may be four feet above the water. Common sense should tell him that he won't see as far as a lookout whose eyes are fifteen feet above the sea. For our navigator the fifteen-mile light has become a thirteen-mile light.

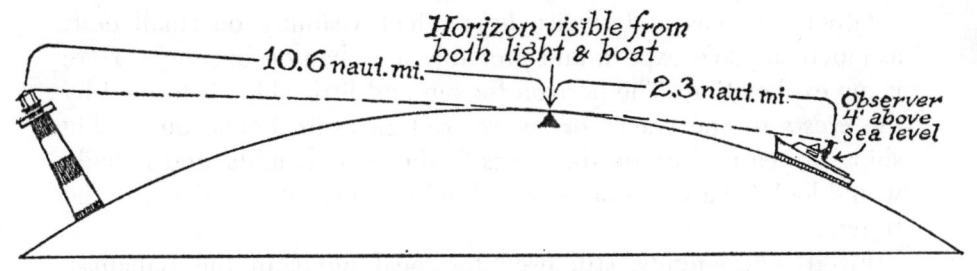

40. *Range of visbility*— *For the lighthouse keeper, 86 feet above the water, the horizon seems 10.6 nautical miles away. For the skipper of the boat, whose eyes are only four feet above the water, the horizon seems 2.3 nautical miles off. They will see each other when they are separated by less than 12.9 miles, the sum of the distances to their horizons.*

When he has learned that, he'll realize perhaps that visibility problems as they usually crop up in navigation are really a double problem. 1.: How far is my horizon for a given height of eye? 2.: How far is the horizon from an object of given height? The limit of visibility is the sum of these two distances to the horizon.

With the aid of tables the navigator now can lay down position lines for lights from whatever height he observes them. He can also work landfall predictions, and use aero beacons whose height is charted, while their range of visibility is not given on nautical charts.

But the seasoned pilot will assign a low confidence factor to all such position lines.

Lights go out of order, though rarely. Some years ago on a freighter between Panama and New York in two four-hour watches we couldn't raise Punta Maisi Light, a seventeen-miler that marks the Cuban side of the Windward Passage. Our radar, though tinkered with by an expert while we transited the Canal, had packed up again. Our captain didn't enjoy the tropical splendor of that night.

Another night, with stars shining brightly overhead, off the Rhode Island shore, I couldn't see the powerful beam of Brenton Reef Lightship although I was miles inside its range. A thin mist, quite unnoticeable in the Sound, had formed after dark.

A shower between you and a light would also blot it out.

On some nights the flashes of a light may seem all wrong, or a fixed light may seem to flash. Explanation: You see the light when you are on the crest of a wave, or on top of a swell; when you get into the trough, the light seems to go out.

Otherwise seas and swells don't affect visibility on small craft as much as you'd expect, and probably less than on big ships. Here is my explanation: The horizon for big and little ships is formed by the *crests* of the waves or swells. But pleasure boats, unlike big ships, are carried up on the crests to the same heights, and nobody would look for a light—or his lost dinghy—when he was down in the trough.

Fixed white lights, still used for local lights in the Bahamas, have misled many a navigator. How is a stranger to tell the light at the harbor entrance from the one on the commissioner's porch?

Sometimes the pilot faces another question: "Is that a light on shore just breaking the horizon, or the masthead light of a boat much closer at hand?" The trick for telling them apart is called bobbing a light. When you first see the light, you lower your height of eye. If you are standing, bend your knees, and a light on the horizon will disappear; a nearby light will stay put.

The main reason for distrusting distances derived from limits of visibility has already been hinted at. The tables, which look so accurate with their decimals of miles, are based on normal refraction. And refraction is seldom normal. We all have seen islands usually invisible from shore stand out clearly on some days. Near a cold or warm front, after the passage of a squall, and wherever air temperature differs greatly from water temperature, abnormal refraction becomes a normal phenomenon.

Above Nassau in the Bahamas flashes an aero beacon, 216 feet above sea level. From my cockpit it should have been visible for

19 miles. Hole in the Wall lighthouse, 168 feet high, on Abaco, fifty miles from Nassau, should have been visible from the helmsman's seat when I got within 17 miles. That should have left a gap of 14 miles in which neither light should have been above my horizon. Yet on several night passages in either direction I have carried one light—not just its loom, or reflection—long after the other light was clearly visible.

Don't let all these warnings discourage you from using the tables. They give very useful circles of position as long as you mentally allow for the width of the doughnut formed by lines of position inside and outside the tabulated range. They let you solve such problems as: "When can I expect to make my landfall?" "How far off course can I be and still find that low island, in the middle of the lake or in the middle of the Pacific Ocean?"

You don't have to depend on printed tables. In their preparation, square roots were used, and few of us would be up to that task. But it isn't necessary to be able to extract square roots. You already know a number of them by heart, and know them with the greatest accuracy. Take any number; multiply it with itself and you get a square number. The root of a square number is the number you started with. Take, for example, four. Four times four is sixteen; the square root of sixteen is four. Then use the following formula:

> To get the DISTANCE TO THE HORIZON
> *in nautical* miles   in *statute* miles
> add 15% (1/7)   add 33% (1/3)
> to the square number nearest to the
> given height (in feet).

For a height of eye of 16 feet, for example, your horizon will be distant about 4½ nautical or 5½ statute miles. Bowditch gives 4.6 and 5.3 miles, but accuracy to the nearest half mile, or even mile is all that's practical.

You are not restricted to exact square numbers for heights. Say your height of eye is 19 feet and you use again the nearest square number (16); you'll still be tolerably close to the values given in Bowditch 5.0 nautical or 5.7 statute miles.

Here, on pages 108A, 108B, to help you is a table of square numbers, their roots, and the corresponding distances to the horizon. This table lets you solve, with ample accuracy, many of the everyday problems in navigation that involve limits of visibility. The beauty of the table is that you can leave it at home and still can reproduce it, or any part of it, whenever you feel up to the task of multiplying figures as large as 19 × 19.

RANGE OF VISIBILITY

Height (feet)		Approx. Distance to the Horizon	
Square Number	Square Root	Naut. Miles	Statute Miles
4	2	2½	2½
9	3	3½	4
16	4	4½	5½
25	5	5½	6½
36	6	7	8
49	7	8	9
64	8	9	10½
81	9	10½	12
100	10	11½	13
121	11	12½	14½
144	12	13½	16
169	13	15	17
196	14	16	18½
225	15	17	20
256	16	18	21
289	17	19½	22½
324	18	20½	24
361	19	22	25
400	20	23	26½

Use height (square number) nearest given height to get approximate distance to horizon in nautical or statute miles.

Example: For an observer 15 feet (nearest square number 16) above the water the horizon will be at 4½ nautical, 5½ statute miles.

The visibility of a bright light 108 feet (nearest square number 100) above the water is limited by its horizon at 11½ nautical, 13 statute miles.

For an observer 15 feet high the light then will break the horizon at 4½ + 11½ = 15 nautical miles, or 5½ + 13 = 18½ statute miles.

I've worked out another method that's sometimes even more convenient. It works the problem backward: How high must an object (your eye, a lighthouse, or a mountain) be to have its horizon at a given distance? The formula allows for normal refraction, and here it is:

> For a DISTANCE TO THE HORIZON given
> in *nautical* miles   in *statute* miles
> the HEIGHT (in feet) must be about
> ¾   ⅗
> the distance times the distance.

The formula works for all distances and heights. Try it. To spot an object on the horizon from 8 nautical miles away, the lookout must be ¾ × 8 × 8 or 48 feet above the water. (Tables give 49 feet.) Or, for a distance to the horizon of 10 statute miles, the height must be ⅗ × 10 × 10 or 60 feet. (For that height tables give 10.2 statute miles.)

Let's work a landfall problem with this formula and let's think big: You are on your way to Hawaii. Approaching the islands you get navigator's nerves. "What if my reckoning is off?" "Will we miss the islands altogether?" Relax. Work out the problem by putting a maximum error on your position, say 60 miles. (You keep your height of eye out of this for extra margin of safety.) The formula gives ¾ × 60 × 60 or 2700 feet. Now you can really relax: the highest point, Mauna Kea, is shown on the chart as 13,796 feet.

Not a chance of your being navigator on a sail to Hawaii? Too bad. But the formula will work just as well for spotting a boat in the middle of your lake, or the radio masts ashore when you come in from fishing.

Here is a related problem, one that has puzzled me for a long time: How high is the sky?

From a rowboat, practically at water level, the sky by day or by night looks like a perfect half-sphere. It doesn't seem to change shape whether you sit up in the boat or lie on the duck boards. By definition the distance to any point on the sphere is the same. Your horizon may be two miles off. The sky then appears to be two miles high.

Now look at the sky from the boat deck of an ocean liner. It hasn't changed shape. Whether you look at it upright, or reclining in a deck chair, it still looks perfectly spherical. But your horizon now is, say, ten miles off. By raising your eyes a few dozen feet, you have raised the height of the sky by eight miles.

From a mountain you may have a view of eighty miles all around. By day and by night, the sky still looks spherical. By going up less than one mile, you have raised the height of the sky to eighty miles.

Can anyone explain that to me?

Now down from the sky and back from Hawaii. I have another question: "Have you ever thought of a cruise, however long, as a lot of short runs?"

Most of them are merely from one buoy to the next when you include under buoys also lighthouses and landmarks ashore. To find the next buoy—or point off a lighthouse, cupola, radio mast, or standpipe—you perform some magic with a plotter on the chart and then steer the course for the required distance. Then more magic, more steering, and all these short legs add up to a cruise.

Simple, don't you agree? Now add a few tricks from the ditty bag of old hands, and you are ready to cruise wherever there are such buoys—in the stretched sense of the word—and charts that show them.

Just follow the buoys. And I do mean follow them; don't cut from No. 2 to No. 6, skipping No. 4 buoy that makes you steer a dog-leg course. No. 4 may mark a sunken rock waiting for your keel. In a dredged channel the missed buoy may squat on the edge of the bank built by all the muck dredged from the channel. Cruising along a coast, think twice before you give up sight of the shore where it forms a bay. It's easy enough to lose count of the chimneys and standpipes even when you see them clearly. (And a new one always seems to have grown since the chart was last corrected.)

You can't run up to a chimney to identify it, but buoys have numbers and letters; get close enough to read them where there is any possibility of doubt. Gongs, whistles, and bells all look alike from a distance. Against the light, red sometimes looks black. You may be able to tell a lighted buoy from an unlighted one by its outline, but to read its identifying flashes in daylight you'll have to get quite close to it.

Prudent skippers don't *think* they have made their buoy unless they are *sure*. Steaming by compass from sea buoy to sea buoy on a miserable, low-ceiling, late-fall day on Long Island Sound, my cold-numbed brain woke me to report: "Long time between buoys, Cap'n."

"We'll give it five more minutes."

At the end of five minutes, sure enough, there it was, dead ahead but still so far it was a mere pencil point on the horizon. Steve, the great navigator-and-helmsman, had done it again. With never another look at the compass, I steered for the buoy.

Then again the little nagger: "Buoy not getting any larger, Cap'n."

"We'll give it five more minutes."

Then suddenly the buoy became much taller right in front of me. It grew a base and then the hull of a submarine. I still wonder what the officer of the deck thought I was trying to do. Ram him?

If you don't find a charted buoy, go looking for it. Buoys do go adrift. (A New York Harbor buoy once single-handed to England, was picked up, identified, and returned to New York with the Admiralty's compliments before it had been reported missing.) But more often, when we don't find a buoy, we have—let's admit it —goofed ourselves.

Doglegs made to find a buoy, to lay a safe course, or to identify a navigation aid add surprisingly little to the total distance run, or the time and fuel used.

A dogleg of (degrees)	5	10	15	20	25
Adds to distance (percent)	½	1½	3½	6½	10

Knowing this, the seasoned skipper doesn't hesitate to run a dogleg. Meeting a tug towing a former forest of logs, he'll change course radically, not just a safe five degrees, or a standard ten degrees, but twenty degrees. That shows the tugboat skipper that he has changed course and isn't just steering sloppily.

The same wise skipper will time how long he has been on the detour. If he has run four minutes twenty degrees to the right of his plotted course, he'll next steer twenty degrees to the left of it. After four minutes he'll be back on the track, and resume the planned course.

The rule of follow the buoys has an important exception: *Shape your course away from danger.* When a string of buoys marks dangers to the right of your course, lay a course well to the left of the buoys. Then wind and current won't get you into trouble before you sight the next marker. Along shore pick a spot well ahead of a headland or lighthouse and plot a course for that point; don't leave it to the helmsman—even yourself—to allow for the ever-changing angle between your intended course and the lighthouse or headland.

At times it might be smart to use the old helm orders "Nothing Right" and "Nothing Left" after the course. Ordered to steer, say, "270 Nothing Left," the helmsman, instead of steering, as usual, as close to 270 degrees as possible (perhaps between 267 and 273 degrees), will keep her to 270 when possible but take all his errors to the right, away from danger, keeping her head between 270 and 276 degrees.

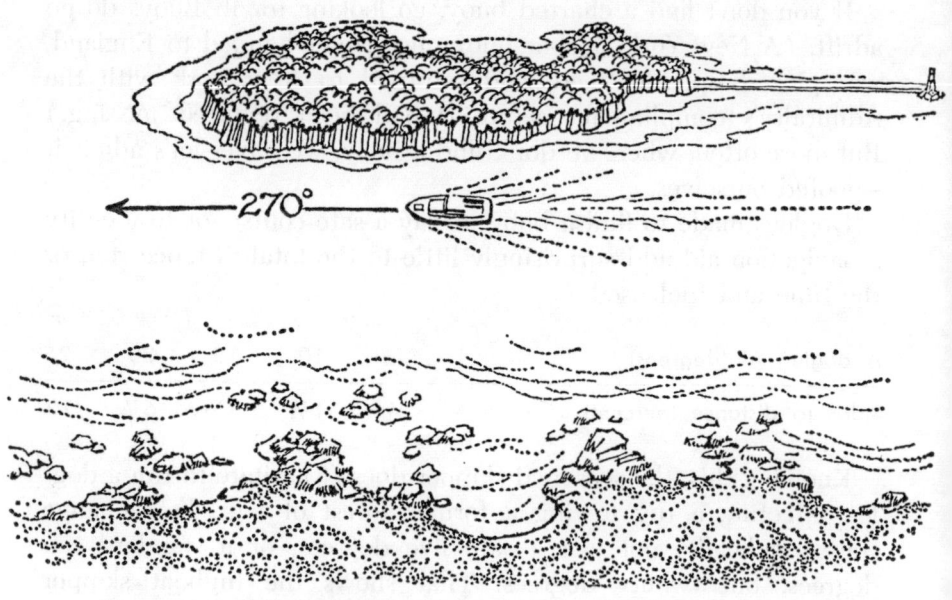

41. *Course 270, Nothing Left (or West Nothing South) would be the proper helm order to keep you off the foul ground.*

On a close-hauled sailboat the helmsman normally is not given a course. He is supposed to steer "full and by," keeping the sails full and drawing, and as close to the wind as possible while keeping her moving smartly. He'll luff up—come closer to the wind—whenever the wind gets stronger, and bring her up whenever the wind shifts more aft temporarily. Headed west between a clear shore to the north and a crappy one to the south, you might well order "West nothing South." The helmsman then, instead of eating out the wind, will sail her a little free at times and keep you off the shoal. And that, after all, is what pilotage is all about.

11 Piloting in Coral Waters

It's a long jump from range of visibility and from lines of position to the kind of navigation you'll need in the coral belt: eyeball navigation. And you *will* need it. Unless you learn to "read the bottom," the cruise through southern waters, dreamed about for years, may be shorter than you had planned.

Some of the best cruising grounds of the world are studded with coral reefs. It isn't that the sea gods were trying to spoil your pleasure. It's just that the reef-building coral animals thrive on the conditions a sailor dreams about: year-'round warm clear water and steady winds. Some corals—singly or in small colonies—are found in all oceans, even in the glacier-ringed fjords of Norway. But the reef-builders live only in waters that seldom get colder than 70°F, and so are restricted to a belt only a few degrees of latitude wider than the tropical zone. To find the right conditions off the United States, you'll have to go to the Gulf of Mexico, to the Bahamas, the Virgin Islands, or the Antilles. By courtesy of the Gulf Stream you'll also find coral colonies around Bermuda and off the shore of southern Florida.

Some species of coral have been dredged up from great depths, but the reef-building kinds are found only in shallow waters. There is a reason. The tiny coral animals that secrete hard shells, which in their multitudes form the massive structures of reefs, depend on a strange partnership with green algae within their own bodies. The algae, as all green plants do in sunlight, take up carbon dioxide and give off oxygen. This helps the metabolism of the coral polyp, which as an animal needs oxygen and has to rid itself of carbon dioxide. Below about one hundred feet of water the sunlight gets too weak for photosynthesis by the algae. The mutually profitable exchange breaks down, and the coral colony dies. So the boatman needn't worry about isolated coral formations reaching up from deep water.

On the other hand, the delicate coral animal, which resembles in miniature its close relative the sea anemone, can't stand exposure to air, wind, and sun. So the reefs usually reach up only to the level of lowest low tide. In all but the calmest weather an obstruction so near the surface should cause the sea to break. But don't count on seeing these breakers in time; sometimes they are visible from shore only.

The coral's food is plankton, that broth of microscopic-to-barely-visible organisms, delivered by oceanic currents, mostly wind-driven currents. Since the coral belt almost everywhere lies within the pattern of the easterly air flow of the trade winds, most coral reefs are found on the *east* coasts of continents and islands. The reefs of Andros and Abaco in the Bahamas, and the most famous of all reefs, the Great Barrier Reef off Australia, illustrate that point. The careful skipper expects reefs on the windward side of any land in the coral belt, and at the edge of any submerged bank.

The reefs often run in bands roughly parallel to the shore. There may be passages through these reefs, but unless you know exactly where these openings are, assume the reef to be continuous. Where there are openings between islands, a stranger will do well to expect coral growth reaching from one island to the next, and only use openings for which he has detailed directions.

While you can count on finding reefs on the windward side near shore, the leeward side may not be free from them. Perhaps a current forks and sweeps around the island to feed a coral colony off the western shore. Or tidal currents may take over the role of food distributor, and you'll find thriving colonies of coral—usually in isolated heads or stacks—on an otherwise clear bottom.

Such isolated stacks are good spots for sight-seeing with a face mask. You'll see there in a small area a variety of corals growing and giving shelter to fishes and invertebrate reef dwellers. You can study them quietly in such a spot without being bounced to and fro as on the exposed windward reefs.

How can you locate these isolated stacks and heads?

The lead is of no use. Look at the log kept by Captain James Cook in *Endeavour*, then off the east coast of Australia.

Monday, June 21, 1770:

. . . A breeze of wind and a clear moonlight night. In standing off we deepened our water from 14 to 21 fathom, when all at once we fell into 12, 10,

Piloting in Coral Waters

and 8 fathom. At this time I had everybody at their stations to put about and come to anchor. . . . Meeting again with deeper water, I thought there could be no danger in standing on. Before 10 o'clock we had 20 and 21 fathom and continued in that depth until a few minutes before 11 o'clock when we had 17 fathom, and before the man at the lead could heave another cast, the ship struck and stuck fast.

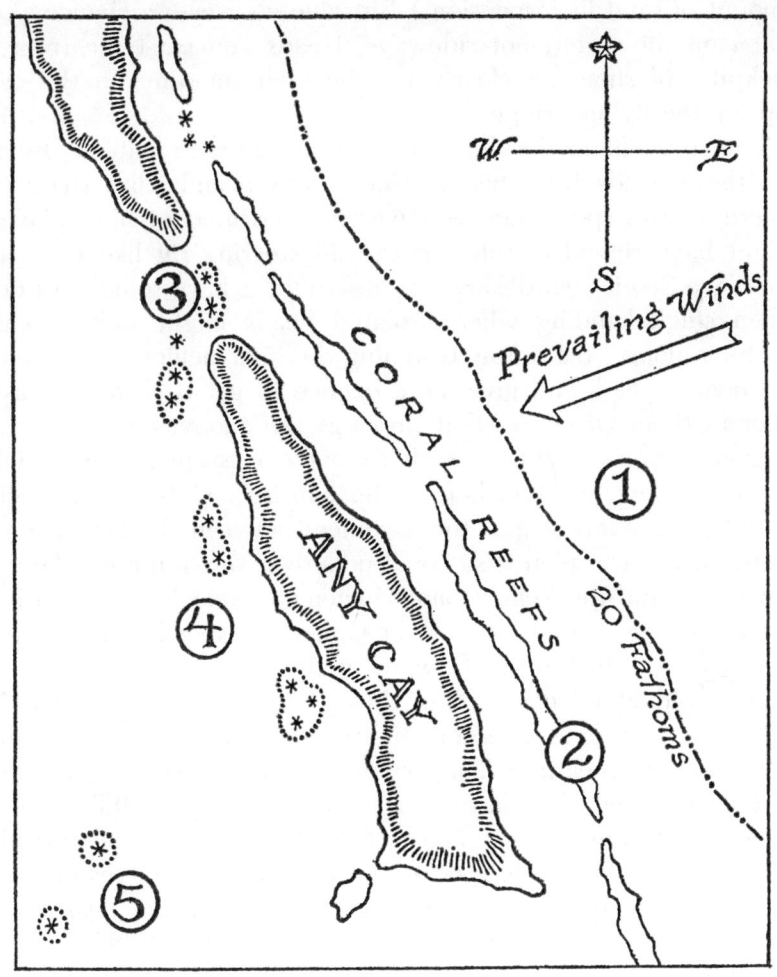

42. *Coral reefs: general locations*—1. *No danger of coral reefs outside the 20-fathom depth contour line* 2. *More or less unbroken reefs along windward (east) shore of any island in the coral belt* 3. *Passages between islands to be considered foul, unless known to be clear* 4. *Current-fed coral colonies on the lee (west) side of most islands* 5. *Isolated, tide-fed coral heads on the banks.*

The sounding pole, handy for feeling your way into sandy or grassy coves, is no better than the lead. The standard echo sounder will show an obstruction only after you've sailed over it.

What then is left? The lookout. Your eyes are the best coral detectors in these clear waters. (They have to be clear. The coral animals cannot stand mud, and most of them tolerate only a small amount of sand in suspension.) But give your eyes a chance: Look *down* on the water, not sideways. Heads you can't see from the cockpit will show up clearly for the man standing on the cabin top, or the flying bridge.

The single-handed sailor has a problem in such waters. He can't see these heads from his steering position, and can't steer from where he can spot them. If I weren't so scared of high places, I might have rigged myself a masthead steering rig like those that the Nova Scotia swordfishermen use. What I have sometimes done, when single-handing where isolated heads might lurk, is called "lashing along." It's simply trimming the sails inefficiently to reduce the boat's speed, and give me a chance to get back to the lashed tiller in time. Of course that prolongs the agony.

Even with a lookout I wouldn't move over suspicious areas when the sun is low, say two hours after sunrise and two hours before sunset. On many trips, for instance between Nassau and the Exumas, you can plan it so you'll pass over the foul area (between the White and the Yellow Bank) when the light is good. With the sun astern, or at least aft of the beam, you'll spot heads that you'd miss seeing with the sun forward of the beam.

I'd avoid at all cost sailing through coral areas at night. The native skippers of Andros sometimes sail inside their reefs at night. But they are cheating: They know the place like the pockets in their pants, and they have a system. Don't try it, it'll scare the teredos right out of your planks. Here it is: They watch for phosphorescence. When fish, spooked by the approaching vessel, scatter trailing luminous wakes, these men know they are near a coral head. For that's where the fish are, not over open bottom. (That's why they are also good spots for setting your fish trap, or for handlining from the dinghy.)

But let's go looking for coral heads under more orthodox conditions, with the sun shining steeply, and preferably over our shoulders. Overcast days are bad. Polarizing sunglasses help by cutting the glare from the surface. If you wear glasses, try clip-ons, or get prescription-ground sunglasses, which are great also for driving a car, not just a boat. For piloting in coral waters get neutral gray sunglasses; all others distort colors, and colors here are important. Not so much for coral stacks. They show up as brownish or yellowish shadows. Some are kind enough to have a ring of white sand around them that make them stand out clearly on otherwise dark green, grassy bottom. Some people explain these white rings as having been grazed bare by animals that live in the shelter of the coral; others say they are caused by tidal currents swirling around the underwater obstruction. I like to think it's mermaids who every morning sweep around these heads to warn sailormen.

I have sometimes used an electric hand lantern at night to spot heads; held at just the right angle, such a lantern shows the bottom very clearly. Not that I'd break my own rule and go reef-crawling in the night. But after a bottom paint job I might want to anchor off after dark, and heads rise right inside some anchorages. On one such night, as soon as I had turned on the switch, a two-foot-long needle fish streaked out of the water and at the light. Some rigging luckily intercepted the attacker. I have used the lantern sparingly since.

Coral reefs grow. The boatman isn't interested in the growth rates measured by marine biologists, nor the nodules and laminations that tell him years, months (moon cycles to be exact), and days of a coral's life. But the boatman should keep in mind that the reefs may have grown since the survey for his charts has been made. Actually, everyone has sailed the Bahamas for years with charts based on surveys made more than a hundred years ago, and found surprisingly little to complain about. The growth rate must be less spectacular than measured by the biologists. Not that they were cheating. But the reefs the sailor comes in contact with, or tries not to come in contact with, are inner reefs where growth conditions are not as favorable as farther to seaward. Also the waves whipped up by occasional hurricanes are more damaging to reefs near the surface than to those deeper down, which are of no concern to the yachtsman. Then too, the reefs are constantly attacked by boring worms and snails, and even nibbled away by fishes such as parrot fish. So they are being worn away, while the corals by budding and branching try to build them up.

Corals are spectacular dangers, and delightful places for underwater nature study, but most of the time the skipper in the Bahamas will be more concerned with the nearness of the sandy and grassy bottoms of the banks. The northern skipper may have sailed in shallower water, but never has he seen the bottom so clearly. At first it scares you. Then, step by step, you acquire a color sense that the native sailors claim to be born with.

The rankest airline passenger can see the inky purple or deep indigo of the deep sea getting lighter as the water shoals. Over sand the colors will run through the ultramarines to lighter blues, then as the water shoals even more, to aquamarine and green. In very shallow water the green will pale to white, and even become pink, until it becomes—as it should—at zero depth the color of the sand ashore.

After perhaps gently bumping a few times, the skipper learns what color of water will carry his draft. That works a while, then crunch—he is aground. Perhaps a cloud shadow has darkened all colors and misled him. When I thought I had learned to distinguish depth by color, I ventured into an anchorage not detailed in the *Yachtsman's Guide to the Bahamas*. At the entrance I was faced with a very light patch on one side, and dark water on the other. Almost automatically I chose the dark side. Wrong! The light water would just have floated us over soft, sandy bottom; the dark water covered hard-packed stuff overgrown with conch grass and was very shallow. All this I found out during the next tide while I scrubbed and painted one side of the hull waiting for more water to get me afloat again.

There is another trick for telling depth. In shallow water, when the sun is favorable, you'll see the shadow of your boat gliding over the bottom. As long as the shadow of your keel is some distance off, all is well. When the shadow and the keel meet, you are aground.

A great source of amusement to others are sandbanks on your course. To a lookout high up these banks are clearly visible in good light; so are the deep leads between them. With the sun ahead, low, or hidden by a cloudy sky, they can be trying, especially where they occur in overlapping bands, or in the shape of horseshoes open on your end.

The chart will show such areas in a general way, but sandbanks grow and recede, and may even pivot with the seasons when the NE winds change to SE breezes. The surprising part is not that they are not exactly where the chart, or the *Yachtsman's Guide* show them, but rather that they stay more or less where the chart survey has found them.

Until recently the charts of the Bahamas were based, as mentioned earlier, on surveys more than a century old. Yet the bars and the depths in the lagoons have changed little. When after a storm you see sand-laden waters pour into the lagoons, you wonder where all the sand that's been carried in has gone. No conceivable storm ever carries it out again, yet the general depth remains about constant. My explanation: Some of the lime in the calcium carbonate that makes up the sand is dissolved in the shallows at

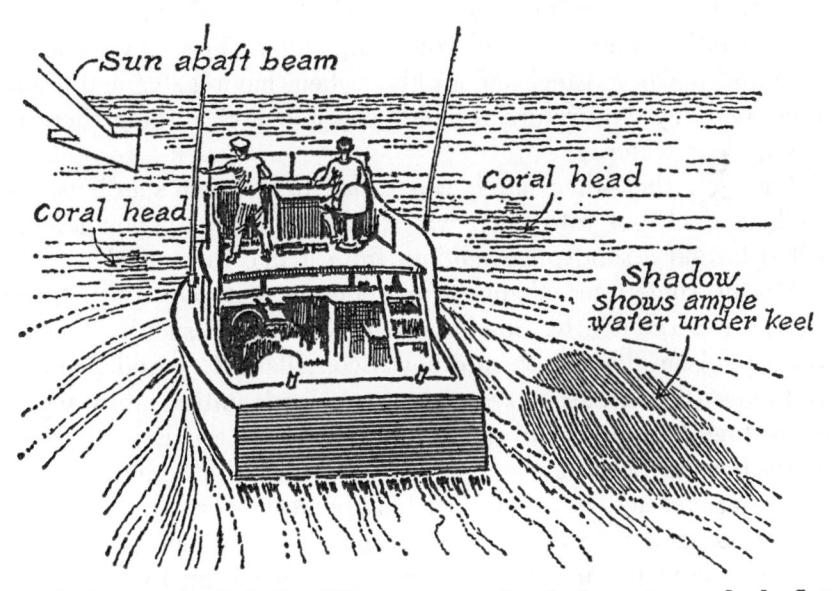

43. *Shadow as depth-finder. When you see the shadow of your keel off to one side, you have a margin of safety; when the shadow of your keel and your keel draw closer together, you are running into thinner water.*

about the same rate as it is deposited. That's my own theory; I can't prove it.

The constancy of depth does not hold over grass; here the water gets shallower as time goes on. The stems of the turtle grass that covers vast stretches of sandy bottom, trap sand that otherwise might be carried farther by tidal currents. Dig in such an area and you'll find a thick mat of stems and roots, and more decaying stems and roots, until you get tired of digging.

Among the underwater meadows, and also over bare sand, you'll see mole hills a foot or two in diameter and perhaps six or eight inches high. They are the tailings of an incredibly efficient sand miner, the sea cucumber. He takes in sand at the bow, extracts organic materials for food, and discharges processed sand astern. This sand is quite loose and not likely to become a hazard to your navigation.

Sometimes you'll find sandbanks—indicated by discolored, almost white water—where the chart shows depth of a fathom or two. Before you write the Hydrographic Office about it, make sure it isn't mud stirred up by a large school of bottom-feeding fish. I have seen them from the ratlines of my schooner, and from low-flying planes; either way they fool you completely. They may be a mile long and make you feel like an idiot when, having steamed around them one day, you return the next day and find nothing there but deep, clear water.

Man, on the other hand, can cause permanent sandbars. You build a dock out into deep water, and before long you'll find it silted in and a sandspit extending from it like the tail of a comet.

Storms sometimes change the underwater topography, temporarily or permanently. Some cays in the Berry Islands shown as one island on older charts are now two; Allan's Cay and Pensacola in the northern Abacos used to be two islands until a storm welded them together; the pond on Norman's Cay, in the Exumas, a few years back a favorite meeting place of deep-draft charter sailing boats, was closed to them by a blow almost overnight.

But navigation in the coral belt isn't all that difficult. The clearness of the water, and the absence of fog make up for the lack of buoys and other aids to navigation, once you know what to look for and keep your eyes open.

12 Master Mariner's Compass

I want a compass on any boat I take out, even if it's only a runabout on a lake. In fact, I'd like two different compasses on any boat I'd have to pilot. Yet I'll make my life easy: I'd arrange it so that I can forget about rules and jingles, deviation diagrams and tables.

If you think me silly for wanting a compass on almost any craft, almost everywhere, answer these questions: Can you be sure never to run into fog? In fog, how long can you steer blind in one direction? How can you carry on by eyeball navigation when it starts to rain kite strings and clotheslines? Do you carry enough rope to anchor everywhere you go? And can you be sure some clown who thinks *he* can see in fog or rain won't run you down while you're anchored? Haven't you read about guys who after fishing all day finally decided to head in, and steamed in any direction but home until they ran out of gas?

With a compass or two you'll also find that good fishing spot again. On a sailboat, however puny, you can figure just how high she points, and when to tack to fetch a given mark, all of which is more fun than just messing around on the same old lake at random. You'll also notice when the wind shifts gradually, as it often does.

Even on the Inland Waterway you'll find a compass useful. Where some shipping channel crosses the ditch you'll be faced by so many buoys, you'd be aground before you have their meaning all sorted out. Not only on the few open sounds you cross, the Albemarle for instance, but on many other stretches you may not see the next marker even with binoculars. Then where do you head? Tom-Sawyering down the Mississippi I'd use a compass; the tugboat skippers do, although they know the river as you know your driveway.

Have I convinced you of the necessity for carrying a compass? Perhaps you always did. But two compasses? Yes, I'd carry another one of a type very different from my steering compass: a hand bearing compass. I have already mentioned its usefulness in taking bearings all around the horizon. It lets you take a bearing over the stern on your point of departure or the last marker you passed and so measure leeway.

It's also handy for steering by the stars. Its prism tilts to let you measure the azimuth of a star just like the bearing on a lighthouse. We'll talk more about that later.

Should your steering compass pack up, it'll give you a spare. Well-run yachts may carry a spare joker valve, a spare corkscrew, and a spare doughnut cutter, but how many yachts, even gold-platers, carry a spare compass?

All these are good reasons for carrying a hand bearing compass. Here is the best: It lets you adjust the steering compass with a minimum of trouble, and serves as a constant check on that adjustment. And having the main compass adjusted is the secret for making the navigator's life easy.

It's all very simple. Free to pivot, a magnetic compass needle (or the card that carries the needle) will align itself everywhere with

44. Hand bearing compass has several navigational uses. Here skipper takes bearing of a mark astern to determine leeway.

the magnetic field. On a beach, away from power lines and metal structures, it'll align itself with the magnetic field of the earth. On a wooden boat without engine and without electrical gear, wiring, and electronic devices, it will still align itself with that field. It will do the same on a steel vessel. But here the field is influenced by the steel plates, the direction in which they were rolled, how they were stored, cut, bent, and welded. The direction in which the vessel has been built, the heading on which she has recently docked or steamed, all influence her field. To this add the attraction of parts of her engine, controls and shaft, electric motors, wiring, and electronic gear that's simply loaded with coils and magnets . . . and you have a field that horribly distorts the field of the earth.

The average pleasure boat falls somewhere between the almost nonmagnetic and the highly complicated structures. Luckily the local field can be measured and compensated for. Usually two magnets, one in the fore-and-aft line, the other athwartships will do it. Some compasses have compensators built in. With those you just twirl the proper adjusting screw in the proper direction to the proper point to compensate your compass for local magnetic influences. With other compasses you place bar or rod magnets near the compass to counteract the local field.

Either way the adjusting is done in a series of steps by steaming on different courses—swinging ship—since the effect of the field to be neutralized varies on different headings of the vessel. Usually one has to fiddle a little and repeat each step. All of it may be tedious but it isn't difficult. The hardest part often is the finding of a reference line such as a range or a set of buoys with deep water all around. A bearing compass makes that part unnecessary.

You proceed in two steps. First you find a convenient spot aboard that is practically free of magnetic influences. On a sailboat that might be on top of the cabin, or perhaps on the foredeck. To find out if the spot is magnetically undisturbed, you move the bearing compass while the boat lies still. Bring the compass close to the forestay, for instance, then move it first left, then right. If the reading of the compass doesn't change, the stay is obviously nonmagnetic. On the cabin top move the compass from side to side, and fore and aft. If the Charlie Noble and deck hardware don't change the reading, you have found a safe spot. Take all your control readings for compass checking, and later for shore or star bearings from that spot. On a power cruiser you may try standing in the forehatch and moving the compass toward and away from the anchor winch and any other metal objects nearby. Or try the center of the fishbox at the stern. Wherever, keep as far from the steering compass as possible. The two compasses will act on each other, and both point wrong.

Having found a neutral reference station, you are ready for the second step, adjusting the steering compass with its built-in compensators or placing external magnets where they'll do the most good. On all courses you'll have a direct and quick check by simply asking your helper what course his bearing compass reads at the time. Correcting is done most easily when the boat steams exactly on a given magnetic bearing, say north, so let the helper give you the course to steer. The little lady takes a bearing on the forestay (or jackstaff) from the center of the fishbox, or on the backstay (or sternstaff) from the center of the forehatch. On the bearing compass she can read the heading to one degree close; you then compare her bearing (or its reverse) with the one shown on your steering compass.

On all but the smallest boats on which a 7½-inch Navy compass would be a bit out of place, I like a steering compass also marked at every degree, not just at every fifth degree. And I'd pick a card that also shows points. Not that I'd like to steer a course called NNE3/4E (or NE×N1/4N); I find 31 degrees a lot easier. But I also find it easier to hold on that first tick—whatever its name—to the left of the triangle between the diamond marked NNE and the big triangle marked NE than on the numeral 31, which looks like 21, or 41, or even 51, or 81 after you've stared at it long enough.

Someday after you have adjusted a few compasses successfully, you'll run into one that just won't come close enough—say to one degree—whatever you do. You have twisted wires, shifted some suspected gear, even replaced some steel parts with brass, and perhaps degaussed the works. What's left? Move the compass. Often a few inches will make the difference. Here too the bearing compass may help. Unship the steering compass, then unscrew the handle of the bearing compass and with its head alone explore the neighborhood. Move it about, left and right, fore and aft, even up and down. You may find a spot much less disturbed than the old compass location yet still within the field of vision of the helmsman. If it happens to be too far away, perhaps a magnifier will solve the problem.

Next to accuracy—and a true lubber's line—helmsman's comfort is most important. If you are the permanent helmsman and of bifocal age, you may find the card just too far away for strainless watching through your reading segments, yet too close or too low for your distant-vision field. Perhaps moving the compass farther away will help you.

There is one problem peculiar to sailboats which by their nature spend a good deal of their lives heeled to one side or the other. Before you declare your compass compensated, that is free of declination error on any heading, sail a few courses first on the port, then on the starboard tack, and compare the reading of your compass with those read by your helper with the bearing compass.

On a freighter with a load of lumber in the holds and the maxi-

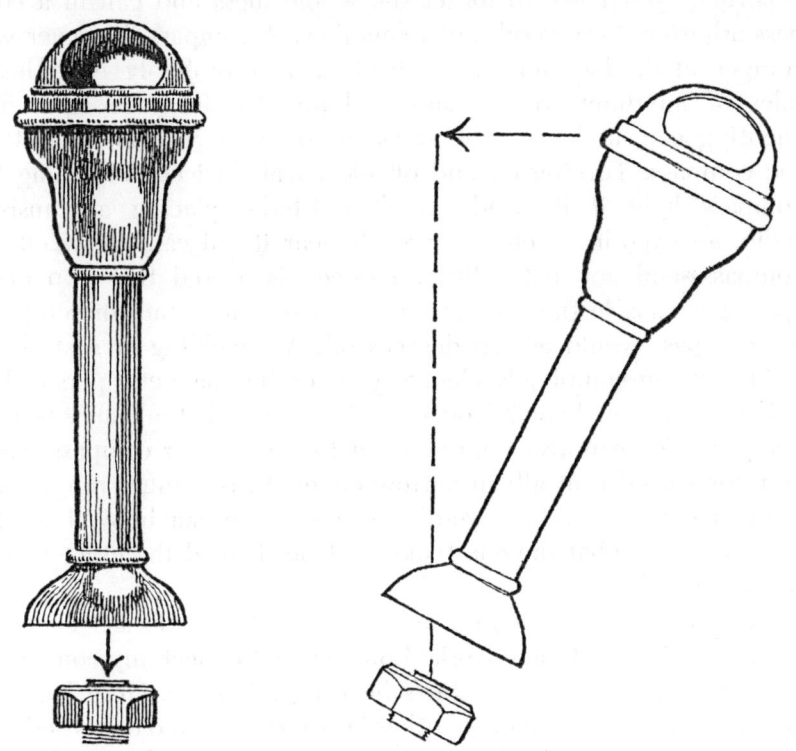

45. *Heeling error. With the boat upright, some on-board magnetism (symbolized by keel-bolt and nut) pulls downward only, does not deflect compass card. When the boat heels, keel-bolt and nut move to one side of the compass, causing deviation.*

mum allowable deck cargo, we settled on a steady ten-degree starboard list that upset only the cook. When the wind changed, or when we altered course and brought it on the other side, she groaned, lurched, and took on a ten-degree list to port. Once I happened to be sunning myself on monkey island when she flipped. I noticed the magnetic compass there jump six degrees while our wake stretched straight astern. We entered this observation in the log, and otherwise ignored it. After all, the gyro compass and its repeater by which the ship was steered were not affected by such magnetic nonsense.

Unless you are up on your celestial navigation, or can borrow a red azimuth table (H.O.260), I don't recommend compass adjustment by the sun. He doesn't stand still long enough to do the job.

Perhaps you'd like to forget the whole mess and call in a compass adjuster. Very good, but remember: A compass, however well compensated, does not stay adjusted. You probably have heard tales of anything from a sailor's knife, to the wire in a new yachting cap, and even the stays in some lady's corset upsetting the compass. Turning on and off electrical devices (including the compass light if its leads aren't twisted), placing a transistor radio, an exposure meter, a wrench near it, all can throw off the compass—and not just a little. I once discovered that two metal spare gas cans in the cockpit had to face in a certain direction, or my compass would go ten degrees off. Arc welding or a stroke of lightning can completely change your craft's magnetic personality.

How will you know? You can always check the hand bearing compass. You can also train yourself to watch your compass where you don't need it at all: in narrow channels, running a range, on a familiar course—say from your mooring to the first buoy. Does the compass read what the chart shows? Does it read the exact reverse on the way back?

I happen to like watching sunset, and—when it doesn't come too early—sunrise. So I have worked out tables to check my compass at those times, whatever the ship's heading might be. Here I expand the tables for use of sailors in other latitudes. It's an old method, and one of the best for checking a compass at sea. But the usual procedure—looking up the sun's declination, then going into the table of amplitudes in Bowditch and from another table there correcting for observation on the visible rather than the theoretical horizon —is awkward. You may find my tables handier.

Master Mariner's Compass

SUNRISE: True bearing of the sun when lower limb is on horizon

LATITUDE	0	25	34	40	44	47	50	52	54
Jan. 1	113	115	118	120	123	124	127	129	131
Jan. 16	111	113	115	118	119	121	123	125	127
Jan. 26	109	111	113	115	117	118	120	121	123
Feb. 2	107	109	110	112	114	115	117	118	119
Feb. 9	105	106	108	109	111	112	113	114	116
Feb. 15	103	104	106	107	108	109	110	111	112
Feb. 20	101	102	103	104	105	106	107	108	108
Feb. 26	99	100	101	101	102	103	104	104	105
Mar. 3	97	98	98	99	99	100	101	101	102
Mar. 8	95	95	96	96	97	97	97	98	98
Mar. 13	93	93	93	94	94	94	94	95	95
Mar. 18	91	91	91	91	91	91	91	91	91
Mar. 23	89	89	89	88	88	88	88	88	88
Mar. 29	87	87	86	86	85	85	85	85	84
Apr. 3	85	84	84	83	83	82	82	81	81
Apr. 8	83	82	81	81	80	79	79	78	77
Apr. 13	81	80	79	78	77	76	75	75	74
Apr. 19	79	78	76	75	74	73	72	71	71
Apr. 25	77	75	74	73	71	70	69	68	67
May 1	75	73	72	70	68	67	66	65	63
May 6	73	71	69	67	66	64	62	61	60
May 16	71	69	67	65	63	61	59	58	56
May 26	69	66	64	62	60	58	56	54	52
Jun. 10	67	64	62	59	57	55	52	50	48
Jun. 22	66	64	61	58	56	54	51	49	47
Jul. 3	67	64	62	59	57	55	52	50	48
Jul. 19	69	66	64	62	60	58	56	54	52
Jul. 28	71	69	67	65	63	61	59	58	56
Aug. 5	73	71	69	67	66	64	62	61	60
Aug. 12	75	73	72	70	68	67	66	65	63
Aug. 19	77	75	74	73	71	70	69	68	67
Aug. 25	79	78	76	75	74	73	72	71	71
Aug. 30	81	80	79	78	77	76	75	75	74
Sep. 5	83	82	81	81	80	79	79	78	77
Sep. 10	85	84	84	83	83	82	82	81	81

NAVIGATION

LATITUDE	0	25	34	40	44	47	50	52	54
Sep. 15	87	87	86	85	85	85	85	85	84
Sep. 21	89	89	89	88	88	88	88	88	88
Sep. 26	91	91	91	91	91	91	91	91	91
Oct. 1	93	93	93	94	94	94	94	95	95
Oct. 6	95	95	96	96	97	97	97	98	98
Oct. 11	97	98	98	99	99	100	101	101	102
Oct. 17	99	100	101	101	102	103	104	104	105
Oct. 22	101	102	103	104	105	106	107	108	108
Oct. 28	103	104	106	107	108	109	110	111	112
Nov. 3	105	106	108	109	111	112	113	114	116
Nov. 10	107	109	110	112	114	115	117	118	119
Nov. 18	109	111	113	115	117	118	120	121	123
Nov. 27	111	113	115	118	119	121	123	125	127
Dec. 12	113	115	118	120	123	124	127	129	131
Dec. 22	114	116	118	121	123	125	128	130	132
Dec. 31	113	115	118	120	123	124	127	129	131

In north latitudes:
Find bearing on line of date, in column of latitude.
Example: Oct. 28 Lat. 40° N—sunrise bearing is . . . 107° T.
For dates and latitudes not tabulated, estimate the bearing from neighboring figures.
Examples: 1. Oct. 31 (between Oct. 28 and Nov. 3) Lat. 40° N . . . 108° T.
2. Nov. 3 Lat. 42° N (between 40° and 44°) . . . 110° T.

In south latitudes:
For bearings *left* of the vertical line, use as for north latitudes.
Example: Oct. 28 Lat. 25° S—use tabulated bearing . . . 104° T.
For bearings *right* of vertical line, *add* one degree to bearing.
Example: Oct. 28 Lat. 40° S—add 1° to tabulated 107° . . . 108° T.

SUNSET: True bearing of the sun when lower limb is on horizon

LATITUDE	0	25	34	40	44	47	50	52	54
Jan. 1	247	245	242	240	237	236	233	231	229
Jan. 16	249	247	245	242	241	239	237	235	233
Jan. 26	251	249	247	245	243	242	240	239	237
Feb. 2	253	251	250	248	246	245	243	242	241
Feb. 9	255	254	252	251	249	248	247	246	244
Feb. 15	257	256	254	253	252	251	250	249	248
Feb. 20	259	258	257	256	255	254	253	252	252

LATITUDE	0	25	34	40	44	47	50	52	54
Feb. 26	261	260	259	259	258	257	256	256	255
Mar. 3	263	262	262	261	261	260	259	259	258
Mar. 8	265	265	264	264	263	263	263	262	262
Mar. 13	267	267	267	266	266	266	266	265	265
Mar. 18	269	269	269	269	269	269	269	269	269
Mar. 23	271	271	271	272	272	272	272	272	272
Mar. 29	273	273	274	274	275	275	275	275	276
Apr. 3	275	276	276	277	277	278	278	279	279
Apr. 8	277	278	279	279	280	281	281	282	283
Apr. 13	279	280	281	282	283	284	285	285	286
Apr. 19	281	282	284	285	286	287	288	289	289
Apr. 25	283	285	286	287	289	290	291	292	293
May 1	285	287	288	290	292	293	294	295	297
May 6	287	289	291	293	294	296	298	299	300
May 16	289	291	293	295	297	299	301	302	304
May 26	291	294	296	298	300	302	304	306	308
Jun. 10	293	296	298	301	303	305	308	310	312
Jun. 22	294	296	299	302	304	306	309	311	313
Jul. 3	293	296	298	301	303	305	308	310	312
Jul. 19	291	294	296	298	300	302	304	306	308
Jul. 28	289	291	293	295	297	299	301	302	304
Aug. 5	287	289	291	293	294	296	298	299	300
Aug. 12	285	287	288	290	292	293	294	295	297
Aug. 19	283	285	286	287	289	290	291	292	293
Aug. 25	281	282	284	285	286	287	288	289	289
Aug. 30	279	280	281	282	283	284	285	285	286
Sep. 5	277	278	279	279	280	281	281	282	283
Sep. 10	275	276	276	277	277	278	278	279	279
Sep. 15	273	273	274	274	275	275	275	275	275
Sep. 21	271	271	271	272	272	272	272	272	272
Sep. 26	269	269	269	269	269	269	269	269	269
Oct. 1	267	267	267	266	266	266	266	265	265
Oct. 6	265	265	264	264	263	263	263	262	262
Oct. 11	263	262	262	261	261	260	259	259	258
Oct. 17	261	260	259	259	258	257	256	256	255
Oct. 22	259	258	257	256	255	254	253	252	252
Oct. 28	257	256	254	253	252	251	250	249	248
Nov. 3	255	254	252	251	249	248	247	246	244

LATITUDE	0	25	34	40	44	47	50	52	54
Nov. 10	253	251	250	248	246	245	243	242	241
Nov. 18	251	249	247	245	243	242	240	239	237
Nov. 27	249	247	245	242	241	239	237	235	233
Dec. 12	247	245	242	240	237	236	233	231	229
Dec. 22	246	244	242	239	237	235	232	230	228
Dec. 31	247	245	242	240	237	236	233	231	229

In north latitude:
Find bearing on line of date, in column of latitude.
Example: Oct. 28 Lat. 40° N, sunset bearing is . . . 253° T.
For dates and latitudes not tabulated, estimate the bearing from neighboring figures.
Examples: 1. Oct. 31 (between Oct. 28 and Nov. 3) Lat. 40° N . . . 252° T.
              2. Nov. 3 Lat. 42° N (between 40 and 44) est. . . . 250° T.
In south latitude:
For bearings *left* of vertical line, use as for north latitudes.
Example: Oct. 28 Lat. 25° S—use tabulated bearing . . . 256° T.
For bearings *right* of vertical line, *subtract* one degree.
Example: Oct. 28 Lat. 40° S—subtract 1° from tabulated 253° . . . 252° T.

You might wonder how useful these bearings are when you missed the actual moment when the lower limb of the sun is on the sea horizon at rise or set, or when it was obscured by clouds. Put differently, can you use these bearings for checking your compass on more than one heading? The next table answers these questions.

CHANGE OF BEARING OF ONE DEGREE

In latitude (N or S)	5	10	15	18	19	21	24	26	29	34	40	47	50	54
Takes minutes	46	23	15	13	12	11	10	9	8	7	6	6	5	5

From this table you'll see that in San Francisco Bay or in Long Island Sound you'll have six minutes before the bearing changes a single degree. In the central Bahamas you'd have about ten minutes. The table is specially useful after sunrise, but can also be used to estimate the difference in bearing before sunset. Knowing in which direction the bearing changes, you can safely double these times by allowing an extra degree in the proper direction. That would be toward the south after sunrise in the examples just given.

Suppose that you have gotten rid of deviation on all headings, and that frequent checks show that your compass is still in adjustment, that no lady with magnetic corset stays has stowed away behind the compass.

That's only half of making life with a compass easy. The other half is to live on the simplest terms with the crazy magnetic field of our planet.

Who am I to call that field crazy? Well, I can show that it's at least behaving very strangely and unpredictably. Let me prove it. Only in selected places does a compass needle point straight north. Everywhere else the needle points in some other direction. That is its privilege. After all, why should it point to the geographical North Pole, when the magnetic pole is more than eleven degrees of latitude—about seven hundred nautical miles—from the rotational pole? But then you'd expect places with equal compass variation to lie on some geometric pattern, and the line that connects places where the compass needle points due north to lie on a neat line.

In the Western Hemisphere the line of zero variation is fairly well adjusted. It runs almost straight through northern Canada, just missing Hudson Bay, then through the Great Lakes, and just off the east coast of Florida, through the Colombia-Venezuela border, to leave South America near the mouth of the Rio de la Plata. But the corresponding line in the Eastern Hemisphere staggers crazily. It runs from Norway to Greece, then loops across northeastern Africa to Tibet, crosses Asia into the Arctic Ocean, curls back through eastern Siberia, bends back to take in Vietnam and Sumatra, then swings east again across western Australia.

Everywhere except on these two lines the compass needle makes an angle with the true north-south line. Where yachts operate, this variation may reach 25 degrees on either side. (It's about 25° West in Nova Scotia, and about 25° East in British Columbia.) But polar explorers have to worry about errors up to 180 degrees; that is, the compass indicates north when it points south.

If you connect points with the same variation, you get a set of curves—isogonic lines—that make the isobars on a weather map look simple. And the variation at any one place does not remain constant over the years. As indicated on nautical charts, it changes by fractions of a degree a year. But don't think that this change remains constant; it varies in amount and in direction in an as yet unpredictable manner. To illustrate the change of the change: In 1580 in London it was measured as 11°E, in 1780 it was 23°W, and is now about 8°W. That's of little importance to modern sailors, who are not likely to use ancient charts. But it keeps armchair navigators from working out the true courses Columbus sailed, although we know his day-to-day magnetic courses.

The variation at any one place also shows daily fluctuations, but they are too small to concern the sailor. The same goes for magnetic storms, connected with solar outbreaks. They'll snarl communications but won't throw off your compass more than one degree, according to the Navy. Here and there on charts or in sailing directions you'll find mention of local magnetic disturbances— anomalies to the magneticians. In shallow water they might be caused by ore deposits. Sailing over a barely covered wreck you might get some of her magnetism mixed up with your compass. But in deep water most anomalies reported by ships' captains turn out on investigation to be caused by something on the ship rather than under water. That sailor's knife again? With the magnetic attraction falling off rapidly with distance, it would take a deposit of super magnets to foul up your compass.

Now let's see how we can live with the fairly constant, though unpredictable variation that turns every magnetic compass in a given area in the same direction, regardless of the heading of the vessel.

If you never cruise far from home, you can make it fairly easy for yourself. Put a second lubber's line on your compass. Then read true—as opposed to magnetic—headings directly from that second line. I don't mean you should take your compass apart and scratch in another line, but put a marker where it'll show true north when the card reads magnetic north. Then you can convert instantly, without jingles, and without arithmetic, true courses to magnetic ones, or magnetic bearings to true ones.

If you plan to cruise some distance from home you'll have to use another method to allow for the changing variation in different areas. Use the compass rose on your chart. The outer rose, as we have seen, always indicates true directions, the inner roses magnetic directions in the vicinity of the chart rose. You don't have to transfer courses and bearings from other parts of the chart to the rose. Just draw a line through the center of the rose and the known direction (true or magnetic) and read off the unknown direction on the other rose (magnetic or true). We have illustrated this method already in the chapter that deals with the tools of navigation.

When you go crossing oceans, you'll use charts that instead of compass roses show only lines of equal variation. Then you'll have to use your head a little, something that's not forbidden in home

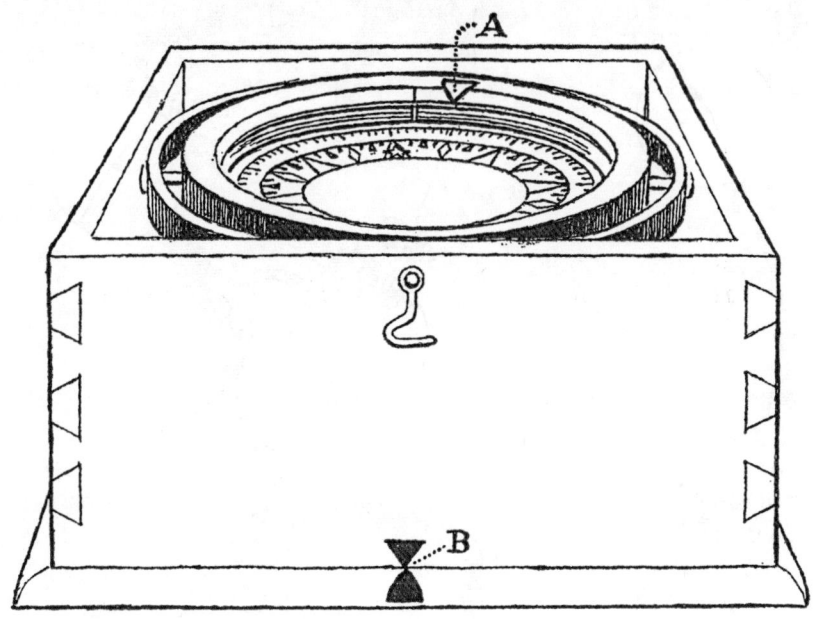

46. *Second lubber's line (A) on compass lets you convert true to magnetic. Markers (B) assure that removable box compass is always placed in same way.*

waters and while cruising. The mathematics are simple enough: You either add or subtract the variation. But which is it? Add or subtract?

Perhaps you know some clever jingles to help you decide. I dislike jingles because I get east and west mixed up, and faced with two choices I more often than not get the wrong one. Call it the law of the key ring. With a dozen keys, I usually get the right one; with only two keys I scratch the trunk of my car with the ignition key, and try to start the car with the trunk key.

So I ignore the jingles and try to visualize the problem. Variation west means the compass points west of north; variation east means it points east of north. Whether to add or subtract in a given situation then becomes quite obvious. Should I even forget whether the variation here should be east or west I try to recall a map of North America with three compasses. The middle compass points true. The one on the east coast points west of north; and the one on the west coast points east of north. I don't try to remember it that way,

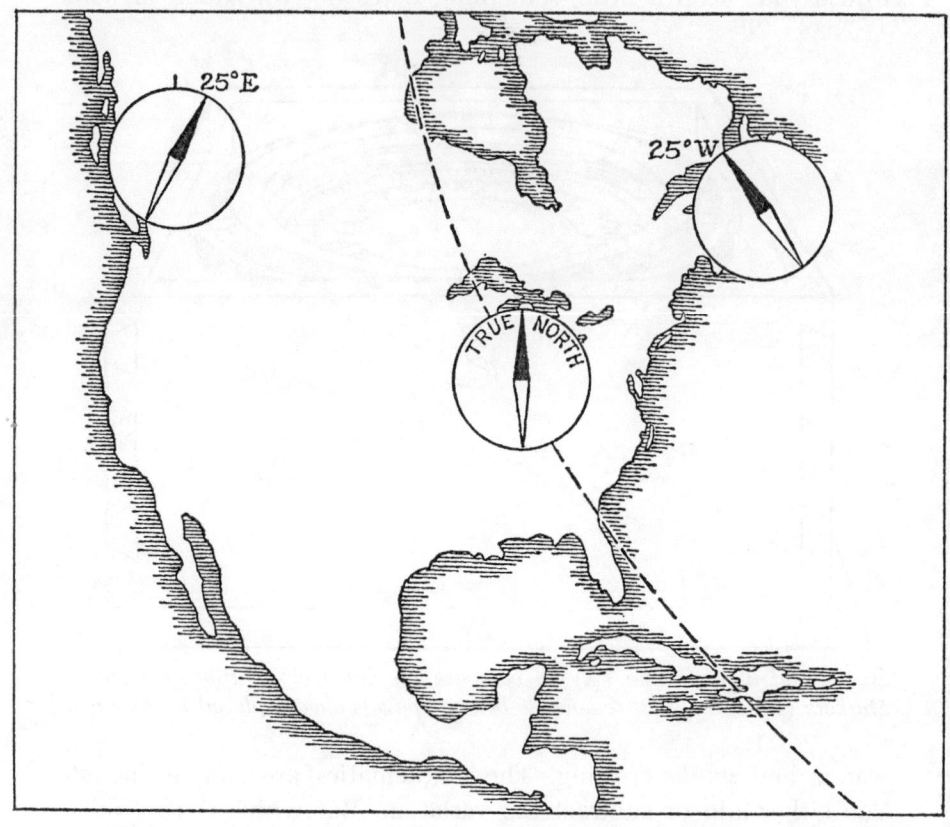

47. *Memory aid for compass correction when applying variation. Along points on the dashed line compass points true. On east coast of North America it points west of true north; on west coast of North America it points east of true north. Note, as a memory aid, how all three compasses point roughly to one point.*

but by the way the needles all point toward one point (more or less).

If by ingrained habit you can convert magnetic courses and bearings into true ones, even while at the verge of *mal de mer*, and dog-tired, you won't need any of these aids.

Neither, according to his method, did a fisherman in Nova Scotia who told me his secret: "Place your compass on a wet glove, keep that glove wet, and the compass will always point true." If that doesn't work for you, you can move to the Bahamas, Greece, Vietnam, or eastern Siberia, where the compass shows true close enough as not to matter.

13 Tides and Tidal Currents

You have been warned by authors of boating books to distinguish between tides—the periodic rise and fall of the sea level—and the currents they cause—flood and ebb. Then the same authors, including this one, forget their own warnings and talk about "tideways" (where the current runs strongly), about their anchored vessel being "tide-rode" (lying to the current rather than the wind), or about their little vessel having been "set by the tide" (pushed off course by current).

In this chapter at least I'll try to keep the vertical and horizontal movements separate. Let's talk about the vertical changes in sea level first.

You know all about the moon and the sun causing these changes. You have been told why the small moon being close to earth, in most places has the upper hand over the influence of the sun, more massive but so much farther away. You know how sun and moon pulling in the same direction, at full and new moon, cause the highest tides of the month. Why these spring tides come two or three days *after* full and new moon, is usually glossed over. But you accept it as a fact, just as you accept the lowest high water coming a few days after first and last quarter.

You know how the changing distance of the moon also governs the height of the daily tides, and how her changing declination (position north or south of the celestial equator) accounts for the differences between night and day tides during parts of each month.

You know that in most places—including the east coasts of

Canada and the United States, for instance—two more or less equal high waters occur within about twenty-five hours, each high water followed about six hours later by low water, two succeeding low waters again of about equal height. You also know that in many places—the west coasts of the United States and Canada, for example—two successive high waters and the two following low waters can be of very unequal heights. And you probably have heard that some coasts—the Gulf coast of the United States, for instance—at least during part of each month have only one high and one low water each day instead of the customary two.

With all this reassuring knowledge it may come as a shock to you to hear that tides for any given spot still cannot be predicted by any formula. Perhaps you can see that the heights depend on local conditions. But also the times of high and low waters cannot even be guessed at.

Along some coasts the time of high water seems to run fairly regularly along the shore. On the west coast of the United States, for instance, high water gets later as you move north. In Seattle it's about seven hours later than at San Diego, less than a thousand miles away. But in a similar distance on the east coast, between Miami and New York, all ocean stations have high water at about the same time. On a given day Miami, Daytona Beach, Charleston, the entrances to the Chesapeake and Delaware Bays, and Sandy Hook all had high water within forty-four minutes. On the same tide the Battery, at the southern tip of Manhattan, was forty-four minutes later then Sandy Hook, only fourteen miles away. It was more than five hours later that the same high water reached Kingston Point, about seventy-five miles upriver from the Battery. Yet in British Columbia, in some inlets high water at the head, fifty or one hundred miles from the ocean, is only minutes after high water at the entrance.

To cope with such unpredictables, the agency in charge of tide prediction (in the United States, the Coast and Geodetic Survey) sets up a tide gauge, and from the swiggles the pen traces during the observation period, calculates what should happen at some other time. Ideally the gauge should record tides for almost nineteen years until moon and sun have run through all possible tide-causing phases, and will start to repeat the cycle. Such records have been made at many reference stations. At other stations a record of only one year, or even one month, is used for calculating the tide tables.

How reassuring these tide tables are. The official tables, or the little cards your friendly hardware dealer gives away, seem to predict the times to the nearest minute, the heights to the nearest tenth of a foot, or about one inch.

Bilgewater. Look closer; the times are given to six-minute intervals. Still very accurate. But these times are calculated only for the very spot where the tide gauge was installed during the survey. Within a couple of miles, within the same harbor, it could be an hour and a foot off. Barometric pressure upsets predictions. On a low glass both high and low waters will be higher, on a high glass lower. The effect is of the order of one foot in height of tide for an inch change in barometric pressure. In many places that goes unnoticed. But ask the people of Sanibel, in the Gulf of Mexico, where the tidal range is small and the beach slopes gently. There are people who have collected shells there until they begin to look like seabirds—head forward and down, neck stretched, tailfeathers out; they know all about the barometric effect.

Then there is the wind: An onshore wind blows waters into bays and river mouths, making both high and low waters higher than predicted. An offshore wind will have the opposite effect.

Once on a cruise on the west coast of Abaco I had planned to settle once and for all the question of tides in that area. We were weatherbound in a little natural harbor; what better time to set up a tide staff and keep a record? Only one thing wrong: With that onshore wind it showed high water all day and all night.

Some people have another factor to worry about. River levels are averaged over the seasons, and tides predicted from that theoretical river level. Then floods and droughts will mess up the tidy-looking calculations.

What is one to do? Throw away the tide tables? Certainly not. But allow for river stages. You can also improve predictions at your own dock by measuring a few tides and comparing them—in both time and height—with the nearest point for which the tide tables give data. The tide will always be high and low as much sooner or later as on the day you measured it. Taking the readings on several days eliminates as much as possible the influences of the weather, about which we can do nothing.

In a strange place, when you ask the dockmaster about times of tides, you won't get the times of high and low water. Chances are he'll give you the times of slack current. To many dockmasters the height of the tide is unimportant; what they care about are the times when they can horse a boat from one slip to the next.

Sometimes we want to know the height of water level at some time between high and low water. There are, of course, tables for that. There are tables for almost everything, and these tables again give a false sense of accuracy.

When it takes about six hours from high to low water—5½ to 6½ hours, perhaps—you can do the calculation mentally. As you probably have noticed, on the rising tide the level comes up slowly at first, then faster, until at halftime between the tides it's halfway between the level of low and high water. The rise then slows during the last half of the rising tide. On the falling tide it first drops slowly, then faster, reaches half level at halftime, then slows in its rate of fall.

Here is a simple formula that lets you calculate the hourly change, whether the level is rising or falling. Call the range of this tide—the difference between high water and low water—H (in *feet*). The water level rises or falls:

$$1 \times H \text{ inches in the first hour.}$$
$$2 \times H \text{ " " " second "}$$
$$3 \times H \text{ " " " third "}$$
$$3 \times H \text{ " " " fourth "}$$
$$2 \times H \text{ " " " fifth "}$$
$$1 \times H \text{ " " " sixth "}$$

You'll see that all you have to remember is 1-2-3-3-2-1 (either mechanically, or thinking of the gradual increase until midtide and the decrease after midtide), and use *inches* in hourly change to correspond to the range of the tide in *feet*.

Here is an example: Range of tide four feet (H = 4).

	RISING			FALLING	
Hour	Change	Level	Hour	Change	Level
	(inches)	(inches)		(inches)	(inches)
0	—	LW = 0	0	—	HW = 48
1	4	4	1	4	44
2	8	12	2	8	36
3	12	24	3	12	24
4	12	36	4	12	12
5	8	44	5	8	4
6	4	HW = 48	6	4	LW = 0

Tides and Tidal Currents 133

You always have a check: At half tide, after three hours, the level should be halfway between high and low, whether it's rising or falling.

Sometimes we have the opposite problem. We sail into a strange harbor and want to know how much below high water the level is now. Binoculars make a good tide gauge here. On a beach, sandy or pebbly, you'll see the wrack left by the last tide. Ignore older stuff higher up on the beach; it has been left by some extreme high tide, perhaps an unusual storm tide. On rocky shores the world over, a black streak of microorganisms marks the high-water level like a ring on a bathtub. On docks, pilings, and trees (such as mangrove and cypress), you can read the state of the tide from such marine animals as oysters, mussels, and barnacles, and from algae and other plants.

Can you predict the times of high and low water without a tide table? There is a method still recommended by old-timers for telling time of high water as so many hours after moonrise. It's a poor method. First, during the greater part of the month the moon rises in daytime or so late at night that most people wouldn't be likely to see it. Second, the method is all wrong. We all know that the sun rises later in winter, when it is below the equator, than in summer, when it is north of the line. In the same way moonrise depends on its changing position above or below the equator, while the time of high water does not. In Boston, for example, on two days on which the tide is high at 11 A.M. and 11 P.M., the moon may rise at 4 P.M. or at 8 P.M.

Another method that still has many followers predicts high water at a given place from the compass bearing of the moon. "Southeast moon makes the sea full," some old-timer may tell you. Don't you believe him. The method is so old and so bad that more than a century and a half ago Captain Nathaniel Bowditch warned pilots against its use in his *New American Practical Navigator*.

The method will work, almost accidentally, on days of full and new moon when high water happens to be at noon and midnight. There, whenever the moon bears south, the sea will be full. That will be, on an average, about fifty minutes later each day.

The same fifty minutes later—you can call it an hour for simplicity —will let you predict tomorrow's tides when you know today's. The accuracy isn't bad; the delay is usually somewhere between thirty-six and sixty-six minutes.

You can work out a complete tide table for your own dock or any other place if you know the time of high water on days of full or new moon. Say you find it's about 8 A.M. and 8 P.M. That makes low water on that day at about 2 A.M. and 2 P.M. It will be about the same on *any* day of full or new moon. On the day after it'll be about an hour later: HW at 9 A.M. and 9 P.M., LW at 3 A.M. and 3 P.M. It'll get later by about an hour until at last or first quarter the tides have switched from full and new moon tides: high at 2 A.M. and 2 P.M., low at 8 A.M. and 8 P.M. Then they again get later by about an hour and will be high at 8 A.M. and 8 P.M. a week later, at new or full moon. If you have a calendar or can see the moon and approximately gauge its age, this very rough calculation will serve you well when no better information is available.

Enough of the up-and-down movement of tides. Let's now look at the horizontal motion, the tidal currents, caused by these changes in sea level. They seem simple enough. Almost anyone would believe that:

1. Since high water is caused by the attraction of the moon and the sun, both seemingly traveling from east to west, high water is later farther west, and so the flood current sets toward the west.
2. The ebb begins at high water, the flood at low water.
3. Places with large tide ranges have strong tidal currents; places with small ranges, weak currents.
4. The flood sets toward the beach, the ebb away from it.
5. Many currents in coastal waters are not tidal, but caused by the wind.

All these statements sound perfectly logical, but *all these statements are false.*

You no doubt remember the drawing in every textbook that shows the earth bulging with high water "under" the moon. No one has ever noticed a current caused by that bulge moving westward. And that's just as well. Take the high water traveling with the apparent speed of sun or moon, about fifteen degrees longitude per hour. Start in Bermuda, for example. An hour later that bulge should arrive at Charleston. That'd make a current of 750 knots. Worse! This morning the tide was high at Ireland Island at 8:34 A.M. Bermuda time, 7:34 A.M. Eastern Standard Time. It was high at North Jetty, Charleston Harbor entrance, at 7:39 A.M., five minutes later. Some current!

It's a different matter in tidal rivers and bays. At Cape Henlopen, at the entrance to Delaware Bay, high water is about 2½ hours earlier than at Reedy Island, fifty miles up the bay. At the entrance to the Columbia River high water is forty-six minutes earlier than at Astoria, twelve miles upriver. Of course, in Delaware Bay the current sets in a northerly direction, in the Columbia River eastward. So there goes the westward flood current.

When I brought my schooner *Lucina* from Nova Scotia, I went through U.S. customs at Eastport, Maine. I left there just before high water, hoping to find slack water and the first of the ebb to help me along. Instead I ran into a strong foul current full of fearsome whirlpools. I had overlooked one of the most basic facts about ebb and flood: Tidal currents don't slack and reverse direction when the tide *level* stands, at high or low water.

This statement, which seems to go against common sense, has sparked countless arguments at every yacht club. By now even the bartender knows the answer. "High water at the club dock means, sir, that the level here is as high as it'll get on this tide. It doesn't say anything about the water level farther up the bay. As long as, above us, it's lower than here, the current is going to run up the bay. It will continue to flood, while the level at the club dock is already dropping."

If you'd let him, the bartender would also tell you that in the same way a higher water level up the bay will cause the ebb current to continue after low water at the club dock, even though the water level there is already rising.

The bartender's explanation is universally true where a tidal basin connects with the ocean through a narrow entrance. It could be a salt marsh draining through a culvert, or San Francisco Bay with its Golden Gate.

In many places the lag between the time of the stand of the tide (at high or low water) and the time of slack water (at beginning of ebb and flood current) is measured not in minutes or fractions of hours, but in hours. At the Golden Gate, for example, the current slacks two hours or more after high and low water. The skipper who listens to common sense instead of the bartender, and arrives there early, may have to fight a four-knot current.

That's a lot of current. A half-knot adverse current (yachtsmen seldom mention currents that have helped them along) would seriously hinder a swimmer, and make rowing noticeably harder work. A one-knot current is enough to spoil the performance of a

136   NAVIGATION

sailboat. A two-knot current affects even powerboats. If you normally cruise at eight knots (9 mph) your speed over the bottom in such a current would drop to six knots (7 mph). That might add

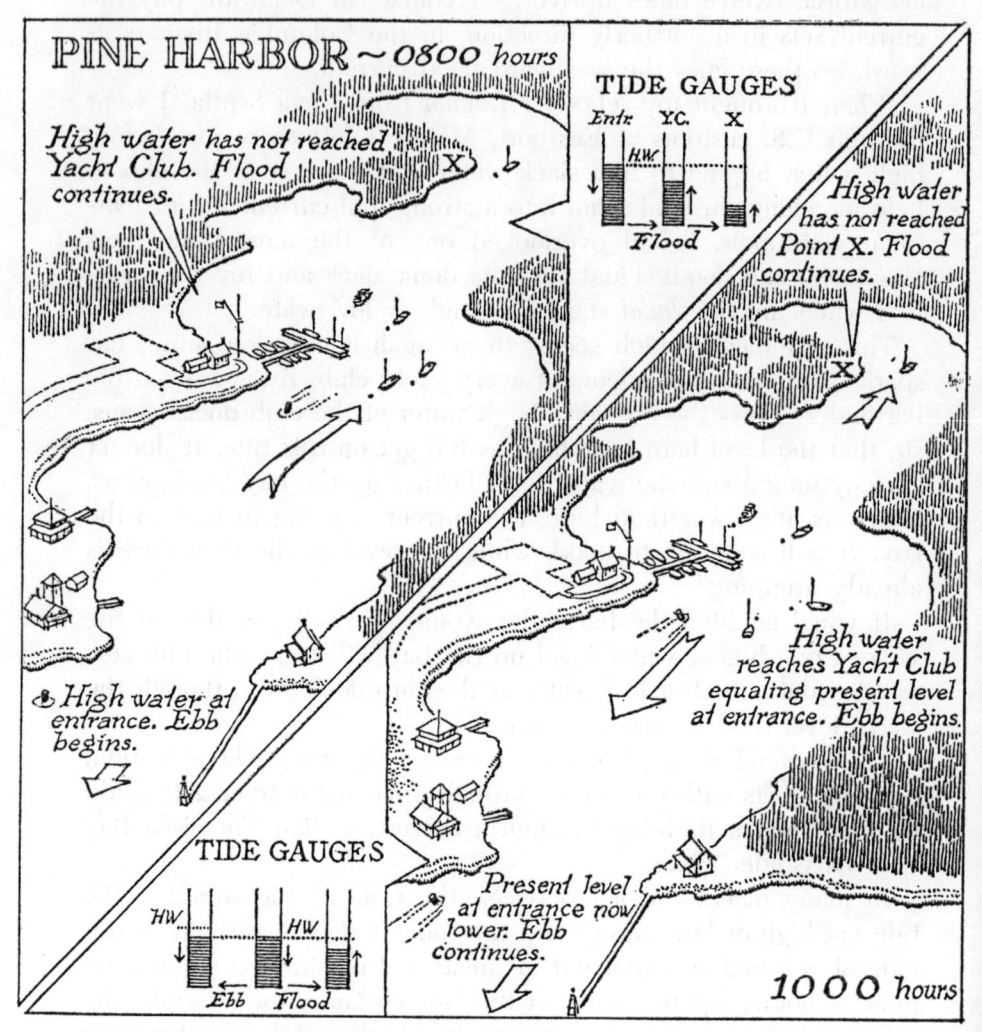

48. *Tidal current does not reverse at times of high and low water. Left: Flood continues in the bay after high water at the entrance. Right: Flood continues in the upper bay after high water at Yacht Club.*

enough time to your trip to empty your fuel tanks short of the gas dock. Increasing revolutions to maintain standard speed, you'll run out of fuel even faster since you'd use more fuel at higher rpm's. A current of more than two knots commands respect from any pleasure craft. Such a current is likely to cause local eddies that'll make steering erratic.

It's often useful to know how long the current will be more or less slack. Here is a table that answers that question. The figures are conservative; at most places the weak current will last somewhat longer.

Maximum current	Weak current (½ knot) lasts
1 knot	90 minutes
2 knots	36 minutes
3 knots	22 minutes
4 knots	17 minutes

Example: Predicted maximum current 3 knots—the current will not flow at more than ½-knot velocity for 22 minutes (11 minutes before and 11 minutes after slack water).

At any given place the strength of the current will vary with the height of the local tides. It will be strongest during spring tides, weakest during neaps. At these extremes the current speed will typically be 40 percent above or 40 percent below average speed.

You cannot predict the average speed of a current from the time of high (or low) water at two places. Dividing the distance from Cape Henlopen to Reedy Island by the time it takes high water to reach that island from the entrance gives twenty knots. Luckily the maximum current in Delaware Bay is about two knots. Even that seems too much when you are bucking it.

In most places the ebb is stronger, and lasts longer, than the flood. You'll find that four out of five of all reference current stations on the United States Atlantic, Gulf, and Pacific coasts bear out this statement. It comes as no surprise where rivers empty into the ocean: Their natural flow adds to the ebb and hinders the flood.

You can't guess the strength of tidal currents from the range of tide. Eastport, Maine, as we have seen, has strong currents; that's not surprising with a tide range of more than twenty feet. But San

Francisco's Golden Gate, with ranges of six feet, has stronger currents. Galveston, with a mean range of only 1.4 feet, has as strong an ebb current as you'll find off the Battery in New York Harbor, where the range is four times that.

You'll find strong tidal currents wherever two bays meet. The link can be natural, as New York's East River (average maximum velocity 4.6 knots), or Washington's Deception Pass (6.6 knots). It can be a man-made channel, as in the Cape Cod Canal (4.5 knots), or just a friendly meeting of two embayments at some headland. At such places an underwater spur will set up disturbances at the surface ranging from a strange popple to a vicious tide rip.

You'll find similar unpleasant conditions where the wind is against the current, say an easterly wind blowing over an eastgoing current.

Watch out also for spots where the current sets at an angle to the channel, as it does at many bridges on the Inland Waterway from New Jersey to Florida. Along the same waterway a current entering from the ocean will often hit you broadside. A not unusual three-knot current will turn your bow four feet in one second.

For the coasting skipper here is another fact about tidal currents: Near the shore, flood and ebb don't usually set toward and away from the land but run parallel to the coastline. Except where bays or river mouths interrupt the coast, you'll find that true from Alaska to California, and from Florida to Maine.

A few miles from shore, in the open sea and in some large bays (the Gulf of St. Lawrence, for example), the current behaves quite differently. On a windless day, influenced only by the current, a boat anchored there would change her heading continuously. In a little more than twelve hours she'd sweep out a complete circle, clockwise, around her anchor. These rotary currents change in strength as they change in direction, but the current never slacks.

Boatmen blame the wind for all sorts of currents, probably wrongly. Longtime observations on lightships stationed off the Atlantic and Pacific coasts of the United States show that it takes at least a twenty-knot breeze to cause a half-knot current; it takes at least a fifty-knot gale to cause a one-knot current. Of course, the wind can upset the neatly printed current predictions. As we have seen, it changes the times and levels of high and low water, and the currents must follow.

In strange waters the coast pilots will warn you of nasty currents.

Tides and Tidal Currents 139

The very names on the chart sometimes give notice. Who wouldn't expect mean currents at places called Pollock Rip, East Chop, The Race, Hell Gate, Something Narrows or Pass, or Devil's Anything?

The tidal current tables published yearly by Coast and Geodetic Survey (one volume for the Atlantic and Gulf coasts, one for the Pacific coast) are a great help. But we can also keep our eyes open. Anchored yachts, leaning buoys, and ripples at dock piles all are current indicators for the observant skipper.

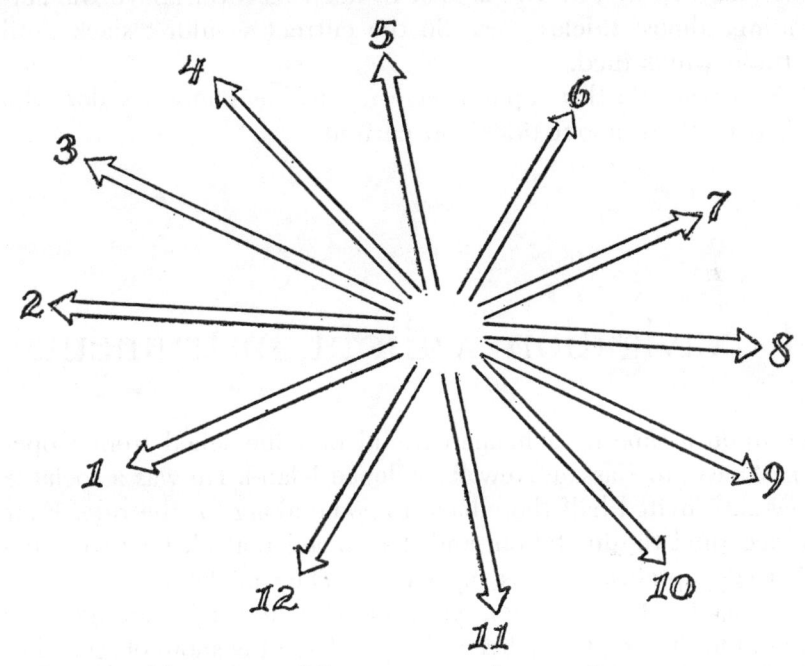

49. *Rotary tidal current—offshore current changes direction continuously, sweeping out a full circle in about twelve hours, numbered from 1–12; length of arrows indicates strength of current.*

Where the current runs fiercely through a passage you may want to use the technique of the tugs that tow logs along the coast of British Columbia.

Five-knot currents are commonplace on some of these runs. The tugboat skipper plans to arrive at such passes well ahead of predicted slack water. Then he waits in a nearby cove studying the passing driftwood through binoculars to get the best time for going through.

Even after a lifetime of tidewater sailing you can run into puzzling currents. The skipper of a ketch did when he tried to beat into the lagoon of a Pacific island. At its only entrance he found a strong ebb. With his engine out of commission, he couldn't stem the current. So he jogged off and on for three hours and tried again. Same current. And it was still pouring out of the lagoon when he tried again three hours later. What was this? Not a tidal current at all. Swells breaking on the windward side of the ring-shaped reef sent enough spray into the lagoon to keep its level above the surrounding, almost tideless, sea. So the current wouldn't slack until the trade winds died.

A long wait. So this captain gave up, as has many a sailor who tried to learn all about tides and currents.

14 Navigation without Instruments

Once upon a time a yachtsman friend of mine sailed from Hopetown, Abaco, to Nassau, New Providence Island. He was a sociable fellow and invited half the village to come along for the ride. Four men accepted the invitation, and it chanced that all four were experienced captains. So was my friend. They all knew the run to Nassau well: Once you got your offing, steer 195° straight for Nassau. On the first thirty-five miles you have the shore of Abaco in sight. Then from Hole in the Wall it's an easy fifty miles to Nassau. The diesels purred. The five skippers took casual turns at the wheel, and made their landfall in record time. Only it wasn't New Providence but Egg Island, thirty-five miles northeast of Nassau. A camera bag that held an exposure meter had thrown off their compass.

This chapter is not about compass work. The point I'm trying to make is this: Without a compass, without any navigational equipment at all, they could have done better. It's unlikely that the wind should have shifted as they passed Hole in the Wall. Watching the compass, not one of these master mariners had noticed that the wind was not where it had been on the first part of the trip. Not by four points. Even if the wind had hauled a bit, the swells would have continued for hours to run with the old wind. Not one of the five singing seamen had noticed that the beam sea was now broad on the port bow.

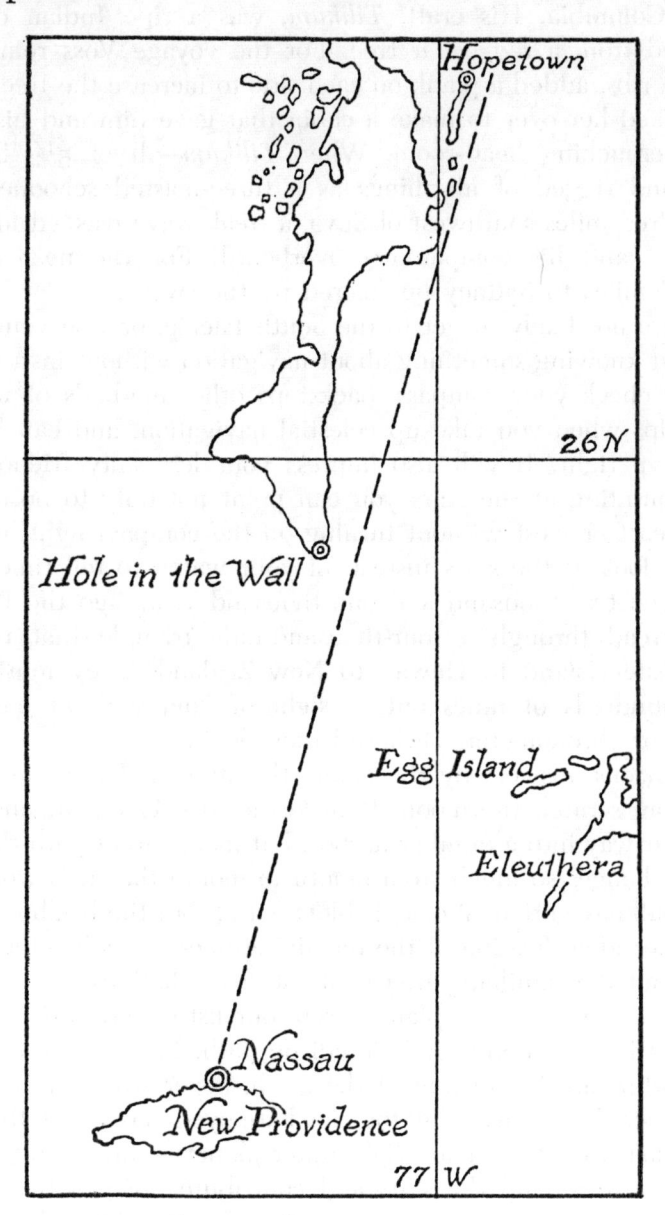

50. *Hopetown—Nassau Course* 195°.

The swells can be most helpful to the navigator. Do you remember J. C. Voss's *Venturesome Voyage?* Captain Voss set out in 1901, shortly after Slocum's first small-boat circumnavigation of the globe, for another sail around the world, starting from Victoria, British Columbia. His craft, *Tilikum,* was a ripe Indian dugout fashioned from a red cedar tree. For the voyage Voss reinforced her with ribs, added a plank on each side to increase the freeboard, and decked her over to make a cabin that gave him and his companion crouching head-room. When *Tilikum*—all of 5½ feet of beam, and rigged of all things as a three-masted schooner—was six hundred miles southwest of Suva, a freak wave washed his only compass (and his companion) overboard. For the next twelve hundred miles to Sydney he steered by the swells.

You are not likely to get to the South Pacific, or lose your compass. But knowing something about navigation without instruments lets you check your compass, backstops other methods of navigation, helps when you take up celestial navigation, and can be fun in its own right. It will also impress your less salty friends that when squinting at the stars you can point not only to north, but exactly east or west without turning on the compass light, or that you can look at the stars instead of your watch to tell time.

Between two thousand and one thousand years ago the Polynesians spread through a four-thousand-mile triangle that reaches from Easter Island to Hawaii to New Zealand. They must have sailed hundreds of miles out of sight of land without compass, sextant, or chronometer. How did they do it?

An obvious answer: by the moon, the stars, and the sun.

You can scratch the moon. It makes a good calendar, and may light your way into a familiar harbor; but its apparent path through the sky changes so much from month to month that it is worthless for eyeball navigation. Worse, it blots out all but the brightest stars and makes identification of the remaining ones difficult after partly wiping out the familiar patterns of the constellations.

We can also strike the planets from our list of navigational aids. Each has its own highly individualistic path. Mercury and Venus, whose orbits are inside that of the earth, never stray far from the sun and can't do anything for the bare-eyed navigator that the sun doesn't do better. The bright outer planets—Mars, Jupiter, and Saturn—move among the stars and contribute little to the instrumentless navigator, except occasional confusion with a fixed star.

There's an awful lot of stars, and a fleet of man-selected constellations. But a knowledge of only a few stars and constellations can help the navigator considerably.

Almost everyone in the Northern Hemisphere recognizes the Big Dipper (or Plow), and from the two leading stars, the Pointers, can find Polaris, the Pole Star. That star is about 4½ times the distance of the Pointer away on the open side of the Dipper. The stars of the Dipper and Polaris are bright enough to be seen even on a full-moon night. There is a check that assures you it's Polaris and not some other star. Polaris everywhere is roughly as many degrees above the horizon as your latitude is north of the equator. On Long Island Sound, in approximate latitude 41°N, you'll always find it about forty degrees above the horizon.

The Pointers don't exactly point at Polaris, and Polaris isn't exactly at the celestial pole but about a degree from it. So at times it could mislead you by one degree east or west.

When you can't see the Big Dipper, Cassiopeia—the big letter M or W in the sky—will help you find Polaris. A line from the outermost handle star in the Dipper to the trailing star of Cassiopeia runs almost exactly through Polaris and the celestial pole. When either of these stars is directly above or below Polaris, that star points north accurately enough to adjust your compass.

Polaris for the rest of this century will slowly approach the celestial pole. In ancient times it was much farther away. Columbus seems to have been unaware of that fact, and reports in his journal that the "needles" when he checked them against the Pole Star were in error.

As you go farther south, Polaris drops closer to the horizon. In the latitude of Grenada, in the Windward Islands (12°N), or of the Panama Canal (9°N) you may have trouble finding Polaris even on a clear night since its light will be dimmed one magnitude by absorption in the atmosphere when it's so near the horizon. It will get harder and harder to see as you approach the equator and there finally sink below the horizon.

You probably have read that no star as bright as Polaris marks the celestial south pole. True. Sigma Octantis—it hasn't even a common name—the star nearest that pole, is of fifth magnitude, visible only on moonless nights. By coincidence it's just about as far from its pole as is Polaris from the celestial north pole. By another coincidence there are two pointer stars missing it by about as much as a line from the Pointers in the Dipper misses Polaris. By a third coincidence the southern pointers are 4½ pointer distances from the celestial south pole. They form the long axis of the Southern Cross (Crux). Their official names are Alpha and Gamma Crucis, which modern navigators have given the cable addresses ACRUX and GACRUX.

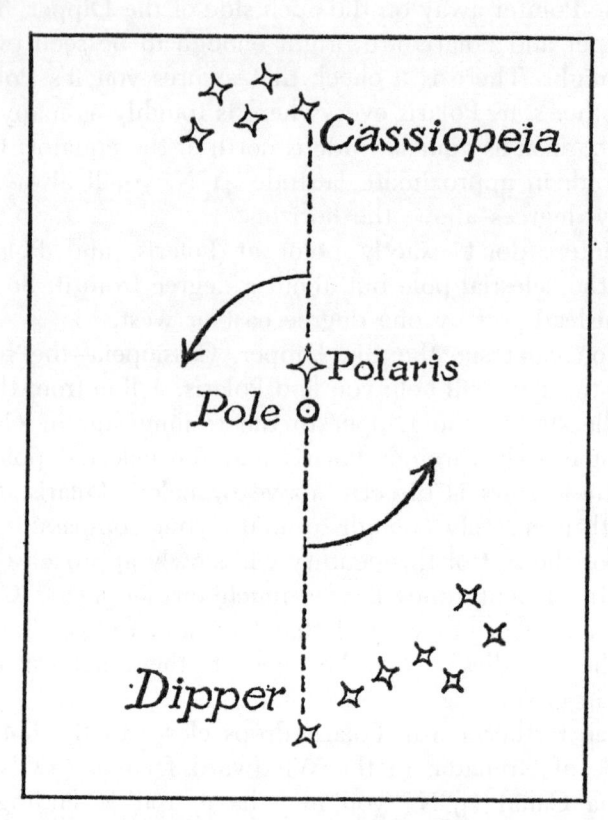

51. *The Big Dipper and Cassiopeia are at opposite sides of celestial north pole. Arrows indicate apparent rotation of constellations. The terms "leading" and "trailing" (of stars within a constellation) refer to this motion.*

Of course the celestial south pole is always as many degrees above your horizon as you are south of the equator. In Sydney, near latitude 34°S, it would be a little more than a third of the way between the horizon and the zenith.

North or south of the equator—at least a few degrees away from it—the poles give you a north and south line. Are there any east and

Navigation without Instruments 145

west lines in the sky? Yes. Seen from the same latitude, stars, unlike the sun, rise and set at the same point of the horizon all year long. A few stars can be expected to rise due east and set due west. These stars—at or very near the celestial equator—do so whenever you see them rise or set regardless of your latitude, and in both the Northern and Southern hemispheres.

You probably already know one of these useful stars. It's the leading (i.e. westernmost—first to rise and first to set) of the three stars that form the belt of Orion. The middle star of the belt

52. *Pointers in the Big Dipper help find the celestial north pole; the stars that form the long axis of the Southern Cross, help find the celestial south pole.*

would do almost as well. Having seen Orion in winter in northern latitudes you may think of it as a northern constellation. Not so; being on the celestial equator, Orion is visible over all the oceans of the world.

There is a hitch, though: During the summer this useful constellation rises or sets during daylight hours. Then another star is just as useful: Zeta in Virgo, the Virgin. It's the star just north (about a handwidth of the outstretched arm) of Spica, the brightest star of

146 NAVIGATION

this constellation, and roughly on a line from Spica to even brighter Arcturus. Find it from a star chart on some summer night. It's worth it. When Orion doesn't rise or set for you during the dark hours, Virgo probably does.

You can carry the star business one step farther and get four points so spread over the sky that you'll be assured of an east-west check every few hours during any clear night.

Some authorities have suggested that the Polynesians sailed

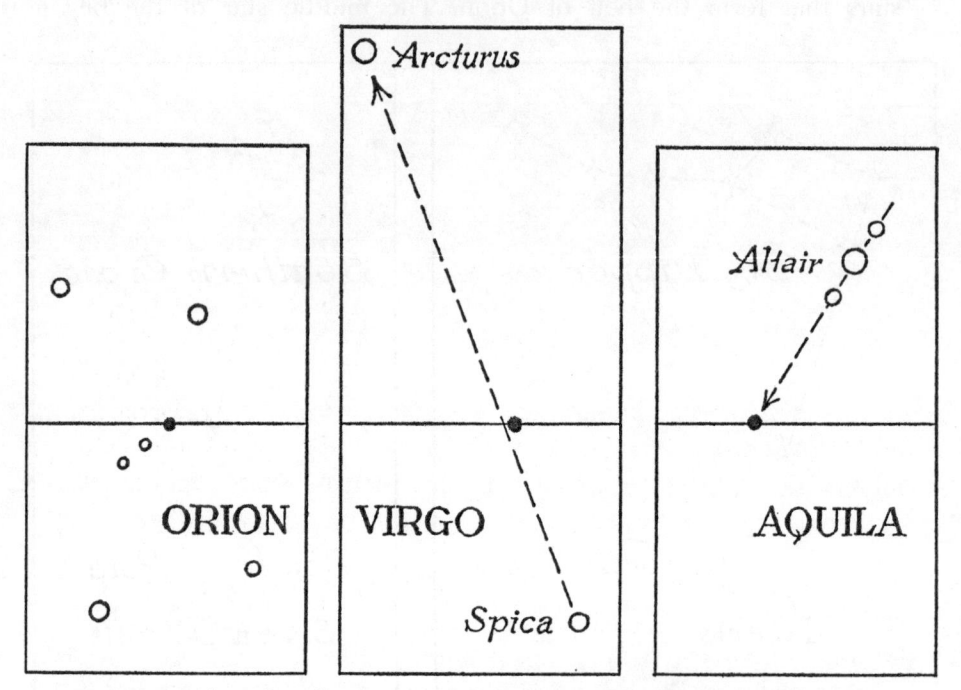

53. *Stars on the celestial equator rise due east, set due west over all the oceans of the world. The leading star in the belt of Orion, Zeta in Virgo, and Theta in Aquila, are such stars.*

north or south until a certain star was directly overhead, then sailed east or west until they sighted their destination. That sounds much like Western navigators running down their easting or westing along the latitude of their destination. But the star-overhead method, still mentioned today in instructions for lifeboat navigation, just doesn't seem practical. Perhaps you can tell when a star is directly overhead when you lie in a hammock ashore. But I doubt that the editors of these instructions have tried the method in a lifeboat at sea, for they suggest the use of a plumb bob as a help. It'll help put a dent in your head, I'd say.

There are simpler ways to find latitude.

Admiral Rodman, some years ago, discovered what he called the "sacred calabash." This instrument, made from a gourd and having some holes in it, was supposed to have guided the Tahitians to Hawaii. Here is how the admiral explained its use: They filled the calabash with water, and held it so that none spilled out of any of the holes (i.e., horizontally). Then sighting through one of the holes they'd look at Polaris. When that star seemed to touch the rim of the calabash, they were in the latitude of Hawaii—about 20°N —could stop worrying about northing, and sail downwind until they made land.

Someone spoiled this beautiful story by measuring the angle between holes and rim. It was all wrong. Even before that some of us had our doubts. Why would seamen surrounded by the ocean use an artificial horizon (the water in the calabash)? Why risk a salt water eye bath, when a stick held at arm's length would do just as well?

In Hawaii you could sight Polaris, and cut a stick that, held at arm's length, would just fit between Polaris and the sea horizon. It would come out about 8½ inches long. When on the return trip you find a good fit again, you'd know you'd be in the latitude of Hawaii.

The Arabs are said to have had a similar device: a stick on a string. The same stick served for all latitudes visited; knots in the string made the observer hold the stick at the right distance from the eye to give the proper angle for every harbor.

Before you rush out to cut a stick, or tie a knot, for your home port, let me warn you that the method isn't very accurate. It's not the length of your arm or string or the crudeness of the stick that causes trouble. It's the fact that the Pole Stars (North and South) are not exactly at the poles and therefore don't quite stand still. If you'd cut your stick, or tied your knot, while the outermost handle star in the Dipper was at the three or nine o'clock position, you'd be about fifty-four nautical miles too far south when the same star is at twelve o'clock; you'd be the same distance north when it's at six o'clock. In any other position of that star the error would, of course, be less. But when the Polynesians, and the Arabs, made their voyages the error was much greater, since Polaris was farther

148 NAVIGATION

from the true pole. Perhaps they allowed for that error by using the stick only when the Dipper, Cassiopeia, the Southern Cross, or some other constellation was in the same position as when they had cut the stick.

Perhaps they used a far more accurate method, one that requires no instrument whatever, not even a stick or string. It seems to have

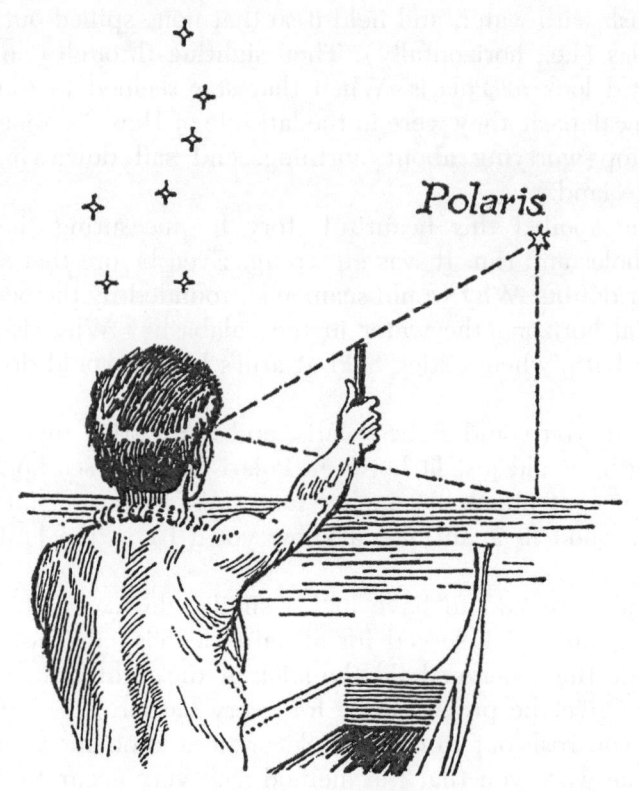

54. *A stick, cut to fit between Polaris and the sea horizon when held at arm's length, lets you find the latitude where it was cut.*

been overlooked by the people who write about Polynesian navigation, and edit lifeboat manuals. Yet it is simple.

In most of the United States the Big Dipper never sets. But as you travel south, Polaris and the Dipper sink lower and lower, until parts of the Dipper dip right below the horizon during a few hours of the night. In Florida, south of Fort Pierce, even Dubhe —the Pointer nearest Polaris—sets. To find Fort Pierce you could sail south until Dubhe just touches the northern horizon but doesn't sink. Then sail west until you see the whistle buoy.

To find a star that will lead you back to your home port look at the horizon directly below Polaris. Watch for a star that touches the horizon in the early morning hours. If you found one that kisses the horizon at 4 A.M., that star would do so again at 2 A.M. a month later, and so on two hours earlier each month. You'll have a guide for several months, then you'd have to find another star, again in the morning. These two stars between them will serve you for the rest of your life.

Of course there aren't enough bright stars at the proper distance from the pole to kiss the horizon at everyone's home port. It would have to be a fairly bright star, because atmospheric absorption, quite apart from haze, greatly lessens the apparent brightness of all stars close to the horizon. If you settle on a star that stays above the horizon by the width of a pencil, a finger's breadth, or a thumb's width, it can be less bright.

Knowing that you are in the latitude of your destination is often not enough. If you were west of Fort Pierce, you'd be on dry land, so you are not likely to turn east where Dubhe kisses the sea, and sail for the Canary Islands instead of heading for the seabuoy. When you are making your landfall on an island, as the Polynesians did, you had better know whether it's to the right or the left of your course. Surely the Polynesians used that old trick of steering on purpose to one side of your destination. Being wind-sailors, they kept to windward of their mark, just as the clipper captains did, and as modern sailors still do. It's easier to slide downwind than to tack back.

The skew course is just as helpful on a modern powerboat. Coming in from fishing offshore, you aim at a point say five miles south of your inlet. When you sight land you confidently turn north. Had you steered directly for your destination, but missed a familiar buoy, you wouldn't know whether to search for it north or south.

We still have the sun as an aid to eyeball navigation. The sun will disappoint you. We have already used it earlier for getting a compass bearing at sunrise or sunset. And that's about all the sun will do for you without instruments.

Of course, at noon it indicates south, or north depending on your latitude and the season, but when is noon? The seagoing navigator without instruments wouldn't know.

Ashore you could measure the shadow of a pole; when it stops getting shorter, it's noon. Or you could in the forenoon measure the length of the shadow cast on a level surface by a vertical pole and make a mark. Then in the afternoon you monitor the shadow; when it gets to be exactly the length of the forenoon shadow, you make another mark. A line from the base of the pole to a point exactly halfway between your two marks runs exactly north and south.

Neither method is practical on a boat. Do you plan to cheat a little and carry a watch for your navigation without instruments? You'll be disappointed if you expect the sun to be south (or north) when your watch, however accurate, points to 12:00 hours. Even without the complication of Daylight Saving Time (which would make your watch one hour fast on sun time) you'll have to make two corrections: one for the difference between our averaged mean sun days and actual sun days which can make noon a quarter of an hour ahead or astern of clock time, and secondly for your longitude, to adjust the arbitrary zone time to local sun time. Eastern Standard Time, for example, based on the sun's passage over the meridian of 75°W longitude, is used from Maine to Ohio. That makes it noon at 11:28 A.M. EST in Eastport (67°W), and at 12:34 P.M. EST in Toledo (83½°W).

Here is a table that lets you find both corrections for any date of any year, and wherever you may be.

TIME OF NOON

To find Standard Time of local noon takes two steps:

1. Find the time of noon on Standard Time meridian for any given date from table below:

Jan.	1– 5	12:04		Aug.	1– 8	12:06
	6–10	12:06			9–19	12:04
	11–15	12:08			20–27	12:02
	16–21	12:10			28–31	12:00
	22–31	12:12		Sep.	1– 5	12:00
Feb.	1–22	12:14			6–11	11:58
	23–29	12:12			12–17	11:56

Navigation without Instruments

Mar.	1– 5	12:12	18–23	11:54
	6–13	12:10	24–28	11:52
	14–20	12:08	29–30	11:50
	21–27	12:06	Oct. 1– 5	11:50
	28–31	12:04	6–12	11:48
Apr.	1– 2	12:04	13–22	11:46
	3– 9	12:02	23–31	11:44
	10–22	12:00	Nov. 1–14	11:44
	23–30	11:58	15–23	11:46
May	1– 7	11:58	24–30	11:48
	8–21	11:56	Dec. 1– 5	11:50
	22–31	11:58	6– 9	11:52
Jun.	1– 6	11:58	10–13	11:54
	7–20	12:00	14–18	11:56
	21–30	12:02	19–22	11:58
Jul.	1–12	12:04	23–28	12:00
	13–31	12:06	29–31	12:02

2. To the time of noon on Standard Time meridian apply the correction for your longitude.

Compare your longitude with that of your Standard Time meridian, e.g.:

Eastern Standard Time . . . . 75° W
Central Standard Time . . . . 90° W
Mountain Standard Time . . . . 105° W
Pacific Standard Time . . . . 120° W

If your longitude is the lesser (east of the Standard Time meridian), subtract the correction below. Noon will be earlier where you are.

If your longitude is the greater (west of the Standard Time meridian), add the correction below. Noon will be later where you are.

Long. Diff. (degrees)	Correction (minutes)	Long. Diff. (minutes)	Correction (minutes)
1	4	15	1
2	8	30	2
3	12	45	3
4	16		
5	20		
6	24		
7	28		
8	32		
9	36		
10	40		

Example: When is noon on April 5 in longitude 83°30′ W?
Noon on Standard Meridian (75° W) from April 3 to April 9 is at about 12:02 P.M. EST according to first part of table. The difference in longitude (83°30′—75°) is 8°30′, which gives a time difference of 34 minutes (32 minutes for 8° +2 minutes for 30′). The local longitude is greater, the place is west of the Standard Time meridian, and noon will be later there, at 12:36 P.M. EST.

If you don't goof, you'll get south accurately at noon. But forget the method you may have learned as a boy for telling directions from the sun, and from your watch at other times. It is based on a simple fact: The sun seems to circle the earth at a practically constant rate, once in twenty-four hours. A circle is divided into 360 degrees, so—dividing 24 into 360—the sun should change bearing fifteen degrees in one hour. Very simple and all wrong.

The sun moves in a circle inclined to the horizon, so the sun's bearing—measured like all bearings along the horizon—rarely changes fifteen degrees in one hour. Let me prove it.

The hourly change in bearing depends on the season and your latitude. Let's look at it from some midlatitude in the United States, say near San Francisco, or Norfolk. In winter, when the sun's path is lowest, the bearing changes ten degrees in the hour after sunrise; between eleven o'clock and noon it changes sixteen degrees. At the beginning of spring and fall—when the sun is on the equator, and you might expect things to be normal—it changes nine degrees in the hour after sunrise, but twenty-four degrees in the hour before noon. In midsummer, when the sun's path is highest, it changes forty-seven degrees in the one hour before noon. In other words, at 11 A.M. the sun bears a bit east of southeast, where the clock watchers would expect it just before nine o'clock.

The method of getting a bearing from the sun is even less useful in the tropics. One only has to remember that there on two days of the year at any one place the sun rises in the east, bears east until noon, then passes directly overhead, and bears west all afternoon until sunset.

Near the poles the method isn't quite so bad. So it is possible that the Vikings, who navigated in high latitudes, were somewhat helped by the sun. Not long ago a Danish archaeologist and the ten-year-old son of a Scandinavian Airlines System navigator solved the mystery of the "sunstone." Some mineral, by showing the polarization of the sky, is said to give the sun's true direction to within 2½ degrees, even when the sun is seven degrees below the horizon. Great, but how did that help them? Did they have clocks?

If you have some means for measuring elapsed time from sunrise to sunset, with a sandglass, for instance, you can get your latitude from the length of day on a given date. The method was known to Pytheas of Massilia, the Greek astronomer and navigator, who in the fourth century B.C. sailed to Scotland and Ultima Thule, wherever that may be.

That method works best near the shortest and longest days of the year, and not at all around the equinoxes when times of sunrise and sunset, or the length of day, differ only a few minutes as you go from latitude 60° North to latitude 60° South.

In the right season, in the right geographical zones, you can even get your longitude by comparing calculated times for sunrise and sunset for your latitude with those shown by a watch showing accurate Greenwich or any other zone time. But that's hardly to be called navigation without instruments.

On the other hand, as a reward for sticking with me through this chapter let me show you a trick for reading the passing of time from the stars. Think of Polaris as the center of a clockface in the sky. The Pointers, or any star in the Dipper or in Cassiopeia, could be your hour hand. But it's a strange clock: It runs backward, anticlockwise. And it moves at half speed, once around in twenty-four hours instead of in twelve.

There is a minor hitch. This hour hand moves against the hollow bowl of the sky, not over the usual flat dial. To make errors from this source small, it's best to use a star quite close to Polaris for an hour hand. Kochab, as bright as Polaris and easily found since it's the only such star near Polaris, will do nicely; it remains visible even on a bright, moonlit night. Being close to the pole, it stays above the horizon all night and every night through most of the Northern Hemisphere, well into the tropics.

If you have glanced at Kochab earlier in the evening—say right after eight o'clock—you can tell time all during that night. Simply double the hours the Kochab hand seems to have moved—backward—around Polaris.

No chapter on navigation without instruments would be complete without mentioning Noah's dove and its successors. But nowhere in the literature have I found a reference to the land-

154   NAVIGATION

finding ability of pigs. A Bahamian skipper first told me about them. "You throw a pig overboard, and 'm pig swim for the nearest land, sure."

I waited for years for a chance to test this method. Not that I was never doubtful of my position, but I never had a spare pig

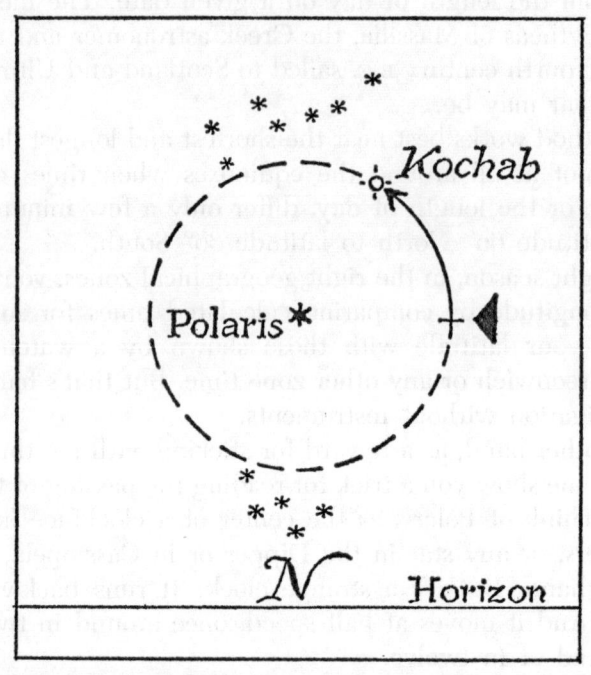

55. *The stars as a clock—with Polaris as center, Kochab acts as hour hand that moves backward, at half the speed of a regular clock. To read time on this clock, double the hours Kochab has moved. Example: at eight in the evening Kochab was at the three-o'clock position. It is now at the one-o'clock position. Elapsed time four hours; it is now midnight.*

aboard. Then one day my great chance came. A piglet slipped off the deck of a mailboat on which I was traveling. He squeaked SOS in pig, and swam a few yards in a circle as if to get his bearings. Then there was a swirl in the water; a shark had ruined the experiment.

15 Using a Star Finder

Perhaps you care no more about astronomy than about the daily horoscope in the newspaper. But the stars can help a boatman, and make his night watches more interesting. You don't have to know Nunki from Betelgeuse (disrespectfully called beetle juice by sailors). You need only a simple gadget to find the brightest stars, identify unknown ones, tell time from the stars, have a pocket planetarium, and—best of all—have an accurate compass wherever you may be.

Old-timers call this useful gadget the Rude star finder after its inventor, Captain E. B. Rude, USC&GS. The U. S. Navy now publishes it and calls it Star Finder and Identifier H.O. 2102. You can buy it at chart agents for the price of a fifth of imported stuff. The instructions that come with it are pure Navy, their language so celestial it might as well be in Chinese. Disregard them; the next pages tell all.

There are other, and cheaper, star finders on the market. Most of them show the night sky as a picture only; the Rude finder lets you read off numbers for the position of key stars. Most star finders are designed for only one area. They may work well around New York or Boston, but are inadequate near San Diego, New Orleans, or Miami; the Rude star finder works anywhere in the world.

It is a simple device: A white disk (with a pin in the center and a degree scale at the perimeter) shows selected stars and their names. In the Northern Hemisphere you'd use the side with the large letter "N" in the middle. Then you'd select from a number of clear plastic overlays, printed in blue ink, the one nearest your latitude. Off Miami, near latitude 26°N, for example, you'd pick the twenty-five-degree overlay and place it on the pin so the legend LAT 25°N becomes legible. Off Rio de Janeiro, latitude 23°S, you'd use the same overlay turned over, and place it on the base on the side with the letter "S" in the middle.

This overlay, like eight others that come with the star finder, shows a geometric pattern bounded by a roughly oval curve. This curve represents your horizon. Stars outside it are below the horizon, invisible. Stars inside the oval are now visible unless blotted out by clouds. With only a few exceptions the stars shown on the finder are bright enough to remain visible on a full-moon night.

Near the center of the horizon oval is a small cross, that marks the point directly above you in the sky, your zenith. Between the horizon and the zenith are other ovals, numbered from ten to eighty. They indicate altitudes. Don't let this term from celestial navigation scare you; altitude is simply height above the horizon measured in degrees. The horizon is at zero altitude, the zenith at ninety. A star shown on the 40° oval would be a little less than halfway between

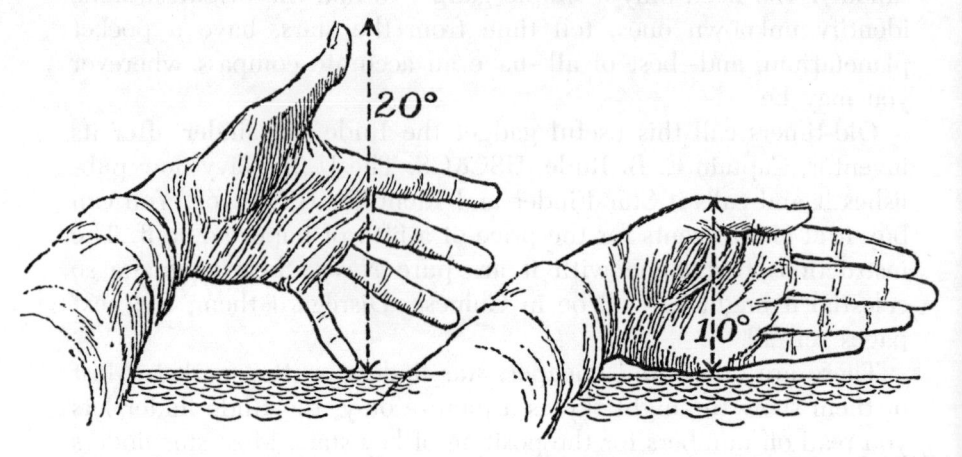

56. *Your hand held at arm's length measures angles in the sky. Each finger covers about two degrees, palm and thumb ten, the spread hand twenty.*

the horizon and the point directly above your head. You won't need a sextant to measure this angle. After a few tries you'll be able to gauge altitudes to the nearest five degrees or better. At first most people tend to overestimate altitudes. This may help you: Your outstretched hand covers twenty degrees, your palm and thumb about ten, each finger roughly two.

More important to the boatman are the curves that form the rest of the blue line pattern on the overlay. They radiate from the zenith, are numbered from 0–360, and indicate degrees of azimuth. If we weren't talking about stars, we'd simply call them bearings. Just as on your compass, the degrees run clockwise from north, making

Using a Star Finder 157

east 90, south 180, and so forth. A star directly under the 180-curve (which happens to be a straight line) will bear exactly south of you.

This line, by the way, ends in an arrow that points to the scale printed along the perimeter of the base of the star finder, and serves for setting it for date and time. For an example, let's set it to 64.

At this setting you'll find Achenar on the horizon oval, on the 200° radial curve. You can see how one can work examples forward or backward. To *find* Achenar you'd look near the horizon, a little south of SSE; to *identify* a star setting in that direction you'd look on your star finder where the 200-curve and the horizon oval meet, and you'd read off Achenar.

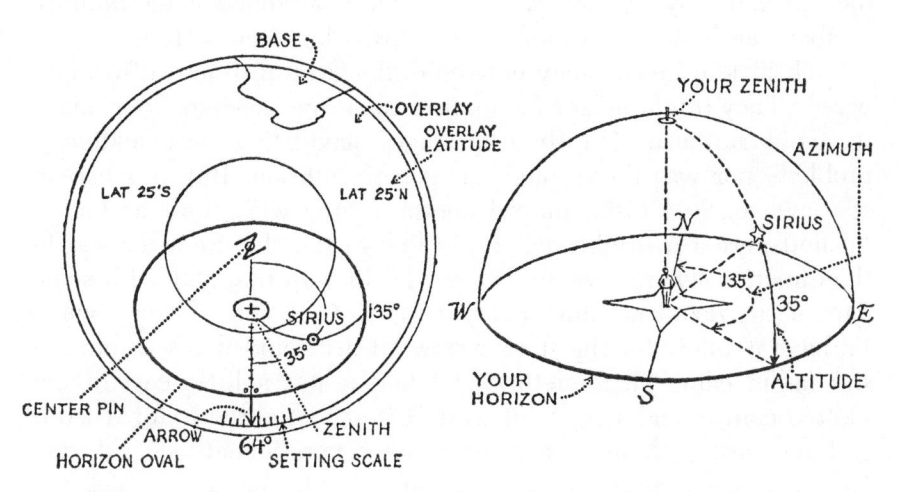

57. *Finding and identifying stars—Left: Rude star finder (HO 2102) set to 64° shows Sirius on 35-degree altitude oval, on 135-degree azimuth radial. At times for which that setting is correct, Sirius in the sky will be 35° above the horizon, bearing 135° true.*

If you recognize a single star and have a fairly accurate bearing of it you can set the star finder from that single star. You don't have to be much of a starhound to recognize Sirius by its brightness and the three stars in the belt of Orion that point to it. Sight over your compass, or better, take a bearing with a hand bearing compass. Say it places Sirius at 135° true. You then turn the overlay until the blue 135° curve crosses the position of Sirius on the base of the star finder. The arrow will point to 64.

One hour later Sirius, now 45° above the horizon, will bear about 150° true and give a setting of 79 for the star finder. That's as it should be: the setting increases by fifteen degrees every hour (once around in about twenty-four hours). The bearing of Sirius having also changed by fifteen degrees in the last hour is rather accidental; for example Canopus, the second-brightest fixed star, in the same time has moved westward only eight degrees.

If the star finder setting increases fifteen degrees in one hour, it must increase one degree every four minutes. That gives us a star clock. By resetting the star finder by the bearing of a star after a lapse of time, you can estimate the time gone by between settings. Simply multiply by four the number of degrees by which the setting has increased, four, to get minutes. If you changed the setting of the star finder by 22°, for example, you'll know that 4 × 22 minutes, or about an hour and a half, have elapsed between settings.

Such little exercises may cut the dullness of an uneventful night watch. They often did for me on interisland passages made at night to avoid sunburn. On these passages navigation was seldom a problem, nor was there much danger of collision. But you had to stay awake. So I often played another game with the star finder. I'd find myself a bright star, fairly low in the sky, more or less in the direction where I wanted to go. I'd line up that star with some part of the boat and start steering for it. Of course, after a while I'd have to allow for the star's westward drift, and that's where the star finder came in. Sometimes I'd find a star a little east of my plotted course, and steer a bit west of it at first, directly for it later, and increasing amounts east of it later yet. Sometimes I'd stay locked on one star for an hour or more before having to pick another. Sure, I had a compass, but watching a star and doing a little star finder twisting won't put me to sleep the way watching a compass does.

Besides a reliable compass bearing of a known star, here are three other methods for setting the Rude star finder. Pick the method you like best. None requires the ability of recognizing even a single star. All three have a few things in common, summarized on page 160.

You can use the *Nautical Almanac* for setting the star finder. Since the stars repeat their courses through the sky almost exactly year after year, it doesn't have to be this year's almanac. Use the ARIES column, the first on the left-hand daily pages; under the date you'll find the raw star finder setting for every hour. For example, under January 25 at 20:00 (i.e., 8 P.M.) you'll find 64° 09.8′, or practically 64°. For minutes after the hour you can use the yellow pages in the back of the almanac, or simply add one degree for every four minutes. For example, twenty minutes after the hour you'd add 20/4 or 5 degrees.

But you don't need an almanac. Here is a table (page 161) that lets you find the raw setting for any time of any date.

You can also set the star finder without either almanac or this table just doing a little figuring in your head, or by scribbling a few numbers on the back of an old yard bill. I may have invented this method, but modesty wouldn't let me call it the "Kals Rule," so I call it the "Rule of Sixty-eight." Just remember that name and the fact that with each passing day the setting increases by one degree for the same time of night, and you are ready to find the setting for midnight of any date.

To get the setting for any other time of the night you only have to allow fifteen degrees for each hour before or after midnight, and one degree for every four minutes before or after the hour. For example: 4:08 A.M. would add 4 × 15 + 2 = 62 to the midnight setting. Or, 10:40 P.M. is one hour twenty minutes before midnight; subtract 15 + 5 = 20 from the midnight setting.

Now that you know all about setting the star finder (and perhaps more than you wanted to know), you may ask: "What stars are shown on the Rude star finder?"

Star finders don't show all the stars visible to the naked eye. The Rude finder shows the fifty-seven navigational stars, the ones a candidate for mate's papers has to know and then promptly forgets. In a lifetime of celestial navigation in all seasons and all latitudes the mate may use perhaps twenty of these stars. But the fifty-seven have been chosen to give navigators a choice, anywhere, evening and morning, summer or winter. The twenty or so brightest stars are all there. Where there was a space bare of bright stars, a few third-magnitude ones have been picked. The second-magnitude stars, of which there are about fifty in the sky, have been severely culled. You won't find Castor, one of the twins, for example, because Pollux, its brighter brother, is so close. For some stars new names had to be coined; Alpha Pavonis, for instance, becomes Peacock. Your old friend Polaris is not shown; its position is marked by the center pin that stands for the celestial pole.

Don't look for the constellations; they aren't there. That's just as well; they'd look very odd. Four of the seven stars that identify Orion for us are there, but when you draw the lines that connect them, you'll find that constellation (and all others) flipped left for right. If you want to identify constellations rather than single stars, you'll have to have a star chart besides the star finder. There is one such in the *Nautical Almanac*, between the daily tables and the yellow pages.

Don't worry about the planets too much. No star finder can show the planets since they keep moving against the background of stars. With the current year's *Nautical Almanac* you could plot the

CORRECTING SETTING OF STAR FINDER

1. *Daylight Saving Time* is one hour fast on standard time. Use setting one hour earlier. For example, at 5 A.M. EDT use the setting for 4 A.M. EST for all methods.

2. *Standard Time* is the time at a certain longitude in or near your time zone. At any other longitude correct for local time. If you never venture more than fifty miles or so from your home port, you can always use the same correction. To correct:

    (a) Find your longitude (to nearest whole degree) from nautical chart.

    (b) Compare that longitude with that of standard time meridian, viz.:

Eastern Standard Time . . . 75° W   Mountain Standard Time . . . 105° W
Central Standard Time . . . 90° W   Pacific Standard Time   . . . 120° W

    (c) For every degree you are *east* of the standard time meridian *add* one degree to raw star finder setting found by any method;
        for every degree you are *west* of the standard time meridian *subtract* one degree from the raw star finder setting found by any method.

Examples:

You are near longitude . . . 73°W   You are near longitude . . 80°W
Standard time meridian (EST) 75°W   Standard time meridian (EST) 75°W
You are *east* of EST meridian 2°   You are *west* of EST meridian 5°
So you *add* to raw setting 2°   So you *subtract* from raw setting 5°

3. *Plus or Minus 360 Degrees.* Sometimes the corrected setting will exceed 360°. Simply deduct 360°. Example: Corrected setting 370°, deduct 360°, set star finder to 10°.

When subtraction is impossible, add 360 to the setting. Example: Raw setting is 5°, correction for longitude (west of standard time meridian) 6°. Borrow 360°, and subtract 6° from 365°. Set star finder to 359°.

Using a Star Finder

SETTING THE STAR FINDER

A. MONTH		C. HOUR		D. MINUTES	
JAN.	9	EVENING		00	0
FEB.	40	6 P.M.	00	04	1
MAR.	68	7 P.M.	15	08	2
APR.	98	8 P.M.	30	12	3
MAY	128	9 P.M.	45	16	4
JUN.	158	10 P.M.	60	20	5
JUL.	188	11 P.M.	75	24	6
AUG.	218	MIDNIGHT	90	28	7
SEP.	248	1 A.M.	105	32	8
OCT.	278	2 A.M.	120	36	9
NOV.	308	3 A.M.	135	40	10
DEC.	338	4 A.M.	150	44	11
		5 A.M.	165	48	12
B. DAY		6 A.M.	180	52	13
Add 1 per day.		MORNING		56	14

The sum of A + B + C + D gives raw setting (to be corrected for local time).

Example: Jan. 25, 8:20 P.M. EST—LONG 80°W

A. January	9
B. 25th (25 × 1)	25
C. 8 P.M.	30
D. 20 minutes	5
Raw Setting (A + B + C + D)	69
80°W is west of 75°W	−5
Star finder setting	64

SETTING THE STAR FINDER WITHOUT TABLES— RULE OF SIXTY-EIGHT

A. By the rule, take ... 68.
B. Add 30 for the number of the month.
C. Add 1 for each day of the month.

The sum of A + B + C gives the raw setting for midnight.

Example: Midnight, Mar. 21

A. By the rule	68
B. March, third month 3 × 30	90
C. 21	21
Raw star finder setting	179

planets for any given date. Even without that you are not likely to be led astray often by mistaking a planet for a fixed star.

Venus, whether morning or evening star, stands out from all fixed stars by its brightness. Mercury, like Venus, precedes the rising sun or follows the setting one. But it never gets as far from the sun as Venus does. Though it is very bright at times, its light is swallowed so often by haze on the horizon, and so dimmed by atmospheric absorption, that most people never have seen Mercury.

Mars, being outside the orbit of the earth, travels widely through the sky. Its brightness varies from almost as bright as Venus down to the level of the Pointers in the Big Dipper. But even if you don't see much difference between so-called blue and red stars, you'll always recognize Mars by its red color. There is no star like it.

Jupiter is most of the time brighter than Sirius, the brightest fixed star, and always brighter than the next brightest star. So it shouldn't give much trouble.

Saturn, the only remaining planet of first magnitude or thereabouts, and so readily seen on moonlit nights, moves so slowly among the stars that it is easy to keep track of. From the spring of 1966 to the spring of 1969, for instance, it has been in the undistinguished constellation Pisces, the Fishes. For the next three years or so it will be in the next constellation, Aries the Ram, an even more barren area of the sky.

So don't worry about the planets. Instead get better acquainted with the star finder. It has more information built into it than you'd ever expect. You may want to explain facts about the motion of stars to someone or make them clear in your own mind. The star finder will help. Compare, for instance, the blue overlays for different latitudes. They range in shape from an almost circular pattern to be used near the poles, to a squashed ellipse for areas near the equator. Either of these shapes covers about half of the sky that's visible at any one time at these places.

You'll also notice that the hole for the pin—the celestial pole—is almost in the center on the near-polar overlay, yet close to the north rim on the overlay to be used just north of the equator. So the Pole Star will appear near the horizon there, and almost overhead in the Arctic. Since all the stars seem to revolve around the pole, you'll find stars under the northernmost overlay change greatly in bearing with the passing of the night, but remain almost at the same altitude. Put differently, most of the stars there never rise nor set. You won't find a single such star under the overlay to be used near the equator.

On the 25°N overlay, used in earlier examples, you'll find Kochab above the horizon whatever the setting. And you can verify that Dubhe, the Pointer nearer the pole, sets at times, while you had learned perhaps in school that it was "circumpolar."

On the other side of the sky, in the south, you'll find stars you had probably thought were visible only in the Southern Hemisphere. The Southern Cross, for example, will be just above the horizon when the star finder setting is about 187, say in mid-May, around 9 P.M.

On the star finder you can also demonstrate that standby of planetarium shows, the change of visible constellations with the seasons.

Set the same overlay to zero, where it belongs at midnight of September 22. You'll find Orion due east, just risen. Change the setting to 90 (midnight, December 22) and Orion will be riding high in the sky, a little west of south. Advance the finder to 180 (as it would be set for midnight, March 22) and Orion will have just set, leaving only Betelgeuse above the horizon. On June 22, all during the night, not a sign of friend Orion; it has set before it got dark and won't rise before daylight has washed out the stars.

Fiddling with the star finder, you'll discover other facts about the motions of the stars. But let me warn you: It's habit-forming, and you really should be polishing the barometer.

16 Celestial Navigation

Unless you plan an ocean voyage, you'll never *really* need celestial navigation. Certainly, it can be helpful in running along the coast, for making a pinpoint landfall after a day's fishing a few miles offshore, and for crossing a large lake. Even on an interisland passage it helps the single-hander: He can go below and let his little ship sail herself, knowing he can find her position again later, regardless of her speed or change in course. Electronic navigation—at least on large vessels—is making celestial navigation less important as more and more aids are added to the existing systems. But there is still another reason for knowing how celestial navigation works: No longer need you be impressed by the mahogany sextant box displayed on some friend's yacht, nor consider him some kind of genius.

There's no black magic in celestial navigation. You could join the inner circle of celestial navigators anytime. If you have enough mathematics to balance your check stubs, and can find the next train home in a timetable, you have all it takes for modern celestial navigation. It's that simple.

It wasn't always so. Mates had to know some spherical trigonometry, and the use of logarithms; and they had to be familiar with formulas for different sights. There was the noon sight, ex-meridian sights, time sights, and equal altitude sights. Long after the invention of the chronometer they had to solve tedious lunars, because shipowners considered chronometers a luxury.

Now a short-wave radio gives you split-second time, twenty-four hours a day everywhere in the world. You can even pick up the time beeps on the hour by listening to your favorite program on a pocket transistor radio. The spherical trigonometry and the logarithms have been poured into prefabricated tables. All sights—the sun at noon or at any other time, the moon, the planets, and the stars—are solved in the same way. And you don't have to be able to tell Orion from the Big Dipper to take a star sight. It's all done with mirrors and our old friend, the line of position.

The mirrors attached to a marine sextant let you see the sun, the moon, or a star while you look at the horizon. A scale shows how far you had to move the arm that carries one of the mirrors to bring the sun or other body exactly on the horizon. So it measures the angle between the sun and the horizon, the sun's altitude. That's all there is to a sextant: a simple device to measure such angles accurately.

The other parts—the handle, adjustment screws, shade glasses, clamp, telescope, micrometer, vernier, and night light—are refinements.

How do you get a position line from such an angle?

Let's forget astronomy for a moment and take an illustration from ordinary pilotage: a lighthouse. With a sextant you could measure the angle between the horizon and the center of the light. Then you could have a table that tells what the angle should be when you

Celestial Navigation 165

are, say, three miles from the light. If your measured angle is exactly the tabulated value, you'd know you are on a circle of position with a radius of three miles, centered on the light. If the measured angle comes out smaller, you'd know you are farther away. If the measured angle is larger, you are less than three miles

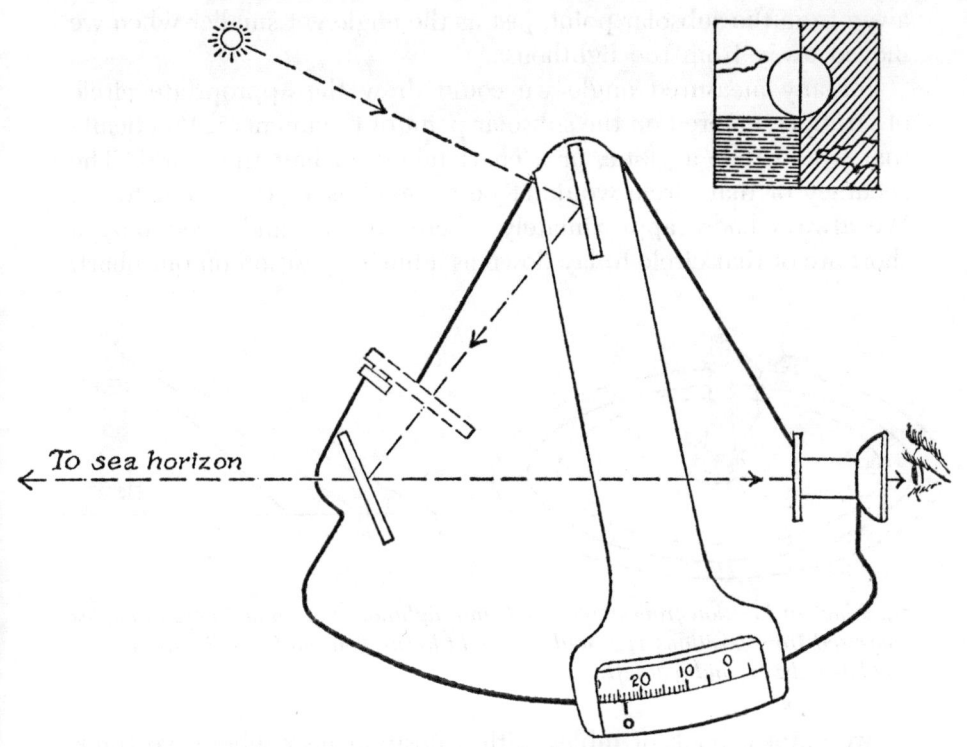

58. *Marine sextant is used for measuring the altitudes of celestial bodies above the visible sea horizon. When the pivoted arm that carries a mirror is in approximately right position, the navigator sees both the horizon and the sun (reflected by the two mirrors). He then moves the arm until the lower limb of the sun kisses the horizon, as shown in insert, and reads the angle on a scale (e.g., 24°). (The dashed rectangle indicates a shade glass without which you could not look directly at the sun.)*

away. The angle would get larger as you keep approaching the light, until standing directly under it and absurdly sighting up through the spiral staircase at the light, you'd measure it as ninety degrees.

Now let's go from the plain lighthouse to a metaphorical one in the sky, say the sun. Obviously at any given moment the sun is directly overhead at one point on the earth. The *Nautical Almanac* gives the position of that point for any given moment. At that point —call it the subsolar point, if you like—and only at that point the sun's altitude is ninety degrees. Everywhere else where the sun is above the horizon, the angle is less. And it gets smaller as we move away from the subsolar point, just as the angle got smaller when we moved away from the lighthouse.

For any measured angle we could draw the appropriate circle of position centered on the subsolar point of the moment. Practically that would take a globe, or a chart taking in half the world. The accuracy of that circle wouldn't be as good as we'd want it to be. We always know approximately where we are, and need only a short arc of that circle to lay down as a line of position on our chart.

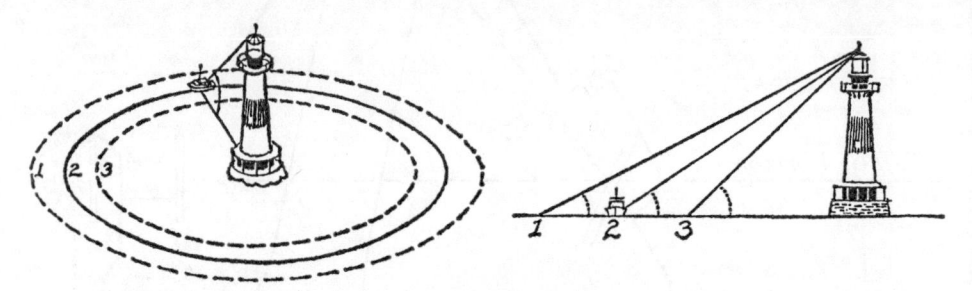

59. *Lines of Position from angles— Given a lighthouse of known height, angles measured from positions 1, 2, and 3 at right locate your craft on circles of position labeled 1, 2, and 3 at left.*

So we enter a book of tables with a position near where we think we are, and look up what the sun's altitude there should be for the moment when we measured it with our sextant.

The tables not only give that angle, but next to it also the bearing of the subsolar point (or the sun, it comes to the same). That lets us plot the line of position, even when the center of the circle is off our chart, thousands of miles away, as it usually is.

Now we cheat a little. We draw the short part of that big circle as a straight line. By the rules of plane geometry this line should be drawn at right angles to the radius, in our case the bearing of the subsolar point or the sun.

If by chance the altitude measured with the sextant is exactly the same as that given in the tables, we are on the line of position just drawn. If the measured angle is greater or smaller than the tabulated angle, we move the line of position toward or away from the subsolar point. For every minute's difference in angle we move it one nautical mile. This simple relationship is the very reason

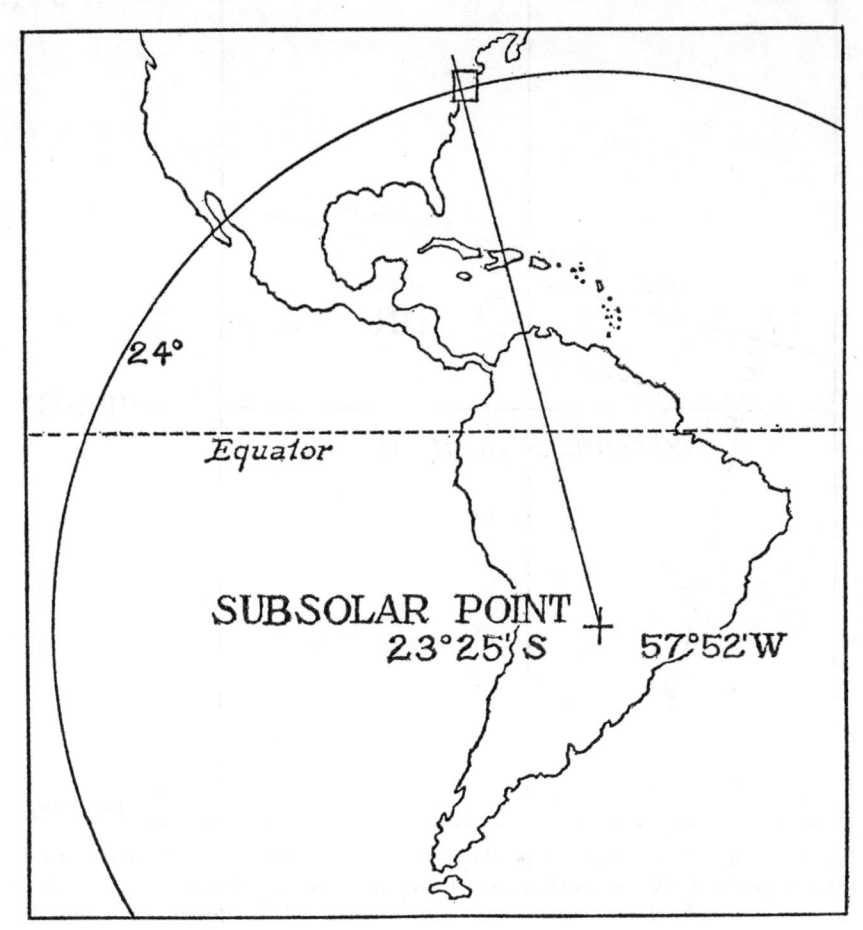

60. *Circle of position from observation of the sun— Center of circle, the point where sun at time of observation was directly overhead, is found in Nautical Almanac. Circle with radius of 24° (24 × 60 nautical miles) connects all points where sun at time of observation was twenty-four degrees above horizon. Small rectangle marks area shown enlarged in next figure.*

why all nations—whether they use English or metric measurements otherwise—use the nautical mile as standard at sea. It's one minute of arc on our planet.

Take my word for it, using a straight line in place of a curved one won't lead you astray unless the celestial body is almost overhead.

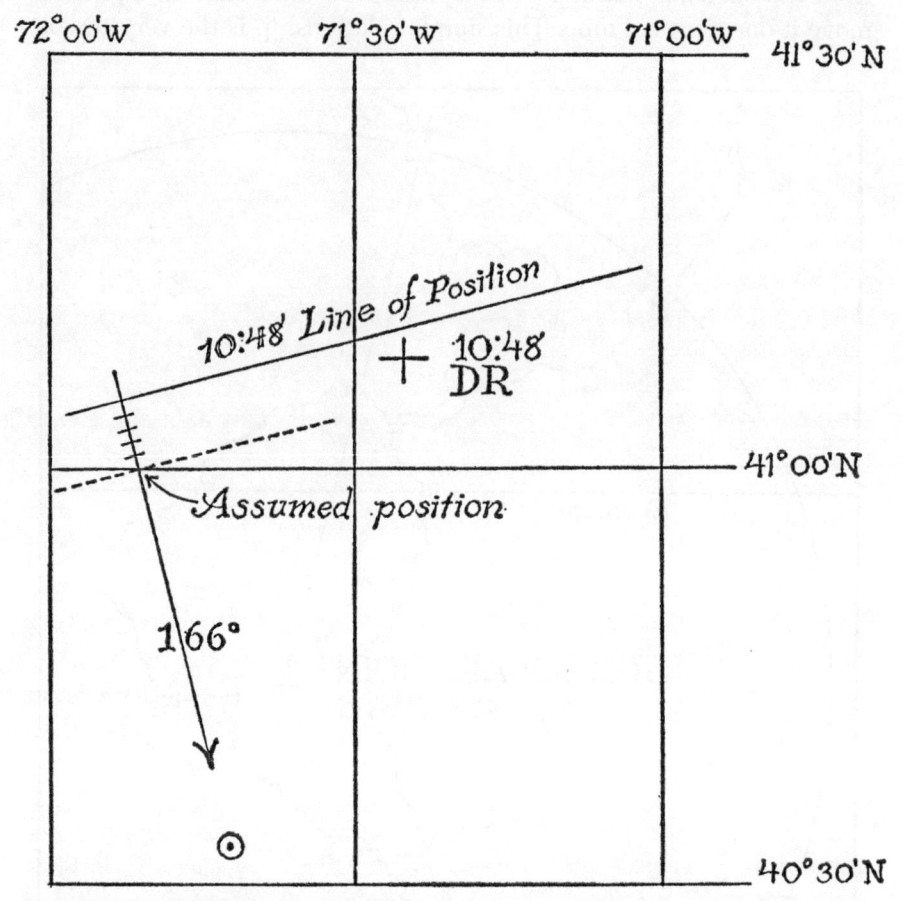

61. *Plotting celestial line of position on chart of your area. To make navigator's tables more compact, modern methods use an assumed position near your dead reckoning position (e.g. the nearest whole degree of latitude). Dashed line—drawn at right angles to the azimuth found in tables—shows line of position for a navigator whose measured altitude happens to be the same as the calculated altitude at the assumed position. Solid line of position shows that your altitude was (5′) smaller than that calculated for assumed position, that you were five nautical miles farther away from the subsolar point (See figure 62).*

Then you can draw the circle on your chart and eliminate the error caused by substituting a straight line.

Working the sight from an assumed position, not your still-

Celestial Navigation 169

unknown accurate one, makes very little difference. You could work the same sight from three latitudes or three longitudes, each one degree from the next, and get practically the same position lines. So your dead reckoning position isn't critical.

I have cheated only a little. I have used the expression "measured" altitude, and unless you are already an expert you may have thought I meant the angle read directly from the sextant. Actually the reading of even a perfect sextant needs some minor corrections. One is for the height of the observer's eye. As we have seen when we discussed visibility, the observer's elevation changes the position of his horizon. And it's from the horizon that he measures his angle. Also under visibility we have seen how refraction in the atmosphere makes a light, or the sun, appear higher in the sky than it really is. Then in a marine sextant one usually measures the angle between the horizon and the sun's lower limb, not the center of his disk. So one has to add a correction for his apparent semi-diameter. All these corrections are readily found in the *Nautical Almanac*. To give an idea how small the change in these corrections is from one sight to the next: The yachtsman who lumps all three corrections together, and always adds thirteen minutes to his raw sextant reading, would never be more than one or two miles out, when the sun is more than twenty degrees above the horizon.

Stars or even planets have practically no diameter, so there is no correction for lower limb. The moon, on the other hand, being so close to us needs an extra correction. But these are details. Perhaps you'd rather read about the general manner of modern navigation.

First, you need a sextant to measure the angle between the sea horizon and a celestial body. That describes a marine sextant. Bubble sextants, used on aircraft, are independent of the horizon using a bubble for leveling. They have been tried on big ships, aircraft carriers and battleships, and found wanting. On yachts they are useless.

Then, you'll need a horizon. That's usually the edge of the sea. When land gets between you and the horizon, you can use a table that shows a correction for that. Or you can take a backsight—that is, face away from the sun and bring it to the horizon, over your head, as it were.

For star sights the horizon is sometimes tricky. You have to wait in the evening until it's dark enough to see the stars, yet it has to be still bright enough to make out the horizon. So, practically, you have only a few minutes at dusk (or dawn) when you can take star sights. There are a few tricks to overcome this handicap. One is to have the sights planned ahead, knowing at what altitudes and what directions to find your stars. You then set the sextant to the expected altitude for one star and sweep the sky in the known direction; the star will show in the telescope of the sextant before you can make it out with the unaided eye. Another trick takes the brighter stars first. Say you have Venus for an evening star. It will become visible when it's still quite light. Next you'd shoot some first-magnitude star, visible while the horizon is still good. Then you'd be ready to nab Polaris in the last minutes of the fading day.

There is another method, discovered by submariners during World War II. They sat in the dark, or wore goggles, to adapt their eyes enough to see the horizon at any time of the night. On some nights, of course, the light of the moon will give you a horizon after dark.

Next, you'll need a recognizable celestial body. The sun is by far the most popular. Next is the moon. The planets Venus, Mars, Jupiter, and Saturn are listed in the daily pages of the *Nautical Almanac* and so can be used readily. The almanac also lists the fifty-seven selected stars shown on the Rude star finder. So you can get the approximate altitude and azimuth before you shoot, or identify a bright star that you have shot through a break in the clouds without recognizing it.

Polaris, not included among the fifty-seven navigational stars, is readily found, always close to true north and approximately your latitude above the horizon. A Polaris sight gives you a line of position that runs East-West, a latitude. That's why many navigators still use Polaris although it's often hard to spot before the horizon washes out. By the way, a Polaris sight is the only sight not worked out by the universal scheme, but by an even simpler method given in the *Nautical Almanac*.

Next, for most sights, you'll need to know where the body—sun, moon, planet, or star—is at the precise time of the observation. You find that information in the *Nautical Almanac*. The abbreviations it uses—GHA for Greenwich Hour Angle, and DEC for Declination —stand for celestial coordinates that correspond to longitude and latitude on the earth. (They are always given in that order, unlike the order for earthly coordinates.) To save space, the almanac doesn't give the position of all fifty-seven navigational stars, but the coordinates of something called "Aries," a sort of Greenwich in the sky, to which all other stars are referred. Very simple.

The white daily pages of the *Nautical Almanac* give the GHA of Aries (also known as the First Point of Aries, or the Vernal Equinox), the planets mentioned, the sun and the moon for every hour. To get positions for any minute or second after the last hour, one looks in the yellow pages in the back of the almanac and adds to the last hour's data, sometimes making small corrections, as for the rapidly moving moon.

Time here is important: four seconds of time could throw your position off by one nautical mile. That's why the radio time ticks are so valuable.

Next you'll need tables that let you convert your observations into lines of position. Without hesitation I'd choose H.O. Publication 249, *Sight Reduction Tables for Air Navigation*. Aviators have no time to fool around. At jet speeds the quickest method is still too slow, and it doesn't help the pilot much to know where he was 120 miles ago. Take my word for it, these tables are the lazy navigator's dream. Many marine navigators still swear by H.O. 214, I think rather because they learned with these tables, than by considered choice. For the sun, moon, and planets you'll need Volume II (latitudes 0–39 N or S) or Volume III (latitudes 40–89 N or S). Although you can work about half the navigational stars with these two volumes, you'll like Volume I for star sights. This last one is revised every few years to allow for slight changes in the positions of the stars mainly due to wanderings of the celestial pole; the other two volumes are good in any year.

Once you get familiar with the arrangement of these tables, you'll find the figures you want—computed altitude and azimuth—about as easily as you find the times and heights of high water in the tide tables.

Then you plot the line of position on your chart. To show the drill followed to give the position line illustrated, here is its calculation in its entirety.

Celestial lines of position are no different from the ones we know from plain old pilotage. Often a single line is all you need. Cruising along the Pacific or Atlantic coasts of the United States, a line running roughly east-west will tell you how far you have come. Knowing that lines of position run at right angles to the observed body, the navigator to get such a line will shoot a body that bears north

172 NAVIGATION

```
1     ☉ Dec 19.  DR 41°07N 71°35W

2     EST 10 48 50         24°00
        + 5 -20             - 2.2
                           +14.1
4     GMT 15 48 30         24° 12'

         45°44.3'
       + 12°07.5
7     GHA  57°52'       S 23°25
8         (-71°52)         (N41)
          -14°
         =346°           S23

11      24°42  -59        1.66
         -25
        24° 17
        24° 12

15              5' AWAY 166°
```

62. *Working up the sight illustrated in figure 58, sketched in figure 60, and plotted in figure 61.*

OBSERVATION
 Sun lower limb symbol, date
  (*left*) .... 1°
 Dead reckoning position (*right*)
 Watch (zone time) (*left*) 2
 Sextant reading (*right*)
 Greenwich Mean Time (*left*) 4
 Observed altitude (*right*)

NAUTICAL ALMANAC
 Position of subsolar point 7
 Longitude (*left*) latitude (*right*)

ASSUMED POSITION
 Longitude (*left*) latitude (*right*) .8

H.O.249 TABLES
 Computed altitude (*left*) 11
 Azimuth (*right*)

LINE OF POSITION
 Difference of altitudes (*left*) 15
 Azimuth (*right*)

°*Numerals refer to lines in drawing*

or south, such as Polaris or the sun at noon. A line of position running roughly north-south along one of these coasts will often tell you how far from shore you are. To get such a line, the navigator would shoot a body that bears roughly east or west, such as the sun in the morning or late afternoon. These are just variations on those two most useful lines of position at right angles to your course and parallel with your course.

We can cross celestial lines of position with any other kind available, for instance depth contour lines, to get a fix. Often without much effort we can get not just a celestial position line, but a fix. This happens whenever the moon is visible in daytime, as it is for a good part of every month. Then we can take a sun sight, and a moon sight, practically at the same time. Slightly less accurate, but very popular, are sights of the sun taken a few hours apart, their position lines carried forward just as in a running fix from bearings of a single object ashore. The accuracy of such fixes depends on the accuracy with which we know the run of the ship between observations.

At dusk and dawn it is customary to shoot a "round" of stars, commonly three stars. It's best to have the bearings distributed around the horizon at roughly 120- (or 60-) degree intervals. Such bearings, as we have seen, give the smallest area of uncertainty. Polaris may be one of the three stars, or you may shoot Polaris as a fourth star, for good luck. Three favorably placed stars can be found for every hour, and in any latitude, in H.O. 249, Volume I.

Three lines of position plotted on the chart will seldom go through a single point; more normally they'll form the small triangle known as the cocked hat. It is tempting to consider the smallness of the cocked hat as a sign of great accuracy of one's observation, and place the ship in the middle of the triangle. Only that's probably not where she really is. Astronomical lines of position, like all others, should be considered as bands rather than as lines. So the small cocked hat becomes quite a piece of millinery.

But under good conditions, with a sharp horizon, a yachtsman who gets his time from the radio will usually come to within two miles of his true position.

Once you can trust your celestial navigation, you can use it in plain pilotage.

One breezy day I sailed my schooner from Eleuthera to the Exumas. Once clear of Powell Point, I trimmed the sails for a course of 230 degrees for the thirty-mile run across Exuma Sound. She steered herself and I thoroughly enjoyed the sailing. But when I made my landfall on the other side, I began to worry. Was that really Shroud Cay, just south of Wax Cay Cut for which I had a chart, or some other cay and some other passage, or no passage at all? There in the southeast, almost abeam, was the moon. I took a careful sight and worked it out. The line of position I got ran smack through Shroud Cay. A native skipper would have laughed at my performance. He knows the islands, which all look alike to a stranger, from their trees, which also look alike to a stranger.

It would seem silly also to one fellow, a chap who'll tell you that he navigated across the Atlantic strictly by ear. I heard that story from a tall redbeard called Shorty. He had lost his crew to the fleshpots of the Canary Islands and signed on this young fellow who had been going to sea for years . . . as pastry cook on a liner. Now he'd learn all about navigation.

Not from Shorty. Shorty taught him basic helmsmanship, how turning the wheel to one side made her go to that side, and how turning it the other way brought her back.

"Now, Captain, please explain to me all about the compass."

"Compass?" asked Shorty as if the sailor had said something very stupid. "You don't need a compass."

The ex-baker looked bewildered.

"You have two ears, haven't you? And you know which is your right ear?"

"Yes, sir," said the apprentice, even more bewildered, tugging at his starboard ear lobe.

"All right then. Look straight ahead and make the wind touch your right ear. Not your cheek, your ear. And whatever you do, don't let it get on your left ear."

For the next four hours Shorty only needed to glance astern at the peaks of Gran Canaria to see that his helmsman followed orders.

Coming on watch again after Shorty's four-hour trick, the ex-baker looked expectantly at the compass. "What course you want me to steer now, Captain?" (I have a hunch he had figured out the compass bit in his first watch all by himself.)

"Same. Keep the wind on your right ear."

The trade winds held, and on every watch Shorty ordered the wind on the right ear.

Once the helmsman asked, "Is that all there is to navigation?"

"That's all."
"And you'll find us some land that way?"
"Of course."

Then one day after ordering him again to keep the wind on the starboard ear, Shorty added, "And call me when you sight Antigua."

Two hours later, the helmsman tumbled excitedly into the saloon. "We made it, Captain. There's land ahead."

"Thank you," said Shorty coolly.
"Aren't you even going to see if it's Antigua?"
"Did you keep the wind on your right ear?"
"Yes, sir."
"Then it's Antigua."
"Don't you want to see some land after all this water?"
"Thanks, I have seen land before."

Shorty finishes this story: "How could I get up? I was sitting on my tables, having been caught working out the sight I had just taken through the forehatch."

PART THREE / EMERGENCIES

17 Running Aground and Getting Off

When you have gently run aground, don't chew on the bulkhead-to-bulkhead carpet. Think instead that you have just joined the ranks of professionals. Think of the *Queen Mary* on the mud in her home port, Southampton, or the battleship *Missouri* high and dry off Norfolk.

In some cruising areas the only skippers who never get stuck are the ones who always stick to their docks. No special providence puts extra water under the keels of writers of boating articles and books. Having poked my bow into places where it had no business, having taken calculated risks, through errors in judgment, and sometimes through plain carelessness, I have left keel marks in quite a few places. So have skippers of boats on which I was merely a guest. And a few times I have stood by while some stranger worked his little vessel off the hard.

This chapter shows some of the tricks that have helped us getting afloat again without outside help. It's about the unspectacular kind of fair-weather grounding in sand or mud. She may bump lightly before she sticks, or just drop her head—or lift it—to let you know that you are on. Sometimes she simply doesn't answer her helm; at other times a towed dinghy hits the transom to give you the bad news.

Until you have become an old hand at running aground, you'll have some almost automatic reactions. Check them. You may want to throw the engine in reverse, full. Don't. You know that to dig yourself really in with a car stuck in sand, you only have to try to back out, goosing the engine. Here the propeller may build a new sandbar. Worse, some of the stirred-up sand or mud may get into your cooling system, permanently. Under sail, your first reaction will be to claw the sails off. Don't. You may need them up again in a minute.

Your best action will depend on many things: the state of the tide in tidal waters; the shape of the hull; size of boat; kind of bottom; number, strength, and weight of your crew; whether you have a mast; whether you have a dinghy, powered or not.

On any boat, in the first moments after grounding there is only one thing to do: Keep her from getting on harder. Put the engine out of gear, or spill the wind from her sails. On a rising tide, or with wind and current setting you toward deeper water, just have a mug of java. When wind or current set you toward a shoal, or when swells or waves make her float at times, get an anchor over the stern as quickly as you can. This is the one time when you should *throw* an anchor. A grapnel or dinghy anchor often is all that's needed.

Then take time to look over the situation. In tideless waters time doesn't matter. On a rising tide, the longer you delay the more likely you are to get off without much effort. Even on a falling tide, a few minutes won't make all that difference. Say the range of tide where you are is four feet; at worst it'll drop one inch in the next five minutes.

Just sounding with a boathook all around the craft from the deck, will often tell a whole lot. In warm waters put on a face mask and jump overboard. A quick swim around the boat will show where she's hung and where the deep water lies. Usually it'll be astern, of course, but sometimes you may have almost swindled yourself over a sandspit; a few feet ahead and you'll be afloat again. At other times—after she has bumped a few times—the only water deep enough to float her will be off to one side. With a dinghy and boathook you can quickly take some soundings. Even quicker, you can walk about.

My last three boats all drew exactly four feet, and just at that depth nature has put a pair of Plimsoll marks on my chest. Water up to my armpits would float us.

While you are exploring the neighborhood, you can make your plan for getting her off, and if you are the type of skipper I hope you are, work out a way to try if the first one doesn't get her free. Before you execute your plan, look in the bilge. If she is taking water, the last place you'd want to be is in deep water.

But suppose she is tight and you want to get her off. It would be nice if I could go on to say: "Try this first; if that doesn't work, try this, and so on. But I can't; it isn't that simple. Most often to get her off two or more things have to be done, more or less at the same time. For instance: Turning her around will often get her free, so will kedging off with an anchor; but sometimes the only way to turn her head is by using the kedge. Changing her fore-and-aft trim may almost float her, but again you may need a kedge to haul her into deeper water.

With this interlocking of methods in mind, let me try to list a few of the ways used by expert grounders and stranders.

Change the fore-and-aft trim. Most boats, power or sail, draw more water aft than forward, and so are likely to be hung up near the stern. Bringing her down by the head is likely to raise her stern and may get her free. With wind or current setting toward deeper water, all you'll have to do is to get all hands, including yourself, to the bow. With the deep water astern, you may lash the wheel amidships, and run the engine slowly in reverse. Pushing off from the bow with a pole may help. But it has to be a sturdy pole; a boathook may break, splinter, and put someone into sick bay. If none of this works, lay out a kedge anchor astern on a long warp. Then with all hands pulling, take out the slack, then more slack and belay. The springiness of the rope will tend to pull her when she comes afloat. If she doesn't get clear, but the anchor rode gets the least bit slack, get it taut again before the next try.

On muddy bottom, rolling her by moving the crew from side to side may break the suction.

Turn her head. Again grounded at the deepest part of the keel, a boat will often come free if you can turn her more or less end-for-end. A sailboat can sometimes be persuaded to start to turn by holding the jib aweather. With the wind aft, you may try wearing ship. Drop the main, push the boom out on the other side, and hoist the sail again. In any boat in warm water you can order all hands and the cook overboard to push her bow around. Have them put their backs against the bow and push from thighs and knees, rather than with their arms.

One of my Bahama-based friends had carried the getting afloat drill to a fine point. At the first sign of trouble his wife and four daughters would jump over the side. If this lightening-ship didn't already get her off, the five girls would push the bow around while father stayed dry at the wheel. But now two of his daughters are married, and one went off to school. The last time I saw him, he was talking of trading his vessel for one of less draft.

An outboard-powered dinghy can be used to turn the bow. You'll find it better to put a fender on the bow of the dinghy and to push, tug style, than using a rope and pulling.

Sometimes, as already mentioned, the only way to get her head turned will be with lots of muscle and a kedge anchor laid out on the quarter on the deep-water side. It's hard work to bulldoze sand or mud with the keel, but that's what gets her free.

Kedging off. Hauling a stranded or grounded vessel to an anchor laid out in deep water is a time-tested maneuver. Throwing that anchor will hardly ever work. Once you have taken in the slack, there's not enough scope left to hold against the strain put on it. A dinghy is the most efficient means for getting the anchor far out, and into deep water. The warp, ready to run, should be in the dinghy rather than being paid out from the stranded vessel. The bitter end of that rope is belayed to the bow or stern of the parent vessel. To get the most scope out, bend another line to your anchor warp; when you take in the slack, most of that second line will come aboard.

Outboard motors and lines astern give all kinds of troubles. So detail a second person into the dinghy to pay out the line and keep it clear of helmsman, motor, and propeller. You may be better off to work under oars. Wind and current may make that strenuous exercise, but coming back, the man in the dinghy can haul himself home hand-over-hand.

Even without a dinghy you can lay out a kedge. Walk it out and have someone feed you slack from the deck. Even a short fellow will keep his air intakes above water in a depth of five feet; a tall fellow with a face mask and snorkel can breathe in six. The anchor carried over a shoulder will keep him from floating; he can pull himself home along the rope.

A fair swimmer can push an inflated inner tube, or other makeshift raft that floats the anchor. Carrying or swimming an anchor out lets the man in the water set the anchor by hand. That saves precious scope, otherwise wasted while the anchor drags along the bottom before digging in.

Whatever method you used to get the anchor out and set, keep a strain on the warp at all times. You may have the pleasant surprise of getting her free with little effort. Just running the engine gently forward (yes, forward) may wash away some of the sand and muck that's holding her. An unexpected inch or two of tide, when according to the tables it should have been already falling, once got me

63. *Walking out an anchor.*

off a sticky wicket. She may also come free when a wave a little higher than the rest lifts her stern.

If you have an outboard-powered dinghy you can make such waves yourself. Have someone run the dinghy near the boat, throttle wide open, but keeping clear of the anchor rode. Slack taken in every time the dinghy's wake hits her may let you walk off your yacht, a foot at a time.

Reduce draft. Here a sailboat has the advantage over a power cruiser. In heeling, a sailboat reduces her draft much more than the more flat-bottomed powerboats. The wind about abeam, will push her over to leeward if you strap in the main sail. Having perhaps turned her around, laid out a kedge astern, or even with just her auxiliary engine ticking over in reverse, you may get the heeled boat into deep water again.

When the wind won't oblige, your crew leaning out from the shrouds may give her the needed list. With a dinghy there is one more method. Guy the boom fore and aft, then lash the dinghy to the boom as if you wanted to hoist it aboard. Fill the dinghy with water or passengers, and with halyard or topping lift, secured above the dinghy to the boom, hoist away. The weight of the dinghy may give the yacht the necessary list.

There is one more method to list a sailboat. Lay out the kedge anchor astern first. Then lay out a second anchor far out at the quarter. The second anchor doesn't have to be in deep water, but it should be set to hold well. Bend an extra line to your main halyard, then take the free end of this line out to your anchor warp, securing it with a rolling hitch. Now haul down on the halyard to lay her over while someone tends the slack on the stern anchor. Unless something carries away, this maneuver will almost always get you off, even when you are several inches short of floating.

Lighten the ship. This is the last resort on power- and sailboats. Often it pays to try it first. The crew ordered over the side to push, may lighten her enough. Even when they are not the pushing kind of crew, send them over the side for a swim perhaps. They can't swim? Hang a line over the side and let them hang on. As far as the boat is concerned, they have lightened her by perhaps 90 percent of their weight even while they hang on. Water too cold? Order them into the dinghy if you have one.

Unless you have a lot of water in the bilge, pumping it won't make much difference in her draft; but it's a good idea anyway to get rid of the water before it gets into the wrong places. Drinking water is another matter. If you carry fifty gallons, you'll get rid of five hundred pounds of weight by ditching it. It'll probably be simplest to let it drain into the bilge, and then pump it overboard. Plastic fuel cans, in fact most cans filled with gasoline, float; dump

Running Aground and Getting Off 183

them over the side on a lanyard. Twenty gallons will lighten her as much as dumping a man overboard. Anchors, especially the storm anchor, account for some easily ditched and retrievable weight; so does anchor chain. Batteries are heavy and can be put into the dinghy. Unshipping inside ballast, if carried, will help and so will canned goods put into the dinghy. But that's a lot of work.

If all your efforts have not brought her afloat, or when the tide has dropped too much while you tried, make her comfortable. A powerboat will normally take the bottom leaning over just a little. A sailboat in the same predicament will seem to lie on her ear.

When there is deep water to one side, shallow water on the other,

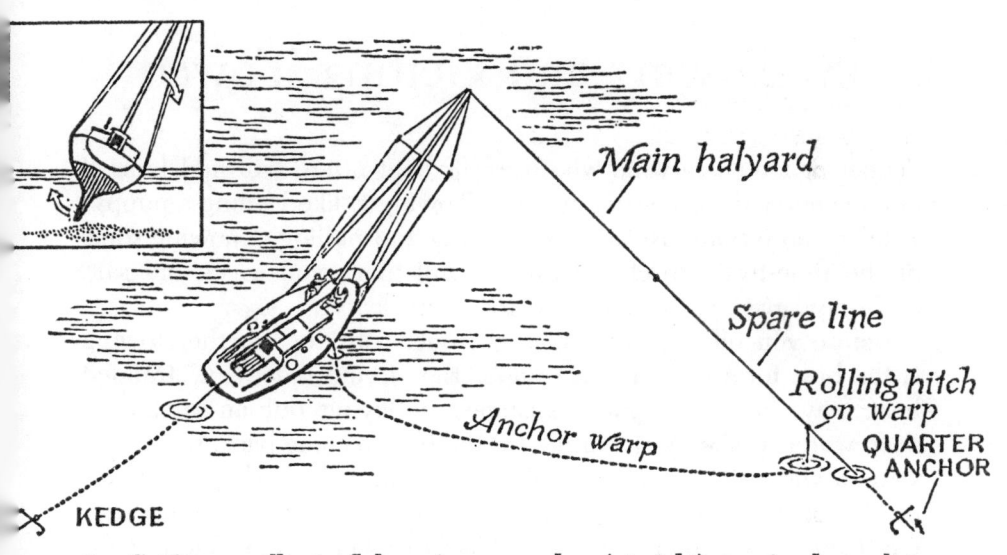

64. *Getting a sailboat off by using an anchor (at right) to give her a list, which reduces her draft as shown in insert.*

make her lie toward the shallow side by giving her a definite list to that side. It may pay to sacrifice a mattress, seat cushions, or life preservers to make a bolster for her bilge to rest on.

I wouldn't attempt to keep her upright with oars, bunkboards, or other makeshift props. If one of them snapped, or sank into the mud, she'd flop over, and might hurt herself badly.

At this point I would not only pump the bilge, but bail it and sponge it dry. It's shocking what a mess a few cupfuls of bilge water can make in one's clothes or tool locker.

Next, I'd close ports and seacocks, not forgetting engine intake and the scuppers of a self-bailing cockpit. However sad your craft looks when the tide has left her, like most boats she'll come upright again unless flooded from above first.

Then, while waiting for the tide to come back or for help to arrive, I'd find some useful task for myself and all hands, including children. It doesn't matter whether you scrape and paint the bottom or make yards and yards of baggywrinkle. Just keep everyone busy.

And then wait, and wait some more.

18 Towing and Getting Towed

Sooner or later everyone who uses his boat often, will find himself at one end or the other of a towline. Towing is like leading a puppy: It takes more than just hitching a string and pulling. Knowing some of the time-tested tricks of towing will mark you as an old salt, and may save parted lines and torn-out cleats.

Before you offer a tow, or accept one, consider whether towing is the best form of assistance under the circumstances. A stranded boat may only need your assistance in laying out an anchor in deep water. If she's just waiting for the tide to come back, taking the women and children home might be a good idea. Perhaps all that's needed to free the stranded boat is your running back and forth (in deep water) to create a wake that'll let her crew kedge her off. Or you might take a line from the mast of a sailboat to keep her heeled to reduce her draft, and let her slide off under her own power. A single-hander might appreciate the loan of your crew for a few minutes more than any amount of power to horse him off.

A sick or injured man could be rushed to medical help quicker on your own boat than by towing his; perhaps one of your crew can follow on the injured man's boat. Calling the Coast Guard for him may be better still.

Rather than towing a boat that's making a lot of water, give her skipper emergency repair materials, lend him a pump, and—if he is short-handed—a man to work it. She might sink if you towed her.

I'll never forget a kind skipper who towed me without a rope.

In dark and rain I was groping my way through the intricate channel to his home port where I had never been before. He jockeyed his boat in front of my bow, reduced his speed to match mine, and from then on all I had to do was to follow his transom. At the end of this tow he gradually reduced speed until we were almost dead in the water. Then he flashed a light at a mooring buoy within easy reach of my boathook, waved, and was gone.

But suppose the situation clearly calls for a tow, or a pull-off from a sandbar. Before you rush into the job, try to find out all you can about the emergency. She might have a broken fuel line and a bilge full of gasoline. Hardly the time to come alongside with your pipe lit. I'd offer to call the Coast Guard. If I had no ship-to-shore telephone, I'd promise to find a boat that had. I'd take her people off, but personally wouldn't hang around for an explosion.

Now suppose you decide on towing. The first problem is to get a line to the disabled boat. There are easier methods than heaving it. Steam under the stern of the crippled craft while you tow a line with a float attached. The float—a life ring or buoyant cushion will do nicely—will keep the line out of your propeller, and make it easy for the other crew to pick up the line from the cockpit (Fig. 65, A.)

In deep water there's another good method. Stop directly astern of the disabled boat, and on the same heading. Watch how the two boats drift. Probably they'll move more or less in the same direction, but one will drift a little faster than the other. In moderate weather pull abeam on the side where the boats will come together rather than drift apart. By leaving shouting distance between the boats at first, you'll have time for a short conference. Just before the two boats kiss, you can pass a line, then pull ahead. In rough water, I'd approach her where I'd drift away from her. (Fig. 65, B.)

When the disabled boat is aground, a dinghy is the safest method for passing the line after the rescuing boat has anchored. It also gives the captains a chance to hold a conference. Without dinghy, consider anchoring directly upwind, or upcurrent, from the cripple. You can fall back slowly on your anchor and still stay in deep water. Let the wind, or current, float a buoyed line to the stranded craft. Every boat yaws when at anchor, and these swings, helped with the rudder if necessary, will bring the line where the other crew can pick it up easily. (Fig. 65, C.) With the wind from the casualty toward deep water, you may gingerly feel your way toward her, relying on the wind to keep you out of trouble.

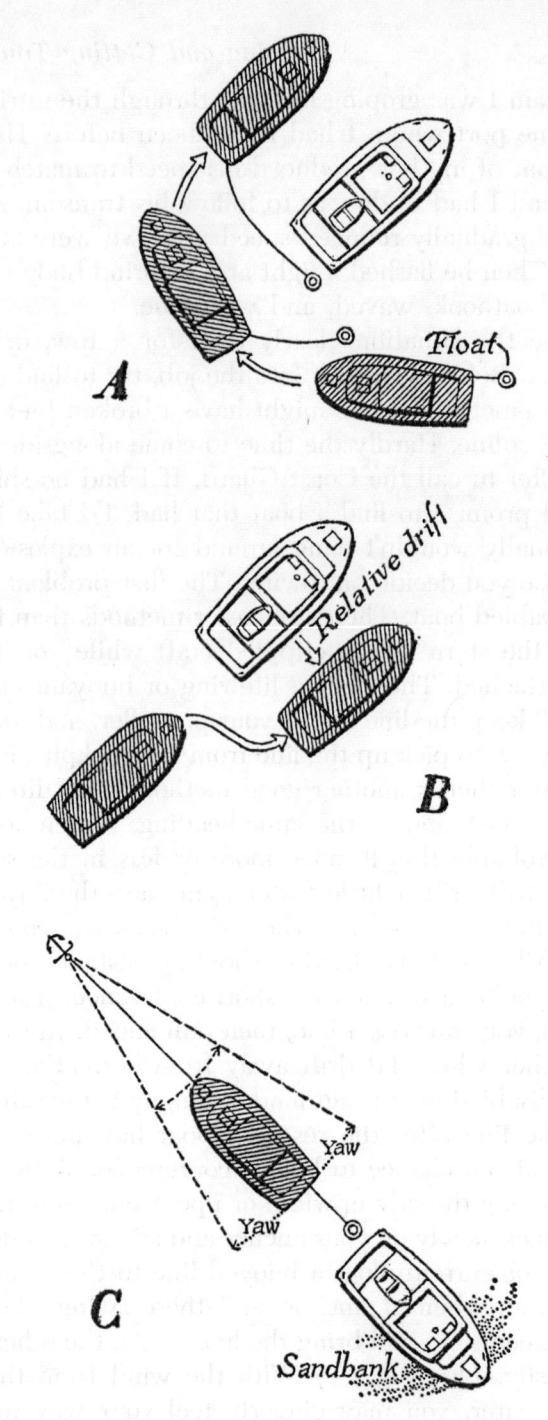

65. *Getting a line to the disabled boat.*

The line passed can be the tow line; more often it will be a light messenger line that lets you haul a heavier line from boat to boat. Rope used for towing water skiers works well for such a line. The tow line is apt to get stretched, perhaps chafed, or even cut, so it's only fair that the vessel to be helped supplies the line. An anchor line will often be used, but make sure the towed craft still has a workable anchor and line aboard. She may need it when you drop her off at the end of a successful tow job, or when something has gone wrong.

If you can, arrange a code of signals. Commercial towing vessels have a whole string of signals. Here is a simple code, without official sanction, but one that will be understood by almost everyone even without a conference. It's based on the well-known danger signal of four or more blasts. For the opposite of danger—everything is going well—try one blast, a little longer than the conventional "I'm directing my course to starboard."

SIGNAL	MEANING
One Blast	I'm ready—take up the slack. Everything holding—take a strain. Under way: Are you all right? Everything O.K. here.
Four or More Short Blasts	Stop—hold it. Trouble at my end.

The boat to be towed will secure the line forward to her strongest cleat, bitt, Samson post, or perhaps anchor winch, and rig chafing gear where the line touches the rail, or goes through the chock. Split hose is good for that; canvas, or even rags, wrapped around the rope and lashed in place with heavy twine will do.

No cleat, in fact no single fastening, can be expected to stand the strain of pulling off a boat that's aground. To distribute the strain over a large area of the hull, rig a bridle by taking the tow line—or one at least as strong—all around the hull. The athwartships lashings, which serve only to hold the bridle in place, can be of lighter line.

The towing boat can also make use of a bridle. If the tow line has to be fastened to a single point, that point ideally should be well forward, as on a tug. But that's rarely practical on a pleasure craft, where the strongest through-bolted stern cleat or mooring bitt will have to do. Tied by her stern, the towing craft will not answer her helm in the usual brisk fashion.

To start a tow, take up the slack very, very slowly, even when the disabled vessel is afloat. Then gently put a little strain on the tow line. Gently. Don't try to steer in any particular direction; just take a strain. This is the most critical moment in towing—cleats pull out, ropes part, and people risk getting hurt.

When you do it gradually, easily, it's amazing what a load you can pull through the water. One man in a rowboat can get a forty-foot yacht going in calm weather. On a friend's boat with a 25-hp engine we once towed a disabled seaplane that drew six feet of water and carried a crew of seven.

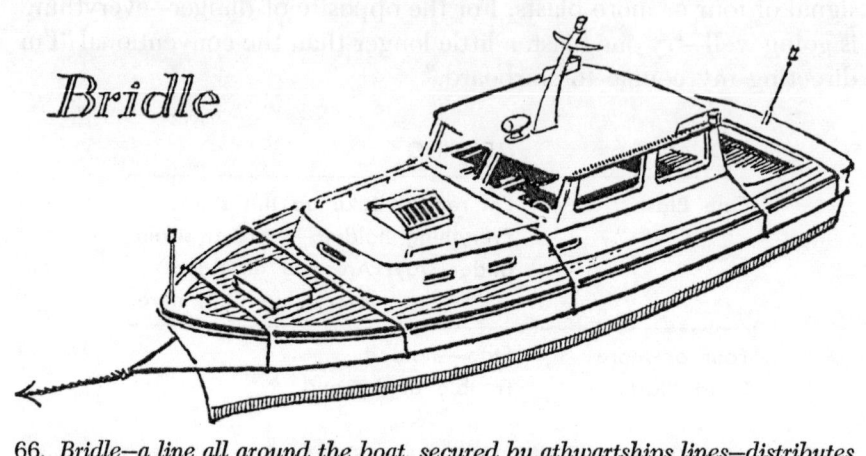

66. *Bridle—a line all around the boat, secured by athwartships lines—distributes strain over large area of hull on boat to be towed; also useful on towing boat.*

Once under way, adjust the length of the tow rope. If there is any sea running, the worst length for the tow line is one which makes the towing vessel climb a wave, while the towed vessel slides down the next one. It would be better to let out line until both boats ride up or down at the same time. Even better, if the length of line permits, leave one whole wave between the boats. And don't forget to rig chafing gear also on the towing boat.

A long tow line will absorb some of the sudden jerks caused by rough water. Nylon, which stretches more than other rope fibers, is the choice of professional towers. In deep water you can get additional shock-absorbing action into the tow line by tying a heavy weight halfway between the boats. The backup weight used to make an anchor hold like a heavier one is ideal for this purpose.

Some boats when towed don't follow in the wake of the towing boat but yaw all over the ocean. You can curb these excursions by streaming a loop of line from the casualty. Anything that floats—oars, cockpit gratings, etc.—tied to the bight will increase the drag on this line and make it more effective. Any towed craft will try to cut corners, so the towing boat will have to take turns very wide.

Detail one member of your crew to watch the tow at all times. Shorthanded you may be able to rig a shaving mirror to watch the tow from the helmsman's seat. Lines under strain become jammed

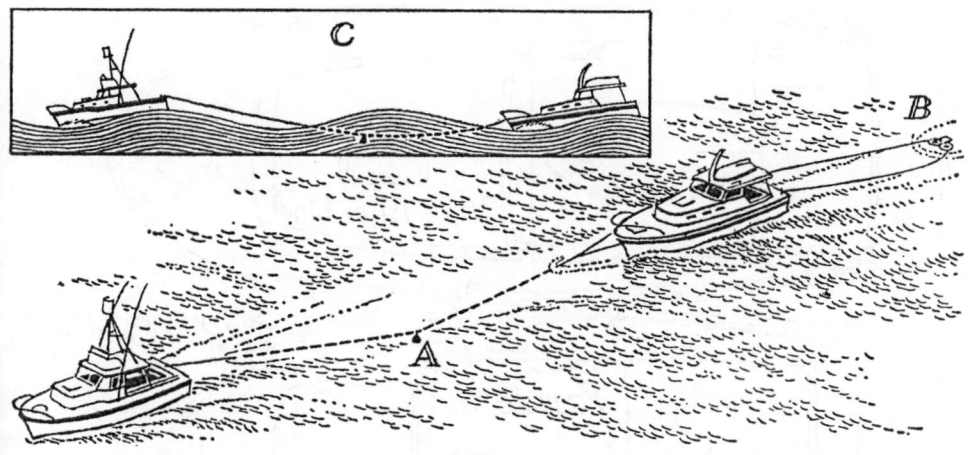

67. *Tips for towing astern*—(A) *a weight tied to line between boats eases shock load* (B) *sea anchor streamed from towed boat curbs her yawing* (C) *leaving one wave between boats helps them keep distance.*

down hard, and both boats had better have an ax or sharp knife handy to cut the line in an emergency.

The problems of the long tow, and the difficulties of controlling the towed boat, can often be overcome by towing alongside. Rig the lines as you would set crossed spring lines at a dock (and breast lines if you like too). Use fenders to keep the damage to topsides to a minimum. In an alongside tow there are no problems of communication, only one boat needs a man at the wheel; steering control is almost normal, so you can maneuver even in narrow channels. Even if you started towing in line in rough water, you may consider not only shortening the tow line, but switching to alongside towing when you get into more protected waters.

190   EMERGENCIES

You may have heard it said that only boats of approximately the same freeboard can tow in this rafting position. Not so. I know of a forty-foot ketch, becalmed on the Bahama Banks, that covered fifty miles under tow from its own dinghy lashed alongside. And what did she use for an outboard? A four-horsepower Seagull.

Towing sailboats has its own problems. Fastening the tow line is not one of them. That can be led through the chock to the mast where it comes out of the cabintop. A few layers of canvas, or even a kapok life vest, can serve as chafing gear. But the towing skipper must remember that sailboats often draw more water than power-

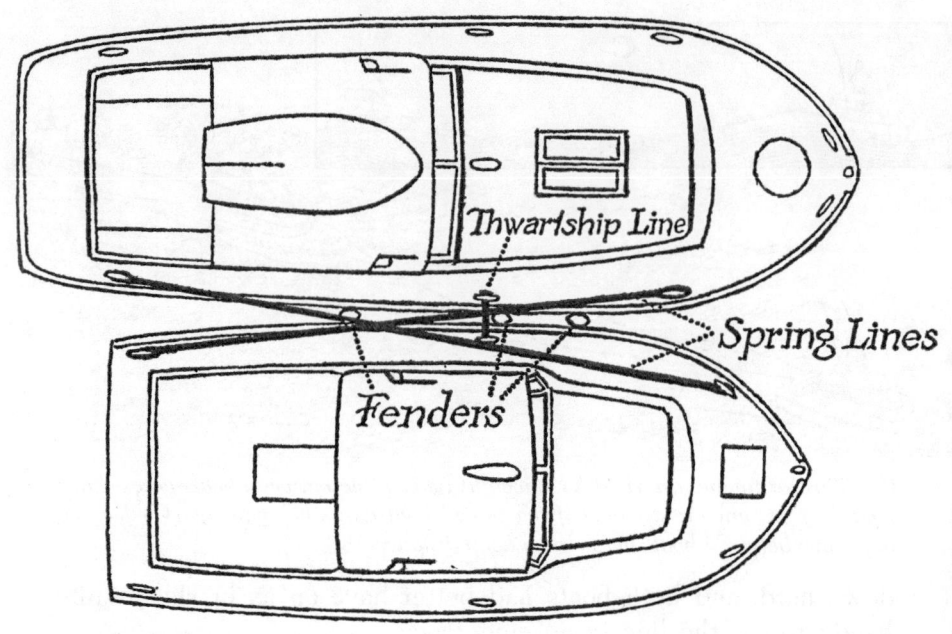

68. *Alongside towing.*

boats of the same over-all length. The cabin cruiser that skims along in eighteen inches of water will have to navigate with care when he tows a sailboat no longer than his own craft but drawing perhaps five feet.

But the real surprise for some powerboat skippers is this: A sailboat has a built-in top speed. And it's a rather low speed. In miles per hour it's about 1.5 times the square root of the boat's waterline length. For a sailboat with a sixteen-foot waterline that works out to 6 mph (5¼ knots); for a twenty-five-foot waterline it's about 7½ mph (6½ kn). Nothing can be done to make a typical sailboat go through the water any faster without drowning her, as it were, in her own wake. The words "through the water" are not just added for bulk. A planing-type hull, which doesn't go through the water but rather over it, doesn't obey this rule. You can also read "through the water" as the opposite of "over the bottom." With a three-knot helping current a boat with a hull speed of five knots may be making eight knots over the bottom or along the shore, but through the water her speed still doesn't exceed her built-in top speed.

The idea of a sort of sonic barrier for sailboats seems strange. I had heard about it and read the theoretical explanations but only halfheartedly believed in it, as some kid may believe in Santa Claus. Then a friendly soul gave my schooner a tow. That was no emergency but a shoreside arrangement to save me a nasty stretch of doubtful-weather sailing. As long as my friend kept the speed down, *Lucina* barely made a ripple at the bow, less than some dinghies I have towed.

"Didn't even know I had you," is how the captain described the reaction of his own craft. Then he opened his throttles a little wider. *Lucina* was at her hull speed and turned into a wave-making machine of unbelievable efficiency. Her stern squatted until her rail was below the level where the ocean should have been. There instead of water was a spoon-shaped hollow. And behind that the water sprayed out in a peacock's tail fifteen feet high.

My friend, watching that, must have found it very amusing; he nudged the throttles ahead a little more. Then he had a surprise. Whatever the setting, his twin 6-110 GM diesel engines wouldn't make his boat go any faster. My peacock's tail absorbed all their spare power. Now any time he wants to start an argument, he just mentions the hull speed of sailboats.

You ought to display special lights if caught by darkness while towing a vessel astern. If you can't jury rig these lights—and you probably can't—play a spotlight on the tow rope to keep other craft from cutting through between you and your tow. Towing alongside at night, with both vessels showing riding lights, may confuse some oncoming skipper, but he is not likely to pass between you and your tow.

Your job as towmaster, or good Samaritan, is not ended until you drop off your charge safely. Don't just let the crippled craft drift, with tow line dangling, to the next dock. It might be better to have her anchor off. If I towed another boat alongside, I'd put my own craft against the dock, not the towed craft. I'd be better able to gauge the approach. We could then stay rafted together, or untangle our lines at leisure.

If a skipper you have helped doesn't thank you as warmly as you think he should have, remember he may be thinking about an explanation of what happened and why he didn't show up in time for dinner at his in-laws. Don't take it out on the next distressed stranger you meet. The way I figure it, a good deed is its own reward. And someday, someone is going to help you when you are in a pickle.

19 Hold Regular Drills

On a passenger liner you go through an abandon-ship drill on the first day out, on a pleasure boat probably never. Liners do run into trouble. But the number of those that have done so is so small you could probably name most of them, starting with the *Titanic*. A single Coast Guard district handles more MAYDAYS from small craft on one summer weekend.

With chances for having to abandon a pleasure craft so much greater, shouldn't every skipper give the matter some thought? This could be the first step: Figure out what you would do, what you'd have your crew—your family and guests—do when. . . .

The second step: Hold a drill. That'll show how well your plan might work. Drills also set up conditioning. After you and your crew have been through a few rehearsals, everyone aboard will perform more efficiently in a real emergency. The drill on a runabout on a lake will be different from that on a yacht that cruises offshore.

On the runabout you'll simply point out everyone's life preserver, make sure all hands know how to adjust and fasten theirs, and caution them to wait for your order to abandon, or have their hair cut by the propeller.

On a large boat you or your mate have pointed out the location of everybody's life preserver when they first came aboard. Now you announce: "When I give the signal, sometime this morning, I want everyone on deck wearing his life preserver, properly fastened." Likely one character will not care for this game. Take him aside and ask him to co-operate "as an example for the youngsters." Or try a different tack—put him in charge of some detail that'll keep him out of the way.

If you carry a dinghy aboard, launch it after the crew has assembled on deck. Better yet let them launch it without your help and supervision. When there's real trouble you may be needed elsewhere, in the engine hatch, at the pump strainer, or on the ship-to-shore. You may be in for a surprise. Your smart wife and your strong son, between them, can't get the featherweight dinghy overboard. A lashing might need to be cut—it shouldn't—"Who has a knife?" "Where is the ax?"

Or you may find the dinghy floating alongside in jig time, but without bailer and oars. "Where are they?" Some clown, a guest of course, may even have let go of the painter, and the dinghy is now rapidly falling astern.

If all has gone well, announce how long it has taken from the time you have given the order until the dinghy was ready to take on passengers. You don't have to go all Captain Bligh about this time business. If it has taken too long, your crew will know it and try to do better at the next drill.

Should the dinghy half fill with water, fine. That gives you a chance to teach the lubbers not to step into a swamped dinghy but to bail her out with a bucket on a lanyard from the deck of the mother vessel. If the dinghy has turned right over, you get a chance to order a right-the-boat drill. Then you may have another surprise. Your pretty, unsinkable dink may also be unrightable until you install a keel with handholds.

Dinghies on yachts large enough to carry them are used for shore transportation, for maintenance, perhaps for anchor work, and even as emergency tugs. So everyone is likely to be familiar with the dinghy's foibles. But life rafts (balsa or rubber) are likely to become permanent fixtures, their lashings glued to the deck by seasonal dribbles of paint. A trial launch may show up more than the clumsiness of your crew. It might be worth more than the price of replacing the bottle of CO_2 it takes to inflate a rubber raft.

There is a dividend to an abandon-ship drill: During the next boring trick at the wheel the skipper is bound to ruminate about abandoning. That's what makes good skippers.

Here are some thoughts, tested in real emergencies.

Rule One: Don't Leave the Ship.

We have all read of ships, big ships, discovered floating peacefully, while their boats and people have never been found. Do you remember Robinson Crusoe? All his shipmates were lost. He alone stayed with the ship, and got enough gear from the wreck to sustain him through the next few hundred pages. Even a wreck awash is safer than a dinghy, and has a better chance of being spotted from the air or from the deck of a passing craft. A pleasure boat's dinghy is a frail thing, and difficult to land even in fair-weather surf.

So I'd get things ready, launch the boat, and muster the crew but stay aboard unless explosion threatened. Often a leak is not as bad as it seems. You may be able to reduce the inflow from the inside, or almost stop it from the outside with a rough patch. A piece of canvas juggled in place from the deck by lines tied to its corners, two of them passing under the keel, can cope with a leak well below the waterline. You may be able to clear the clogged pump. A bucket brigade can handle an amazing amount of water, perhaps long enough to beach your craft and so save her. A fire, however frightening, can be brought under control if you stay aboard.

Rule Two: Don't Swim.

Even with a life vest most people can only swim a short distance; the best swimmer is helpless against any sort of current. To land unhurt on a steep or rocky shore is almost impossible for a tired swimmer.

Don't let the temptation to jump overboard overcome your good judgment. If you have a dinghy or raft, don't swim and don't let anyone, however good a swimmer, try to swim for it even with a life preserver.

Rule Three: Stay Near the Stricken Craft.

Again she'll be easier to spot than a dinghy or raft. A fire may burn for hours, but its smoke may bring help. The wreck awash, or sunk in shallow water, even the oil slick from one foundered in deep water, may attract attention.

Also, fires can burn themselves out; feared explosions may not happen; leaks can reduce themselves to trickles. In short, you may be able to get back aboard. The best way to make sure you can is to keep your raft or dinghy tied to the yacht with a long line (except when there is danger of an explosion). Otherwise the yacht presenting a greater surface to wind or current may sail away from you.

Rule Four: Take What You'll Need.

That's another argument against swimming for shore. How much can a swimmer carry?

You'll have to make quick decisions about what to take, what to leave. You can't afford to be the old lady who, trying to find a packet of old love letters in her trunk, missed the last lifeboat. As part of your own mental abandon-ship drill, think about it now during your peaceful watch.

Getting all hands off and landing them safely is only part of your job, unless you operate on a lake surrounded by lived-in cottages. Then you only have to apologize for trespassing, and ask to use the phone to call a cab. Most shipwrecked sailors aren't that lucky. They have to carry their own means for attracting help, and for surviving without too much hardship until rescued, or until they have made their way back to civilization.

What you'll need will depend on the waters you cruise, the season, the size of your boat, and the number of your crew. You'll find some of the gear I'd like to carry listed in the chapter on wrecking. To be useful all this stuff should be with you when you land. Some of it must be kept dry. Individual waterproof containers are easily improvised, but who can assemble all that gear in an emergency?

That's again where drills come in. You can detail a member of your permanent crew to get these things every time you hold a drill. Better yet, you can keep all the stuff in a ready-box, perhaps a picnic cooler with the lid taped tight. Then at drill time that member of your crew or someone else you designate, only has to hunt for the things not permanently stowed in the box, say foul-weather gear, and drinking water.

Periodically at these drills, or at other times, you'll check the contents of the emergency locker. Test the flashlights, light a match or two, look at expiration dates on drugs, and see if pills haven't turned to powder.

At the time of an abandon-ship drill or at any other time, you can hold two other drills: Man Overboard and Fire.

In order not to strain weak hearts, a man-overboard drill should be announced beforehand, I think. Be as realistic as you like, but don't just have someone yell, "Man overboard!" Announcing the drill beforehand also gives you a chance for giving some instructions. You may explain that a person in the water is hard to see, so the object you'll throw overboard will be neither bright nor large. A gallon jug, almost full of water, is better than a cardboard box that riding high drifts with the wind. No one, with or without life preserver, is to jump to help the supposed victim. Instead a life preserver is to be thrown to—not at—the casualty. Ideally that ring or horseshoe has a water light attached for night use, and releases yellow smoke for visibility in daylight. Until released from that duty, whoever has thrown the buoy keeps the bobbing head (or bottle) in sight whatever goes on aboard. If possible have this lookout take position in front of the helmsman and point at the victim with outstretched arm, so the helmsman can concentrate on handling the boat.

Under power the helmsman if he saw the fall may have turned sharply to get the propeller clear of the victim. He should now complete the circle.

If the boat is still steaming on a straight course, read that course. Drop a float overboard. Then start a tight circle (most boats turn more readily to one side than the other) until you are back at the float or cut your own circular wake. At that point start steering the reciprocal of the original course. This maneuver will bring most boats back quicker than stopping and reversing; try both methods on your boat and time them.

On a sailboat the reverse method, even without sails set, will probably not work at all; most auxiliaries have very poor steering control in reverse. Under sail your best action will depend on the point of sailing. Heaving to (by hauling the jib aweather and strapping in the main), tacking, jibing, dousing sail and starting the engine, all may be the best maneuver at the right time. You may want to try them all to see what your boat does in a given situation.

Under power or under sail, a few drills will need your supervision. Then one day you can test your crew: You are the man overboard; they are on their own. I wouldn't want to be in the drink myself at such a test; I might get hungry before they'd pick me up. No, I'd stay aboard just watching, and perhaps timing, the drill.

Once near the victim, you should come up to windward of him to give him a lee. That's the recommended practice. But watch your drift. Your boat may be bearing down on the poor exhausted soul and hit him. In a drill you may find the gallon jug suddenly bobbing up on your weather side.

To bring the victim aboard, one man or preferably two, with life vest *and* a line tied securely to the boat, should go overboard.

Now besides the helmsman-engineer we have needed at least one and perhaps two extra hands to handle the emergency. What's a single-hander to do? He just can't afford to fall overboard. Even with a proper safety harness and lifeline, if he fell overboard from anything but a sailboat moving slowly, he'd have the devil's own time getting back aboard. Handholds and steps at the stern may help him a little. A dinghy towed astern—frowned upon most of the time—is easier to get into than climbing onto a sleek hull with high freeboard.

I know. I had just taken over *Boheme* where she'd been anchored for several months in the Bahamas. I scrubbed the cabin. When I needed rinse water, I tied a short rope to a bucket. Then the rope slipped out of my hand. I hadn't taken the time to tuck in an eye-splice, or even tie a figure-eight knot at the end of the rope. Never one to let a ninety-eight-cent bucket get away, I jumped after it. The current was stronger than I had expected, and it was quite a swim back. Have you ever tried to swim carrying a bucket? I tossed the bucket on deck and looked for an easy way to get aboard. There wasn't one. Porpoising out of the water, I could barely touch the rail. The rudder was no good for climbing either; I promised myself to put some cleats there later. Although I was in good condition, I was getting quite exhausted by then. What to do? Her anchor, of course. But the chain was studded with sharp little barnacles. No thank you. I could have swum ashore to borrow a dinghy, but how'd I look dressed at the most in a plastic bucket? I finally managed to reach a piece of line on deck, and to tease it over the side. Under way, I could never have made it.

So single-handers do—or should—wear a safety harness at all times and snap its short lanyard to some solid support. Not a bad idea on any boat, especially when you leave the comparative safety of the cockpit. And don't jump after buckets.

Again you can time the drill conspicuously, and afterward think how you could improve not only the time but the whole technique. If you don't want to waste time on a good day, how about holding that drill when it's not fit outside to go far from your anchorage?

That would also be a good day for a fire drill.

Sorry, Captain, again you'll have to do all the thinking, even more so than at the other drills. That's the price of command.

First, you may recall that the experts talk about three classes of fires. Class A is for wood, paper, cushions, and lamb chops; Class B for liquids such as gasoline, diesel fuel, and the alcohol used in

69. *Safety harness.*

some galley stoves; Class C covers electrical fires caused by overheated wires and short circuits. You may not want to teach your crew the classes. But recall to them that water should never be used on liquid fuels because it spreads the burning liquid, which floats atop the water. Alcohol fires seem to be an exception. Unlike gas and oil, alcohol mixes with water, and diluted alcohol will not sustain a fire. But there is some danger that water may chase still-undiluted alcohol into the bilge or some other hard-to-get-at place. Ashore, water should not be used on electrical fires because of the danger of electrocuting the fireman. When you are in a marina, plugged into shore current, that's still true. From the batteries used on most boats (12 or 24 volts) electrocution may be unlikely, but water may make a partial short complete, and almost certainly will ruin electronic gear such as radios and direction finders.

So perhaps you'd be smart to forbid the use of water on *any* fire. Instead carry extinguishers that can be used on all fires, such as carbon dioxide and dry chemical types. (Carbon tetrachloride has been disapproved by the Coast Guard for years because of the lethal fumes it gives off.)

Then I'd impress on my crew that they are not expected to be heroes. Better to throw a burning cushion overboard than trying to smother the fire by sitting on it.

Next I'd stress that the first moments often decide the outcome of a fire. Have them call you at the first whiff of smoke.

At an actual drill I'd let every member of the crew handle a fire extinguisher and—without actually squirting—aim it at the *base* of the make-believe flames. They should actually fetch and unship the extinguishers. It's amazing how people don't see the extinguishers they almost bump into all the time, how brackets corrode, and how paint cements them in place. If the extinguishers have gauges, check them at every drill. Show everyone the master switch that should be pulled in any electrical fire. If the automatic bilge pump is on a separate circuit, show them that switch too. And have all the switches clearly marked OFF and ON.

Everybody by now knows about gasoline-air mixtures being explosive. Anyone who has tried to adjust the carburetor on a balky outboard also knows how critical the mixing ratio is. Isn't it surprising that so many boats explode? There must be an awful lot of fools handling boats, or at least on boats.

Take one that blew up in Nassau while fueling. The captain had taken all the recommended precautions while gassing up. But below the girls got bored and decided it was a good time to brew a cup of coffee. One lit a match, and WHAM! The smartest thing might be to send everybody on errands, and let the dockmaster and you take care of fueling.

But then there is the skipper who turned off all electrical equipment, closed hatches and ports, kept the nozzle to the filler pipe to avoid a static spark, filled slowly to prevent bubbling, left room in the tank for expansion, and did everything just right. After airing out the boat he sniffed and inspected everywhere, and found the flame on his kerosene-operated refrigerator burning brightly. That could also have happened with an alcohol box, or one that runs on bottled gas where, at least, the pilot flame is always lighted.

This L.P. gas is hot and clean fuel, but unfortunately heavier than air. Leaking gas accumulates in low parts of the boat, in the bilge, for instance, where ignited it'll cause a spectacular explosion. You, of course, know this. But does the cook and everyone who might make himself a cup of coffee?

Undoubtedly the galley is the greatest fire hazard on a pleasure boat. Perhaps as part of the drill you should spend a few minutes there, even if normally you shun the place. There's not only the hazard from fuel, but also oil in the deep fryer—even the grease in the skillet can catch on fire. Is the overhead protected against such flareups? Can the cook reach an extinguisher (or at least the baking soda) and shut off the fuel without getting burned? Can the cook get out when things go out of control? Does she know how to handle flareups of kerosene-pressure stoves? Will she not refill an alcohol stove until it has cooled off? Is the stove secured so that a sudden roll will not upset it or the pots? Should you have an asbestos mitten in the galley? (The usual cotton oven mitts, to my mind, are a fire hazard in themselves; so are pot holders.)

The engine hatch is the next most fire-sensitive spot.

No oily, or even clean, rags should be stored there. Any grease dripping or thrown from a bearing should be scraped off, and the spot cleaned. The drip pan under the engine should be dry.

All these things can be checked during a fire drill. More important: Can everyone get out wherever the fire? Can you get to at least one extinguisher without getting cut off by fire?

You needn't make heavy weather of all these drills. But hold them regularly, and especially at every change in your permanent crew, and when you replace your early season's friends with another batch of freeloaders.

Children will enjoy the drills if you make a game of them. The grown-up girls are more likely to be mutinous. You can point out to them that we carry a spare tire and jack even where there are service stations on every other block. And cars out West carry water bags, although nobody really expects to die of thirst between Los Angeles and Las Vegas.

20 Learn to Float

Half of all the drownings in the United States happen within twenty feet of safety. The Coast Guard estimates that 50 percent of all Americans cannot swim fifty feet. Even a fair swimmer can stay afloat only so long, perhaps not long enough to be picked up from a boat however well she's handled.

What to do? Forget about swimming. Learn to float and teach it to your crew.

I'm not referring to flotation devices. Of course, it's an excellent idea to have children wear life vests at all times near the water, not just under way, but also dockside. But what about adults? Most of them, it seems, would rather risk drowning than be seen wearing life preservers. And yet, some personal rescue devices can be worn quite inconspicuously; one even comes built into an ordinary-looking sport shirt.

But apparently these devices don't get used enough. Coast Guard statistics for a recent year show nine out of ten people who found themselves in the water after some boating mishap did not wear a life-saving device, or have one within reach. Not surprising, since according to the same source more than a third of all these mishaps came without warning.

But there is a way to save yourself. It doesn't depend on any mechanical device, and anyone can learn it, easily. The late Fred Lanoue invented it, and called it drownproofing. He had worked on the system for years. His object: to keep a person—even a cramped or injured person—afloat in salt water or fresh, not just in a pool but in rough water.

The method got national attention in the forties, when Mr. Lanoue, by then teaching swimming at Georgia Institute of Technology, put on a demonstration that made *Life* magazine.

It was quite a demonstration. Imagine the pool at Georgia Tech with photographers all around and flashbulbs popping. About sixty swimmers were in the water. Swimmers is perhaps the wrong word.

They had been carefully picked from the school's worst performers in the water. Anyone who dared jump into deep water, and could swim thirty feet, turn around, and come back alive was eliminated as too expert for the test. Some students had never made it across the pool; a few had never been more than five feet from the rail. To simulate cramped and injured people, about half the test subjects had their hands tied behind their backs, or their legs tied in a Buddha position.

Without touching sides or bottom of the pool they stayed afloat for an average of four hours and forty minutes. The group with tied wrists actually lasted longest: Average quitting time was almost 5½ hours. After eight hours, at the end of the test, one-quarter of all the starters were still floating, more of them tied than not.

One fellow had given up after only ten minutes. Only six of the quitters felt they had reached the limit of their endurance. Some, mostly thin fellows, got cold, although the water was kept at 80°F, the air between 90° and 100°. Almost as many subjects simply got bored; others had unbreakable appointments. The major cause for dropping out was the need of a bathroom.

Lanoue's method for floating obviously works.

It's different from the one used by the fat man in a pool, face and toes out of the water, and smoking a cigar. That method works only in calm water. If it gets rough, water will run down your nose and throat, down into your stomach and lungs. Also while most women and children, and some well-padded men will float on their backs, in fresh water most men will not. And I have noticed this: Once kids know how to swim they easily learn to float on their backs; until then they lack the confidence that seems necessary to keep them afloat in that position.

Lanoue's system is based on a different principle. With some air in their lungs, women, children, and ninety-nine out of a hundred white men are lighter than water. (Strangely, a much larger percentage of colored men are heavier than water.) In salt water everybody floats, I believe. Even when lighter than water, one has to be almost totally submerged to float. An alligator can breathe in that position, but we float hanging in the water with only the back of our head exposed. Not much good for breathing.

Your head weighs about fifteen pounds. In tests even the best swimmers lasted only two minutes carrying a fifteen-pound weight above the water. A dog-paddler, or water-treader who tries to keep his head up may not last even that long.

Lanoue lets you work only enough to bring your mouth above water to inhale, then lets you sink again to the natural floating position for a rest. (You exhale under water through the nose.) Little effort is needed to get your mouth above water for so short a time. A lazy raising of your arms, and then pushing down on the water will do it, or a slow scissors kick, or frog kick. He lets you breathe as often as you like. At first that will be every few seconds; when you get used to it, you'll rest most of the time just below the surface, and come up for air at ten- or twelve-second intervals. The lazier you are about that, the longer you'll last.

70. *Natural floating position of man in fresh water; only the top of the head is out of the water.*

Sometimes floating isn't enough; you want to get somewhere. And here too Lanoue's method shines. His travel stroke is just an extension of the stay-afloat technique: the same lazy arm and leg motions, the same breathing cycle. The only new thing to learn is a glide in the middle of each set of motions. The average beginner who has mastered the stay-afloat drill swims a mile after two more lessons. Several hundred Georgia Tech students swam the mile after only one more lesson, although they had never made the forty-four-foot width of the pool before. Mr. Lanoue used the mile because that's the distance an average swimmer covers in the time allotted to this test, one hour. His object is not just to cover the mile, but have the pupil fresh enough afterward to swim another mile, or yet another.

The Marine Corps teaches Lanoue's travel stroke at Parris Island. It tests recruits for the mile fully clothed, then for seventy-five yards with full equipment.

Every freshman at Georgia Tech has to pass the one-hour-float and the one-mile-distance tests. You may say, "I'm a bit past the freshman stage of physical fitness." Mr. Lanoue has had a few pupils like you, types who didn't look as if they'd make it. National magazines, other than *Life,* have sent writers to do articles about his method of drownproofing. Either magazine writers are specially poor physical specimens, or the editors handing out the assignments had an unsuspected sense of humor, and sent the worst available men to Mr. Lanoue. Yet every one of these writers stayed up one hour, and swam one mile.

Where can you learn the technique? It's now taught at many colleges, some of which have classes for outsiders. Check with the swimming coach if there's a college near you. Some YMCA and YWCA coaches also give the course. Some fellows learned drownproofing in the Navy or the Merchant Marine; if you'll join the Peace Corps, they'll teach you.

If you can't find an instructor, perhaps you can learn the technique all by yourself. If you already know how to swim it shouldn't be too difficult, especially if you have mastered the scissors kick. Unless you are a hermit you shouldn't have much trouble finding someone to teach you that kick while you hang onto the rail of a pool, or the swimming ladder of your boat. I'm a longtime frog-kicker myself. But that stroke has drawbacks. First, I find it difficult to do it as languidly as the Lanoue method requires. Second, if you get a cramp in one leg, half a frog kick isn't as effective as half a scissors kick. In fact, you get so used to frog-kick with both legs in unison, that you may find it hard to kick with one leg only.

What if you can't find a coach, and now can hardly swim at all? You still can teach yourself to float. I'd start almost within reach of the swimming ladder of my boat with someone standing by on deck with a boathook. And I'd start wearing a face mask and snorkel. The water should be deep enough to cover you up to your mouth when you stand upright. Better yet if it's over your head, and just leaves the upper end of the snorkel out of the water. You then needn't fear to drown, even if your supposed rescuer falls asleep.

Learn to Float   205

On hard bottom you can get yourself above the surface, in water well over your head, by just pushing off from the bottom.

Mr. Lanoue would not have approved of my suggestion for starting with face mask and snorkel. The air in the mask acts as a buoyancy device, the very thing we don't want to become dependent on. Worse, inside the mask you won't learn the important technique of exhaling through your nose under water. But it's better than not learning to float at all.

The mask frees you of the fear of imminent drowning, and lets you learn the basic resting position of hanging limp in the water. Also you'll learn to feel air—as opposed to water—on the back of your head. With your eyes dry and under water you can also watch your arm and leg movements.

Once you have learned the trick of hanging limp—a matter of a few minutes—and proved to yourself that you won't sink to the center of the earth, you are ready for the next step. Slowly raise and extend your arms, then swing them down, and watch yourself coming up. This is the time to straighten your neck and exhale (when you don't wear a mask). Never push so hard that your chin and shoulders come out of the water; that would be wasted effort.

You can also raise both forearms to your forehead, then spread your arms sideways, as shown in the illustration.

With either method—lifting arms and dropping, or lifting and scratching the surface of the water—what's needed is a little pressure lasting a long time. Says Herb McAuley, who had been Fred Lanoue's assistant since 1947, and now is swimming coach at Georgia Tech: "Our big problem with non-swimmers is that they want to stroke from the elbows instead of the shoulders, and try to jump up instead of easing up."

When your arm motions by either method bring your mouth above water, hold your arms behind your back and try to bring your head up using leg kicks.

Once either legs or arms—or a combination of both—let you breathe when you straighten your neck, discard the snorkel. Let out some of your breath (never all) on one surfacing, and take another shallow breath on the next. That's not Lanoue's method, but it works with the face mask. Don't try to let air out and to take on more in one coming-up.

As soon as you have convinced your reluctant brain that you'll float, can live for a few seconds without breathing, and can get to the surface at any time by almost effortless motions of arms, legs, or both, try it without face mask. With your newfound confidence you can work on getting used to water in your eyes, and practice exhaling through the nose during the time it takes to raise your head. You won't have any trouble stroking to get into a breathing position. But you must learn to exhale under water, *before* you get to the breathing position. Then you'll be ready to inhale as soon as your mouth gets above water, and let yourself sink again shortly

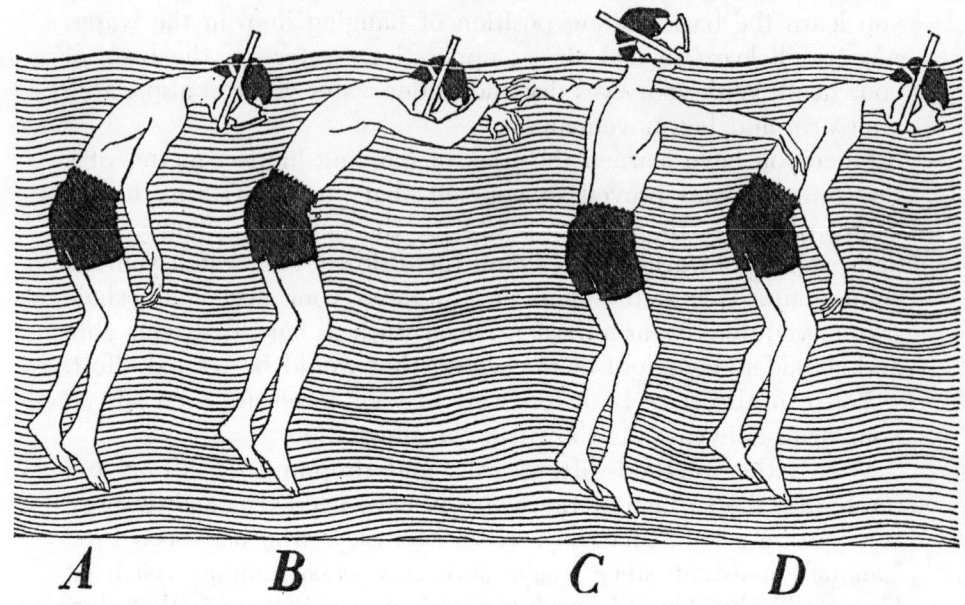

A   B   C   D

71. *Learning to float, using face mask and snorkel. (A) Rest just below the surface, letting arms and legs hang limp. (B) Slowly raise arms as though fending off a blow to your forehead. (C) Extend arms and feel yourself rising in the water. (After you have discarded mask and snorkel you take breath when mouth gets above water, having expelled most of the last breath through the nose, under water.) (D) After each surfacing hang limp for another rest.*

thereafter. The short time is important; don't stay up for both exhaling and inhaling.

You'll still have to learn to master panic if you get a coughing spell, say after taking a gulp of salt- or chlorine-loaded water. You'll find that you can cough under water without taking in any more water. If you keep up the regular movements, and spit out or swallow the water, you'll be back to normal breathing after two or three surfacings.

If the water is rough, face away from the waves.

If you find yourself sinking, or find you don't stay up long enough to get an adequate breath, push down with your hands, to keep yourself up. Pushing from the elbows will perhaps do it; pushing from the shoulders gives far more lift. Most people in bathing suits won't need that movement, certainly not in salt water; but in rough fresh water fully dressed you'll need the extra stroke.

72. *Downward push of forearms will give you extra lift when needed; pushing from shoulders, rather than elbows, gives more lift yet.*

When you have learned to float, and feel that in warm water you could do it almost indefinitely, try to get somewhere. Angle your kicks and arm strokes backward rather than downward. Then —when you feel yourself going forward in the water—lie still and horizontally until your forward momentum is spent in that glide. Then stroke for the next breath. For safety, have someone row along in the dinghy while you practice this distance float.

After you have learned to float, and perhaps to travel some distance, don't let it go at that: Teach the technique to your family and crew.

21 Distressproofing your Boat

Most boats are designed and built to take it. Properly handled, a well-found boat almost always can take as much punishment as her crew, and more. But emergencies show up her weak spots.

Take the last cruise of the *Santa Cruz*, a forty-nine-foot deep-draft sailboat, designed for a world cruise. The original plans showed a schooner rig, but the boat my friend Ralph Zimmerman bought had been ketch-rigged with a gaff mainsail and a jib-headed mizzen. In St. Petersburg, on the west coast of Florida, Ralph outfitted her and stocked her for an around-the-world voyage. Everything was on board and ready, except for a few items to be picked up in Panama. She carried no radio transmitter, in Ralph's book a device of little value on long ocean passages.

To give his crew and craft a shakedown, Ralph entered *Santa Cruz* in the St. Pete–Havana Race. Besides the owner-skipper and his son, Bill, she carried a crew of three keen amateurs.

She started to leak as soon as they hit open water. By the time they were abeam of Key West, they pumped fifteen minutes out of every hour. The skipper wasn't worried. His *Zarak* had leaked at least that much after a few months of idleness in the Pacific. And now *Santa Cruz* had been idle for a long time. He expected the dried-out planks above the waterline to take up soon. When he started across the Gulf Stream, the leak became worse, finally requiring continuous pumping.

If he hadn't been in a race Ralph would probably have turned around then, and gone into Key West. Though he had little hope of beating many of the other twenty competitors, he didn't want to deprive his crew of the fun in Havana. He inspected all through-hull fittings and, finding nothing wrong, carried on. A later search showed a leak just above the waterline where the planking runs into the stem. That would explain the leak's getting worse when they hit the rougher water of the Stream. But stopping that leak didn't appreciably lessen the work needed at the pump.

Distressproofing Your Boat 209

Nearer Havana than Key West, the pump gave up. There was no other pump worthy of that description aboard. Spare diaphragms for the pump were one of the items on the short list, to be sent to Panama.

After dropping the mainsail to ease the motion, and thereby reduce the leak, Ralph organized the crew into a bucket brigade. Then he pressed the starter button for the diesel engine. Nothing happened. The battery, although above bilge level, had been splashed out of commission. The engine couldn't be started by hand

73. *Ketch* Santa Cruz *starting on her last voyage.*

because the mizzenmast had been stepped directly in front of the flywheel with no provision for a crank.

So Ralph ordered the main rehoisted to make a quick run for Havana while maintaining the bucket work. But the main had other plans. It pulled out the pin rail taking the coils of peak halyard aloft.

Meanwhile the sea had kicked up to a point where Ralph wouldn't let anyone go up the mast. The *Santa Cruz* carried on under jib and mizzen in the dark. The crew worked as hard as they could with their buckets, but the water gained. The vessel became noticeably loggy.

Closing with Cuba's shore Ralph flashed distress signals, and fired red rockets. When the first set of signals brought no response from the land, he wore ship and made a second pass, firing more rockets and signaling S-O-S with the spotlight. Then a third pass. By this time the water stood eighteen inches above the cabin sole.

Heading for what had seemed the entrance to the yacht harbor, Ralph found himself sailing alongside a reef. Unable to bring the loggy vessel into the wind, lacking searoom to jibe, Ralph ordered the anchor dropped. It found no bottom.

Seconds later a sea set *Santa Cruz* on the reef. Two men managed to get to shore to call for help. The others were rescued, but *Santa Cruz* pounded herself to pieces on the reef.

If such a catalog of troubles can beach a man of Ralph's experience—he had sailed *Zarak* from Chicago to Tahiti and back—what are we poor souls to do who may only have a lake or sound to teach us seamanship? We can't very well hold drills for nasty leaks, broken pumps, dead batteries, and halyards gone aloft. But we can think about emergencies and carry spares of one kind or another for most of them. I'd start—as I start most things—with blank paper on a clipboard. Then I'd dream up emergencies in different parts of the boat and jot down what I'd carry to handle them.

I might be thinking about inrushing water. Patching materials would include plywood, sheet copper, or more flexible, easier-to-cut lead, heavy canvas and tacks to attach these materials. Hammer is already aboard. I'd also carry some caulking cotton, though an old shirt wedged into a crack will do just as well. Then I'd think about all the through-hull connections in my boat. Not that they are apt to leak; but when a hose lets go, can I shut off the water? Shutoffs that aren't used regularly have been known to freeze in the open position. Bungs or even corks of various sizes may save the day. A few pieces of straight-grained softwood will let you whittle stoppers that wrapped in cloth, and driven in hard, are very effective. Hoses of all sizes used aboard and universal hose clamps are other obvious spares.

Then I might think about pumps. I wouldn't want to rely on a single pump, however efficient. Also I'd check the installation of the suction pipe. Some builders place it to one side of the bilge.

When the boat is aground or heeling, the pump may suck air with the bilge half full. Also a pump sucking from the deep part of the bilge will not reach water when she's down by the head. Have you got a spare pump that can get rid of that water before it ruins gear stowed forward?

Then I'd think of spares for the pumps, and tools to take them apart and put them together again in a hurry. And how about strainers? On almost every new boat some shavings have escaped the yard's vacuum cleaner, and will get into the pump, perhaps clogging it. Then there are the labels of cans and bottles stowed in the bilge. People still get caught by that one. Perhaps some coarse-mesh screen attached with a hose clamp to the suction hose will keep the pump clear. Better yet, build a thrumbox. That's a simple screened box built into the bilge from which the pump sucks filtered water. A lift-out directly above it, or an easily removed board in the deck sole lets you clear the sieves rapidly without any tools.

Speaking of pumps: Your engine can be made to act as an emergency pump by simply disconnecting its normal water intake hose and putting that into the bilge. Use a strainer, even if it's only a rag tied over the end of the hose. If the hose won't reach the bilge, how about carrying a coupling and a spare length of hose that will? And how about a few plastic buckets, just in case?

Perhaps you carry the engine manufacturer's on-board spare kit. Fine. But their sets of gaskets are usually just that: one complete set. Every time you remove the head or valve cover you risk spoiling a gasket and needing a new one. So I'd carry a few spares of the most often needed gaskets besides the kit. The kit will include injectors for diesel engines, ignition parts for gasoline types. But to keep cost down, they don't give you a spare fuel pump. I'd get one. Even if you can't replace it on the water yourself, you'll find someone in every marina who can do the job in a few minutes, if you have a spare pump.

If that job, or any other engine job you are likely to run into, requires a special tool—an offset wrench, an extra-long or thin-wall socket—get it.

How about copper tubing? Two or three sizes will handle all engine repair and emergency plumbing jobs. A few feet of each, a cut-off and flaring tool, plus a few fittings will put you in business. You can become an expert in cutting off and flaring in a single try. Short ends of tubing, flattened and swaged with a pair of Visegrip pliers, also keep wire rope from raveling. Two or three such ends slipped over such wire can be used to make an eyesplice or what amounts to a short splice.

Still in the engine compartment: How can we deal with an oil leak other than at a gasket or copper fitting? Probably we can't, under way. But with a large supply of engine oil, you'll often be able to nurse a bleeding engine home.

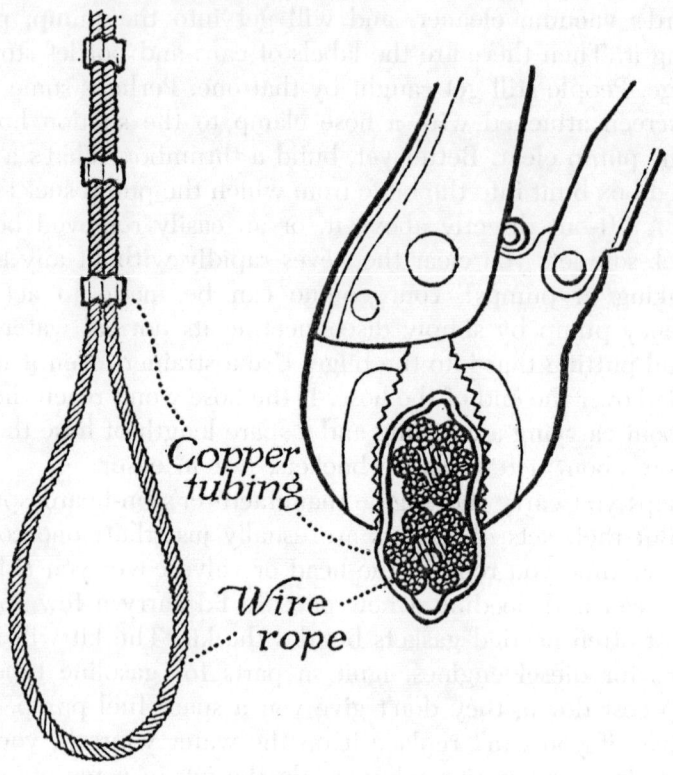

74. *Short lengths of copper tubing, somewhat flattened, then crimped with Visegrip pliers make neat eyesplice in wire rope.*

I'd have a long look at my battery installation. Will water in the bilge put the battery out of action, perhaps before you can get off a MAYDAY on your radio? Can a light left on carelessly in the head overnight make starting impossible? A gasoline-powered charger may be the answer; or two batteries as long as the chief doesn't let both batteries run down at the same time. Here is another idea: For a real emergency carry a dry-charged storage battery. The acid that goes into them is nasty stuff, but comes packaged safely enough. You are supposed to let the battery stand for fifteen minutes after filling. In an emergency you'd fill it, then by the time you've got the cables off the old battery and hooked to the new one, it'll have enough oomph to start the engine or run your ship-to-shore. When the emergency is over you can top off the acid that will continue to drop for a while as it soaks into the porous plates. Dry-charged batteries come dated since they lose their charge gradually. They can be recharged on a slow charger ashore after you have added the acid, so perhaps you can make a deal at your gas dock to exchange your battery before the date runs out.

Are all batteries securely fastened? A lead battery gone adrift can not only cause a spectacular short circuit, but crack, and spill acid that eats through metal and wood alike. It can also by sheer pounding loosen some fastening and get you close to sinking.

I'd certainly carry spare shaft, key, and propeller on a cruise.

Most skippers won't bother with spare lights. Under way, an electric lantern may warn other vessels of your presence at night. White flares—they don't mean distress—are even better. On a cruise I'd carry at least a kerosene anchor light, and a can of fuel.

Steering trouble is a frequent cause of distress calls. Shouldn't you carry extra control cables, pulleys, and fittings? On a sailboat steered by tiller, a spare might be a good idea. Mop handles aren't strong enough as a rule. Can you rig some fitting to the rudderhead to steer her by ropes? An ingenious skipper will be able to jury-rig even a lost rudder from whatever is at hand, but why not think about that now?

Sailboats have their own problems. Almost everyone carries palm and needle, which are all right to keep a small tear from splitting clear across, but not everyone is up to mending a long seam. Perhaps iron-on tape applied to both sides of the sail will get you home, and not mess up the sail any worse than poor stitching. There's also a very strong self-sticking tape that's been used for everything from wrapping turnbuckles to splinting broken legs. It might work on a sail too, although I've never tried it. Before I'd ruin two panels of a good sail with my inexpert stitches or any kind of tape, I'd try something else first. I once sailed to the nearest sailmaker with a gaff sail folded double to make it into a jib; to make up for that, another time I set a jib in place of a torn gaff mainsail to get to a man who'd repair it properly.

214   EMERGENCIES

Every sailor knows that a broken boom can be "fished" with bits of lumber and some lashings. But it might be simpler to sail home with a loose-footed main after casting off the lashings from the boom and somehow controlling the sail by the sheet-block fastened directly to the sail.

Rigging spares are a must, even if you only sail on a small lake. A turnbuckle, some rigging wire, and a half-dozen rope clamps

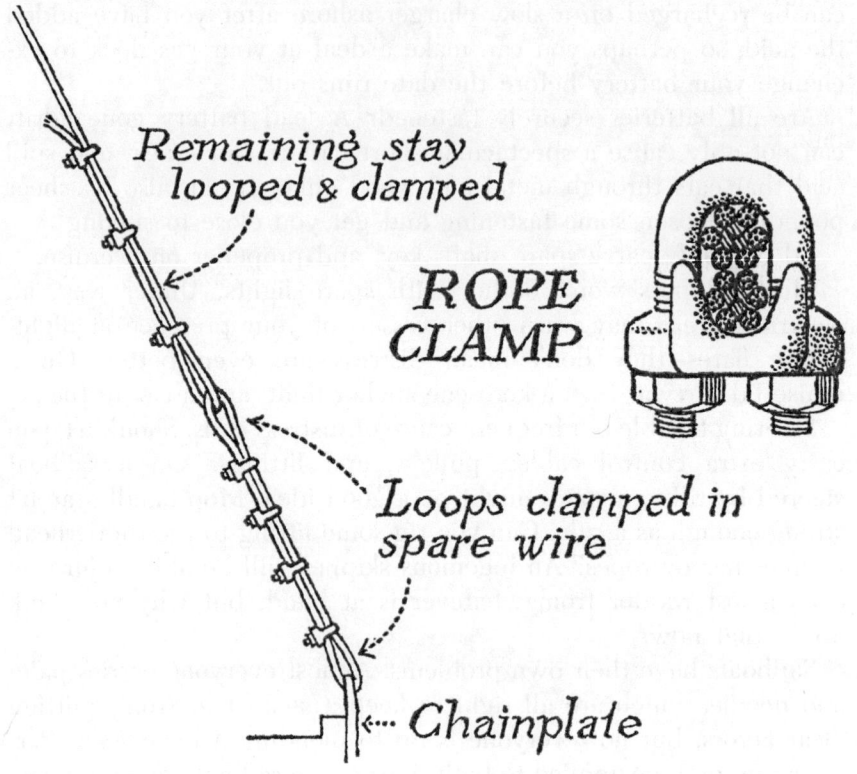

Remaining stay looped & clamped

ROPE CLAMP

Loops clamped in spare wire

Chainplate

75. *Rope clamps and rigging wire let you repair rigging under way.*

that fit the wire you use will not only get you home after a stay has carried away, but may save an expensive mast.

Halyards gone aloft can be most unfunny. Single-handed in a rough sea in the Bay of Fundy, I had a jib halyard part on me. Without the jib *Lucina* wouldn't sail anywhere but downwind. Since then I have always had a spare block and halyard at every masthead. Whatever halyard gives trouble is quickly replaced by this spare rig; it could also serve as a temporary stay in case of rigging failure. In port I have used the spare halyard to hoist a bosun chair for periodic inspections and maintenance aloft.

The navigation department is often short of spares. We have seen Captain Voss in mid-Pacific without compass, and I have suggested a hand bearing-compass as a backstop. Even more famous, Captain Slocum had to make a blind landfall after his goat had eaten his chart. That's not likely to happen to you, but charts have blown overboard. If you carry both detailed and cruising charts, they'll pinch-hit for one another. Quite unfamous is a certain single-hander who lost his reading glasses overboard, and without them could neither read his charts nor *Yachtsman's Guide to the Bahamas.* He did make some port though, and when last seen had a spare pair of glasses and also a chart glass.

Don't worry that carrying spares is going to take the adventure out of boating. Even when you carry all the spares you can think of, and spares for some of the more important spares, Neptune is going to find more problems for you.

22 Successful Wrecking

The wrecking in this chapter isn't the kind that uses a lantern tied to a donkey on the beach. It's about wrecking your own craft without outside help. In a successful wreck no one gets hurt. All hands get home poorer, but wiser.

By that definition the *Santa Cruz* in the last chapter was a successful wreck. Not only her skipper and crew, but anyone who reads about her interlinked chain of mishaps can learn from her sad end. That's why I brought her into this book. Now let me tell you about another wreck.

Just before dawn on a clear June morning a small schooner ran on a reef on the west side of Crooked Island Passage. Her helmsman had fallen asleep.

I was the helmsman. I was single-handing my *Lucina*. A crew wouldn't have prevented the disaster. I hadn't realized I was getting sleepy, and wouldn't have called out the next watch.

From Clarence Town, about two hundred miles southeast of Nassau on Long Island, to Mathew Town on Great Inagua Island is a deep water passage of roughly 150 miles. To make one of the three possible in-between anchorages in daylight, I had started from Clarence Town in the late afternoon. At first my gaff-rigged schooner could just lay the course without making much progress in a sea a bit popply over shoal water. My friend Max, who started at the same time bound for Haiti, did even worse. Just before sunset I noticed Max heading back to port, obviously disgusted. At that time I was about a mile to windward of him. Had it been the other way around, I too would likely have headed back.

Then the wind shifted more to the south, and fell light. I went on the offshore tack. Old *Lucina* sailed herself with the tiller in the comb, as she had done many times between Nova Scotia and the Bahamas, and on many cruises in these islands. I cooked dinner, puttered about, and read. I was well rested and not in the least sleepy.

Thirteen miles from Clarence Harbour, by taffrail log, I tacked. The sea then was slight with the usual long easterly swell. Jupiter dominated the clear moonless sky. To pass the time I got out my Rude star finder and looked for some of the lesser lights.

There are no off-lying dangers on the east coast of Long Island. But gradually losing my offing, and allowing for a possible onshore current, I kept looking for signs of land. Venus rose. By her light I saw the shore clearly outlined, perhaps three miles off.

That's the last I remember, except for a vague dream that I had come about again, and now had thousands of miles of clear sailing, all the way to Africa. I woke with a start, surrounded by breakers. No response from the tiller. The engine box flew open, lifted by inrushing water. I had an overwhelming urge to jump overboard, to get away.

Yet I knew one should always stay with the ship. I had another reason for staying: It was still dark. Landing on a beach through surf can be difficult enough; landing on rocks might be impossible. All I could make out of the shore was a dark mass, perhaps fifty feet high, topped by a vague silhouette of scrub. To seaward the water was boiling whitely in several spots. On either beam an almost unbroken line of white water marked the barrier reef on which the schooner seemed wedged. Shoreward heavy breakers told of an inner line of reefs. Then a zone of breaking surf and froth. But no high plumes of spray.

"Perhaps there's a bit of foreshore, not sheer cliffs."

No point in pumping: the crests and troughs of the swell ran right through my little ship. To ease the sideways strain, I lowered the mainsail, and put a quick lashing around it. The very next wave, a little higher than most, licked up and snapped the boom.

The cabin was a shambles. Water rose and fell rhythmically four feet. Mattresses and bunkboards, papers and cookpots, securely stowed a few minutes ago, pumped up and down all around me. In the trough of a wave I reached for the two waterproof containers prepared for an emergency. One held distress signals and matches, the other—an ammunition box—the ship's and personal papers and more matches. I lashed both boxes to the mainmast, just above the cabintop.

Lucina was in a bad way: Her bulkheads worked visibly; wherever I touched I could feel sliding, shearing motion.

"Better get ready to abandon."

The dinghy, a light eight-foot fiberglass job with built-in flotation, was lashed—keel up—to the cabintop. It was a good dink for visiting around the fleet in harbor, and for hauling stores, usable with care for laying out an anchor. It was decidedly not a surfboat. With some struggle I managed to launch it without swamping.

Then out of nowhere came the voice of my youngest daughter, when I had asked her years ago what she'd do in a certain emergency: "I'd just stop to think what an intelligent person would do in my place."

An intelligent person would try not only to get to shore, but prepare to get back to civilization. That means some drinking water, shoes, clothes for a scramble through brush, and an ax or machete to clear a trail. When I reached for the ax, always kept handy for an emergency, it was gone. So I'd have to go below for the machete.

The shambles in the cabin had become chaos. The companion ladder lurched at me. I threw it overboard. The table torn from its stowed position attacked me. I hurled it after the ladder. I braced my feet against the bunks to hunt in the surging water, under floating charts and limp clothes, for the machete.

Just then a wave, higher than the rest, raised the water right over my head. A stab of pain in my right calf. I couldn't move my leg.

The mainmast had jumped out of its step. All the weight of mast and rigging now levered against my leg, pinning it against the bunk riser. The whole ship pulsated, but the bunk was still solid. I couldn't reach a pry.

"If she rolls now, or slides off, I'd be in a fine fix." My hand fumbling for a tool to free myself found the machete.

Just then the schooner rolled.

A crunch, and the pain seemed to double. Then suddenly my leg was free, though numb and painful at the same time.

76. *Schooner* Lucina *on a reef in the Crooked Island Passage.*

It had become light enough to see the shore clearly. There was a beach. A bather wouldn't have chosen it: coarse, steep, surf-swept, and probably covered at high tide. I loved the sight of it. The only flaw: The reef between us seemed almost uncovered in the troughs. I knew the tide was now on the rise. The longer I could stay on *Lucina*, the more cushion I'd have crossing it. Even with one leg out of commission, I should be able to swim that far.

Then I noticed the ladder and the table on the beach, just a little to the north.

"What would an intelligent person do now?"

Prepare for a long stay on the beach, hoping for rescue from seaward if his leg wouldn't carry him to the road.

So I turned adrift a plastic water can wrapped in a life preserver to protect it from the reef. A second can for good measure. I put some food in the dinghy, next to the document box. I drifted off a life preserver carrying more food and the distress signals.

"Water, food—shelter next."

The sun would be directly overhead and I'd need shade. I released a canvas cockpit awning with wooden battens. It'll make a splint for my leg, bandages if I get cut up on the reef, and a signal flag besides.

The first-aid kit in its waterproof box—not just the usual Band-Aid, eyecup, and tongue depressor affair, but thanks to a sailing doctor, stocked with antibiotics and pain-killers—was below. I might need it badly, but I didn't dare risk getting trapped again. So I'd also have to do without fishing gear and canvas shoes. Out of the broth below I fished flip-flop sandals, a few more cans of food, a waterproof flashlight, and a bottle of insect repellent. I already had an all-purpose knife. I stuffed all this gear into a seabag to which I tied the last spare life jacket for added flotation.

With a dry crack the foremast snapped at the cabintop.

I dressed for my swim. During the night I had worn only shorts. Now I slipped into foul-weather gear to protect my skin at the reef crossing. I also got my face mask, for protection and to help me find a deep passage through the inner reef. I didn't wear swim fins; I'd always lost them in surf.

It was only a matter of minutes now before the schooner would break up. I had grown so used to the crashing breakers around me that now I could hear old *Lucina*'s small dying noises. Part of her foredeck carried away, dumping an anchor. I floated a buoyed line toward shore as a lifeline for possible boarding later. But swirling water draped it in a hopeless tangle around a piece of elkhorn coral.

I couldn't think of anything more to do. I sat in the cockpit, one hand on the lashing that held the dinghy oars.

The after bulkhead of the cabin opened up. I could see the whole length of the ship. Where the stem should have been, there was dark green water. Before I could get sentimental about losing my old friend *Lucina*, and all my little treasures, the mainmast started to twist.

I grabbed the oars, set my face mask, and got into the dinghy. The first stretch, between reefs, was easy going. At the reef line I backed water with all my strength, to pass on the next wave. I thought I had made it, but suddenly the dinghy stood on end, and pitched me out—still on the ocean side. Through my mask I could clearly see the coral thicket smothered in bubbles. There was a clear pass a little south of me. I swam for it, not sparing my aching leg. Before I reached the opening, another breaker caught me, pressed me against the coral. On the next curler my head hit solid coral. "I should have wrapped it." Again I was swept outside the reef.

Finally on the fifth try I made it across and onto shore. I had lost my foul-weather pants and my shorts. The jacket was in ribbons, but my body was barely scratched. My right foot was bleeding from several cuts, but my leg seemed less painful after the salt-water bath.

For the next half hour I limped along the beach, making piles of the stuff I had thrown overboard. It was all there and more: a pipe and a sealed tin of tobacco volunteered, a shirt drifted in, I found my wallet, and nearby, half-buried, my shorts.

Retracing my steps along the beach looking for more salvage, I noticed blood on the shingle. Far more blood than the cuts on my foot could have left. Then only did I realize that I had gashed my forehead just above the right eye.

I took stock: I was in pretty good shape, and could last on the beach for some days in comparative comfort. But I had no daytime signaling gear, and nothing to fight boredom. I should have brought reading matter or perhaps pencil and paper to design my next boat.

But I didn't need any of these. Before I had time to look for a sign of a trail, four brothers from a nearby settlement happened to come down to the beach. Within a couple of hours I was back at Clarence Town, where the government nurse patched me up. The leg wasn't broken; three weeks later I walked normally again. I had no insurance on the schooner. The stuff salvaged didn't amount to much, but I sold the dinghy for the price of a portable typewriter.

One moral of this story is obvious: Don't fall asleep, especially not on the onshore tack. But I hope you'd draw another conclusion:

Successful Wrecking

You may not have as much time as I had, so get together an abandon-ship kit, geared to the area you cruise and the season, and inspect it periodically, as suggested in the chapter dealing with regular drills.

The checklist below may help you plan your own kit.

BASIC SURVIVAL KIT

WATER: Most important. Plastic screw-top containers float even when full, stow well, and are useful aboard, too.

FOOD: Should be concentrated and varied. Ship chandlers and surplus stores can supply emergency rations. Metrecal and similar weight-control products come in liquid and powder. One-half pound Metrecal powder in one quart of water makes one day's minimum ration, supplies nine hundred calories.

SHELTER: A tarp of canvas, or tough opaque plastic, will keep off spray, rain, and sun. It will double as rain-catcher, emergency sail, signal flag. Don't forget warm clothes, foul-weather gear.

MEDICAL: A good first-aid kit in waterproof box—should contain effective pain-killers, antibiotics. Your doctor will advise and write the necessary prescriptions.

SIGNALS: Very pistol and caps, flares (don't skimp on quantity, see text), matches, signal mirror (war surplus), waterproof flashlight, or, better, lantern. All packed in waterproof containers.

NAVIGATION: Charts and instruments to suit area cruised; a compass.

COMFORTS: More matches, smokes, reading matter, games, insect repellent, hand line for fishing, ball of marline, needle and thread all in waterproof container that can also hold ship's and personal papers, valuables, travelers checks.

MISCELLANY: Ax, bushknife, or machete, sturdy utility knife, oilstone, dip net (handle can be improvised), canvas shoes, small rope (¼"–⅜") for tent-building and many other odd jobs.

NOTE: A special waterproof locker that can be removed quickly without tools can be built to hold most of these things. Or a canvas seabag, buoyed with Styrofoam or cork, can be kept handy at all times. Make it a ship's rule to replace anything taken from the survival kit.

To remind one of things not in the kit, yet needed, cut tags in the shape of missing articles. These tags, attached to the survival kit, can be "read" in the dark.

Let's look at one more successful wreck. Here is the official report filed in Nassau:

Sloop BOHEME, 4.38 Tons Net, British Registry #311362, W. S. Kals master, dragged anchor during severe thundersquall about 2200 Monday, February 4, 1963, off western shore of Ship Channel Cay, approximately two miles south of Beacon Cay light. Struck Rock. Broke up in morning of Thursday, February 7, flares, blinkers and other signals having failed to bring help. Crew (one) taken off rock Sunday, February 10, at 1700. Wreck presents no danger to navigation.

My *Boheme* had been anchored since morning in six feet at low water, over sand, with a thirty-five-pound anchor and about ninety feet of ⅜ chain. This anchorage is protected almost all around the compass by Ship Channel Cay, an off-lying rock, and submerged bars. Weather forecast: nothing unusual. Some distant lightning at sunset.

Sometime after 9 P.M., loud thunder. I double secured the anchor by taking two turns around the Samson post aft of the winch. I then closed hatches, dogged ports, and doused the kerosene lamp. Before my eyes were adjusted to the darkness, the first gust hit. Broadside. *Boheme* heeled sharply; the dinghy hit the port quarter. *Boheme* dragged anchor and, crunching the dinghy, fetched up against the off-lying rock. She came to rest lying on her port side, high and dry.

A sailor might estimate the velocity of the first gust from this: The mainsail, secured by five stops, was blown out into bladders between the lashings. The weather bureau has no record of the gust. On nearby Highborne Cay, after the first gust had shaken the building, someone looked at the anemometer, which then recorded a steady 55 mph. The yacht *Sealanes*, anchored at Royal Harbour, thirty miles north of me, had its wind gauge stick at 110 mph.

Damage to the vessel was astoundingly light. Two planks above the waterline stove in between frames. I could fix that myself with tools and lumber aboard. Meanwhile I'd patch it with sheet lead. The squall had hit at low water, or nearly so, with a three-foot rise to come by first light. The anchor must have caught again; the chain was bar-taut. I lashed two manila lines to knobs on the rock to hold *Boheme* in place. "We'll be all right in the morning." That was Monday night.

Tuesday, just before dawn, when *Boheme* was already upright but not yet quite afloat, another squall hit, with heavy rain and rough seas. Several waves broke over the rock and right over my head while I was sitting there, holding onto some gear, under a tarp. Most of it washed away.

During the squall the sloop had torn herself loose and shifted position. She now had her starboard side against the rock; the anchor chain was limp. She had chafed herself in several spots. I made her fenders from spare lumber and the mattresses. To refloat the sloop, now stranded at high water, without outside help proved impossible. Ship Channel Cay was uninhabited, Beacon Cay light is untended; the nearest help would be at Highborne, seven miles to the south.

I had no radio transmitter. I set a gaff topsail on a pole and began my watch for passing vessels. I had lost one box of flares but still had another. I had tried to buy a Very pistol and shells before leaving Nassau, but the chandlers were out of them. I had a kit of pen flares with several spares, a powerful electric lantern, a sun mirror, and those standbys of castaways: fire and smoke.

Yachts on the popular run from Nassau to the Exumas would come close enough to see me; so might native fishing sloops working the shore. But Tuesday the weather was miserable. Boats stayed in harbor. Small private planes which might fly low enough to see my distress stayed on the ground.

My hope then lay with the mailboats and interisland freighters that would keep running on schedule through Ship Channel, barely two miles away. I lit a fire, and kept it burning day and night. By squirting kerosene on it I'd make it flare up, then by drenching it with seawater I'd get an impressive column of smoke and steam. I had spare batteries so I could use my signal lantern freely. I dotted and dashed—three shorts, three longs—even at westbound vessels, hoping a passenger in the stern might see the flashes. But I spent my best efforts on eastbound ships. I started to signal when they were still a good distance off. The lookout wouldn't report the first signal. He'd want to make sure. Then he'd call the mate, who'd want to see the signals for himself before calling the captain. And the captain would want to see them for himself before he did anything about them. What did I expect him to do? Certainly not change course and take his vessel into shoaling water to come to my help; only that he'd report on his radio having seen fire, smoke, a white flag, and S-O-S flashes. It'd be something to talk about amid the endless chitchat of the ship-to-ship gamming.

I husbanded my flares, using them only at night. The pen gun (probably better than nothing in a fisherman's kit) was not up to the job. The flares rose no more than twelve feet or so, and fizzled after a couple of seconds.

At night I also set a pressure kerosene lamp behind the topsail which rippling in the breeze made quite a display.

No luck until Wednesday afternoon at three-thirty. Then a schooner yacht on a Nassau to the Exumas course came close enough that I could have bet she had been designed by Alden. She kept coming closer, until through my seven-power glasses I could see two men and two girls passing binoculars from hand to hand looking at *Boheme* and at my rock. I didn't spare the signals that time, you can be sure. Also the sun was just right for mirror signals.

All I needed was a boat—a big outboard might have done it—to drag the vessel off. At high water a few men could probably have bulled her back into deep water. Within the hour the schooner would be in Highborne, and report me if they hadn't already done so by radio.

They didn't report me. Neither did eight eastbound commercial vessels I had counted by midnight Wednesday. No low-flying planes.

Early Thursday a swell out of the west attacked my rock. It must have been caused by a disturbance far off, in the Gulf of Mexico probably; the local wind at the time was out of the northeast. Almost coinciding with high water, the swell lifted *Boheme* and then dropped her again on her rock, lifted and dropped. No craft can take that for long. A fastening at the quarter let go first; soon the transom was loose. Then a stem fitting failed, and the mast came down. The house washed off. Her bottom was holed, and within an hour *Boheme* was a wreck.

On the swell-caused alongshore current, gear drifted by: a rack with all dishes still in place, a shelf with the books neatly arranged, sailbags. It was a great temptation to jump and rescue some of the gear, in spite of the current. "Don't be an idiot, Steve, you've got all you need to survive."

In fact I had more than that. And just as well. For there was only one single plant on the rock. I don't know its scientific name, but have learned to call it "survival weed." It's edible; better yet, its fleshy leaves are full of water fresh enough to quench thirst. It grows all through the tropics right above the high-water mark. I was careful to leave that single plant for someone less fortunate than myself. For I had not only gallons of water, but also rum, scotch, gin, and vermouth.

I saw only one species of animals on the rock: hermit crabs. They are edible if you don't mind their looks, but matching the size of the rock the specimens here were little runts. I had not only had a good supply of staples aboard but such delicacies as canned asparagus tips and smoked oysters. I still had those. But I lived mostly on survival rations supplied by Horlick's which I had planned to test for a boating article: Verkade lifeboat rations and bars that boiled made delicious curry, and beef stew.

I wasn't bored either. Between lookout and signaling duties I had time to read and plenty of stuff to read. One book stands out in my memory: Björn Landström's *The Ship*, a delightful, illustrated book about which I was supposed that week to write a review for my boating column. I did.

Out of lumber from the wreck I made a catwalk the whole length of the rock hoping to attract attention of a plane. The rock wasn't quite big enough to spell out the word HELP, but the message seemed clear enough. The boards also made walking my island easier. Except for one spot, about two feet by four, which became my bed-sitting room, it was spray-eroded limestone, all jagged and spikey.

I was seen by a native sloop, the *Star* out of Foxtown, Abaco, crawfishing around Beacon Cay, and taken off the rock Sunday afternoon after six nights and almost six days in solitary.

The wreck of *Boheme* was due to a single cause: a failure in communications. The moral is clear. Have a radio. Don't use my excuses: economics, shortage of space, and lack of batteries. Even a good walkie-talkie would do in many places, provided you can get your message through on the crowded citizens band. Carry regular flares, lots of them. Better yet, carry a Very pistol and lots of shells. And don't forget yellow flares, shells and smoke bombs for use in daytime.

And keep out of first gusts.

PART FOUR / LIVING

23 About Comfort

Are you a good sailor? According to the dictionary that's a person who doesn't get seasick. By that standard Lord Nelson, for instance, was a miserable sailor; he retched his way from apprentice to admiral, and retched right through the Battle of Trafalgar. Yet people still look on freedom from seasickness as a sign of manliness, like beards and coarse language.

Bilge!

Tests have shown that any normal adult can be made sick by motion. Doctors now talk about motion sickness, rather than seasickness, since the same unpleasantness also strikes on land, and in the air. You'll find its victims on planes, cars, buses, trains, elevators, carrousels, and even on camels.

Some people seem barely touched by motion sickness in a gale at sea; others get queasy on a river ferry. Newborn babes are said to be free from this ailment, but since they dribble from their scuppers most of the time, how can you be sure? Four out of five older children get sick when they travel. Also when they travel they eat a lot of popcorn and lollipops. Very old people are reported relatively free from *mal de mer*. Women are more liable to suffer than men, fat people more than lean ones. The sickness hits all races of man, and doesn't spare animals. The expression "sick as a dog" was probably coined on shipboard. Very likely by a dog.

Apprehension of getting sick can bring on the symptoms: Some people get troubled while their liner is still lying at the pier. One study claims that fear adds to the chances of an attack, but a friend who uses the paper bags on every plane trip reported after a bumpy flight: "I was too scared to be sick."

Deaf-mutes and other people with inner ear troubles could not be made sick on a test stand. But illness, even a simple cold, can make a non-sufferer join the rest.

Luckily, most of us work up some resistance after a few trips. In a typical Atlantic winter crossing one out of every four first-time passengers fed the fishes; only one out of six second-time crossers hugged the rail. In a group of air cadets the sickness rate from first to fifth flight dropped 75 percent. But ashore we again lose our sea legs. I have seen even old hands on a freighter more or less upset on the first day at sea after a time in port.

And then there are the unlucky ones. The one man in twenty who on the first day out wishes he'd die, and on all following days regrets he didn't. You won't find many regular sufferers afloat. They are likely to change to more stable jobs, or take up steadier hobbies. But there are always the Lord Nelsons: A sea captain told me that since his apprentice days, thirty years earlier, he rarely spent a day at sea without tasting his breakfast twice.

Unlike other diseases this one has been around for a while. Witness: Cicero, fleeing Rome, a few leagues out to sea decided he'd rather return and *have* his head cut off.

You'd think that medical science would know all about the mechanics of the trouble. All you'll find is double-talk: altered and affected nervous centers—effusions of blood to the brain—regurgitation of bile into the stomach—irritation of the liver with increased secondary bile excretion. I like best the explanation of a French doctor who attributes it all to what could be translated as "visceral chafe." The truth is, the exact mechanism is not known. Most likely the main trouble center is in the inner ear. There we have a wonderfully engineered organ, the labyrinth. Three looped canals—one in the vertical plane, one fore-and-aft, and one athwartships—give us a sense of balance and acceleration.

The canals are studded with tufts of hair, and filled with liquid. When we change position, or speed up or slow down, the liquid moves as in a carpenter's level and bends the hair. Nerves carry the message to the brain, where it's read as an awareness of our position or change in motion.

When our boat rolls, pitches, corkscrews, or falls into the trough, the sloshing liquid flashes a signal, *Something wrong around here*. This explanation won't win a Nobel Prize in either medicine or literature, but at least it explains some known facts. Remove the labyrinth from the ears of an animal, and he loses his sense of bal-

About Comfort 229

ance; he also becomes immune to motion sickness, just as some ear-trouble sufferers are.

Undoubtedly messages from your eyes also help to upset your stomach. On a freighter in a gale in the Pacific our master gyro compass acted up. The second mate removed its cover. The bumps, grinds, and twists of the compass sent him to the rail for the first time in his life. In fact the compass was rock-steady; it was the ship that danced all around it. No matter, everyone who came to the chartroom and saw the naked gyro, had to leave in a hurry.

Your senses of taste and smell can also make matters worse. Blowing out a fuel line, head-down in the bilge, while your boat rolls

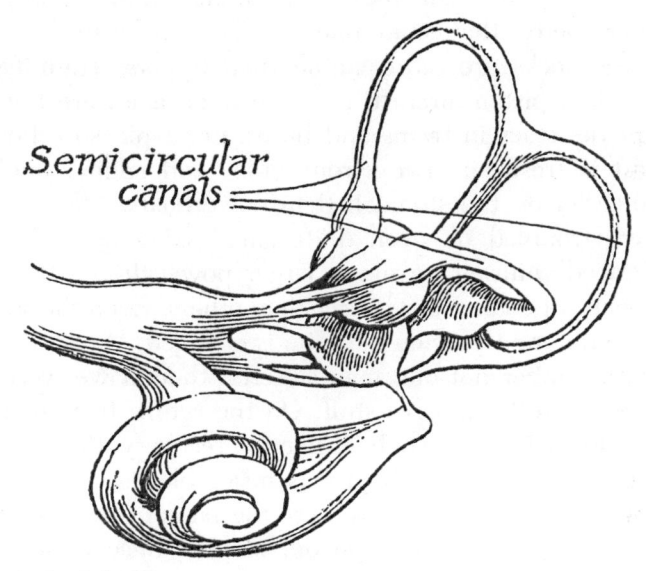

77. *Labyrinth of the ear.*

in the trough, will do it. Even a suggestion of a taste can precipitate a crisis. It's considered great sport to ask a green hand—I mean literally green—"How would you like a nice greasy pork chop?" and watch him make a break.

The symptoms of motion sickness are only too well known to all sufferers. It may start with yawning, mouth-watering, cold sweats, a need for air, a light headache, or half a butterfly in your stomach. Some people suffer from dizziness, hellish headaches, and visual disturbances. The high point is a backfire from the stomach. That brings quick relief to some people; others carry on in wave after painful wave, when there's no more ballast to jettison. Depression and a total lack of interest in life are as much part of the sickness as the effects of earlier miseries.

Probably nobody has ever died directly from seasickness. But—without practicing medicine—a savvy skipper will keep this in mind: The symptoms of seasickness may mask some serious other condition, such as intestinal block or appendicitis.

There used to be as many home remedies for seasickness as there were sufferers who had found their sea legs. Some of the cures may have helped if you believed in them strongly. Light meals, and light drinks before departure are still recommended. When you have a choice, you can reduce your discomfort: Large ships normally are better than small ones; midships is better than bow or stern; lower decks are more stable than uppers. High-flying jets are better than piston aircraft, seats between axles are better than those over the axles in trains and buses. On a pleasure boat you'll suffer least in fresh air, away from galley and engine smells. Sailboats are easier on the stomach than powerboats. Many a sailboat man, never troubled on even quite small sailboats in large seas, has "disgraced" himself on much larger power-driven boats.

Some boats, of course, are kinder than others. Even the same craft will behave differently when her trim is changed. On a Liberty ship loaded with lumber not one man suffered though we were punching into some pretty massive stuff. On the return trip, loaded with steel rails, the ship had such a snappy recovery that every man jack, from captain to mess boy, was miserable.

Until World War II sedatives were the basis of most serious seasickness remedies. They put you out of your misery, but unfortunately they also put you out—more or less. Out beyond usefulness, and beyond pleasure too. Since then a family of drugs—Dramamine is the best-known one—has helped thousands to work and enjoy themselves. The wife of a Nassau charter boat captain was such a poor sailor, she even got sick on a sailboat in calm water. Now, taking the pills, she stands her watch at the wheel, and besides cooks and bakes under way. Five-course dinners with hot rolls!

Although considered harmless enough to be sold without prescription, these drugs don't agree with everyone. I even know a fellow who got sick ashore when he took a pill before boarding his vessel. That perhaps is unusual. More common is drowsiness, and the label of one of the drugs warns in small print: DO NOT OPERATE

AUTOMOBILES OR DANGEROUS MACHINERY WHILE TAKING MEDICATION. A fast boat isn't an automobile, to be sure, but isn't it a dangerous piece of machinery?

Before you hand out these pills like pretzels, make sure your patient is not on some other incompatible medication. When in doubt, ask your doctor.

Rest and fresh air helps many people; work takes their minds off their stomachs and almost cures others. If everything else fails, try this ancient prescription: One hour's rest in the shade of a tree . . . and stay off carrousels and camels.

Now suppose that with or without pills everyone aboard is upright and pink-cheeked. What else does it take to make a happy ship? I'd rank a dry ship next. I'm not talking about the hull being so tight that the bilges get dusty. I feel about minor hull leaks as I do about rattles in a car: As long as I know what causes them, they don't bother me much. I'd put up, for example, with a leaking stuffing box knowing the trouble isn't likely to get worse and can be set aright in a few minutes. But I'm allergic to leaks in the living quarters of a boat. Perhaps I was "sensitized" on one cold, rainy weekend spent on a friend's boat. The boat had recently been shipped from England to the Pacific coast. Somewhere, perhaps in the Panama Canal, the seam compound in her teak deck had bubbled, and now water dripped on the table, into my bunk, and down the neck of the foul-weather suit I was forced to wear even below.

With plywood and fiberglass decks, leaks aren't as common as they were under canvas-covered or painted decks. But one rule still holds: The drip is rarely under the leak. Water will find strange paths and always drip where it'll annoy you most. In the Islands, during a captains' get-together, we discovered that the only leak in the cabin was always over the captain's bunk. There's an explanation. Boats there swing to their anchors most of the time. They'll head into the regular easterly winds, and so present the starboard deck to the sun most of the time. However often you wet them down, the planks on that side will shrink. And the captain traditionally gets the No. 1, the starboard, bunk.

To stop pinhole leaks often takes a long chase with filler and putty knife. When no pinholes or hairline cracks are to be found,

I'd suspect a deck fixture—winch or cleat, perhaps—and take it off and reset it in a puddle of bedding compound.

The skipper of *Seabeast* finally gave up struggling to get his side decks tight. Here's his solution: He fastened a hammock over each bunk, not the usual Pullman net, but pieces of plastic to hold the water until he'd empty them.

If you own an old hooker that seems to leak in every deck seam, there is another solution. It's called "Dinner Key Teak" after the marina in Miami where it is said to have originated. It's as far from teak as you can get on the economic scale. It's roofing felt, laid down sanded side up in gunk. I know that sounds perfectly horrible, but it makes a neat, tight, skidproof deck after it's painted.

Leaky ports can make hideous one's nights aboard. Usually it's the fault of the rubber gasket, which has lost its springiness. Even if you can get the exact replacement gaskets, there is a better material for them. I first learned about this from Captain Clint of *Inca*. It's square flax packing, made for use in stuffing boxes, and available in every marine hardware store or boat yard shop. Get the size that fits the groove, tamp it down with a sharp knife, and make a diagonal butt-joint. The packing, given a dab of waterproof grease perhaps once a year, will outlast your interest in any boat.

Hatches and coamings are frequent sources of irritating leaks. Rebuilding them is quite an undertaking. Depending on their finish, I'd try paint, thick varnish, glue, or epoxy before tearing them apart or letting a yard do the job. If that treatment doesn't work, I'd be tempted to run a tape clear around the coaming. That could be a strip of thin sailcloth laid in varnish or glue, and later painted. Such taping has also stopped many leaks where the cabin trunk joins the deck.

When you have waterproofed the main living area, don't give up. A few drops of rain running down the inside of the hull can ruin your best check-cashing suit in the hanging locker, or turn your dry change of clothes in a bunk drawer into a soggy mess. The waterproofing for a drawer can be extended to also keep out sloshing bilge water. Fiberglass the inside of the drawer, but also make a hood over the rear part of it.

Even after you've made all storage compartments rainproof, don't give up. Fresh water seeping into the boat anywhere, but especially in poorly ventilated parts of the boat—behind the ice box, for instance—won't interfere with your comfort, but it will start dry rot. This fungus infestation will spread, and turn sturdy boat frames to mush. You may have seen a marine surveyor looking for signs of it. He uses an ice pick that won't go far into sound wood, but buries itself in a rotten timber. Or perhaps he used a hammer which gives a clear, ringing sound on sound lumber, while rotten wood has no more resonance than a loaf of soggy bread. In an advanced case of dry rot, water will squirt out of the wood where the hammer has hit. Your nose is a good dry rot detector, and—unlike ice pick and hammer—leaves no marks. People say dry rot smells moldy; to me it smells rather like gasoline.

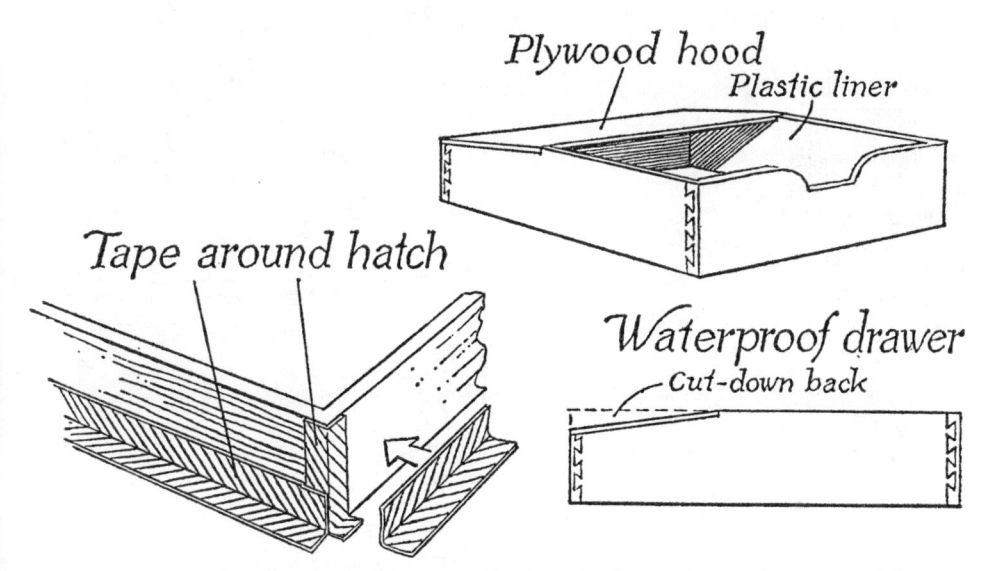

78. *Waterproofing a hatch coaming (left); splash-proofing a drawer (right).*

Good ventilation will keep down dry rot and mildew too; it will also get rid of galley odors and the wet-dog smell of drying clothes. Directional cowl ventilators, self-draining cowls, half-cowls, clamshells, mushrooms, light-admitting spray-proof vents, and louvered cabin doors are standard equipment on most pleasure boats. These devices work best when the boat lies into the wind. Perhaps a whirligig—a wind-powered fan, as it were—will improve the ventilation of your boat if you keep her dockside.

Stifle the urge to shut off ventilation when you're cold. Condensation will form, and you'll feel even colder when it gets clammy.

234 LIVING

When you use alcohol, kerosene, coal, wood, or butane for light, heat, or cooking, you *must* provide fresh air, plenty of it. The flame competes with you for the oxygen in the cabin, and the flame will win.

I've done some boating on the East Coast long after most yachts were laid up for the winter, and on the West Coast right through the winter, and I have come to like coal for heat. My choice

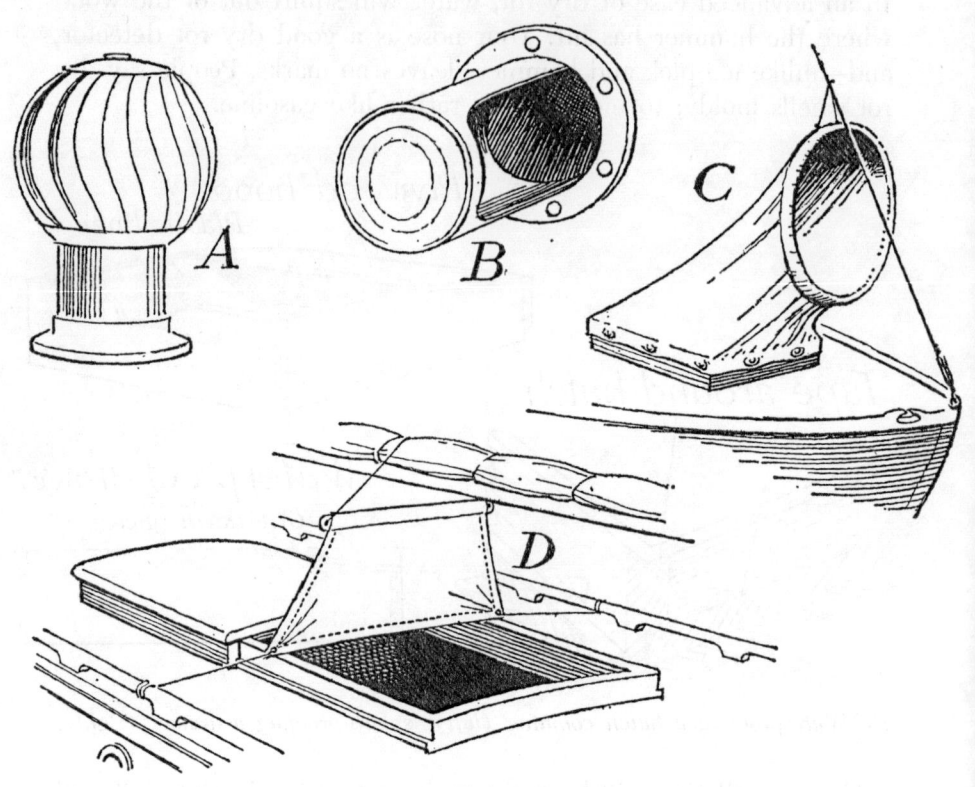

79. *Improving ventilation below*—(A) *whirling ventilator* (B) *windscoop on port* (C) *ghost* (D) *windsail over hatch.*

would be a cast-iron stove that will burn wood *or* coal. Here are my reasons: You can get a good wood fire going in very little time; also you may not find the right grade of coal everywhere, but you can always beachcomb slow-burning wood, or get scraps of hardwood at any boat yard. Wood is fairly clean, at least until you get to disposing of the ashes. For a banked fire to keep the cabin toasty all night without attention, nothing beats coal. Hardwood

About Comfort 235

briquettes are handy and readily available, but they don't have the staying power of coal. Don't let the briquettes get soaked in seawater. After they have dried, without crumbling or any change in appearance they seem to become fireproof.

I have used kerosene in pressure stoves and lamps and like it, but the heaters working on the same fuel always seemed to foul the air.

When it's cold, ventilation is necessary; when it's hot, ventilation *is* comfort. When you lie to a dock, ventilators, ports, even an open forehatch are often not enough. You can increase the efficiency of ports by adding scoops that catch a breeze, that of a hatch by rigging a "ghost," a canvas or nylon tube to funnel fresh air down.

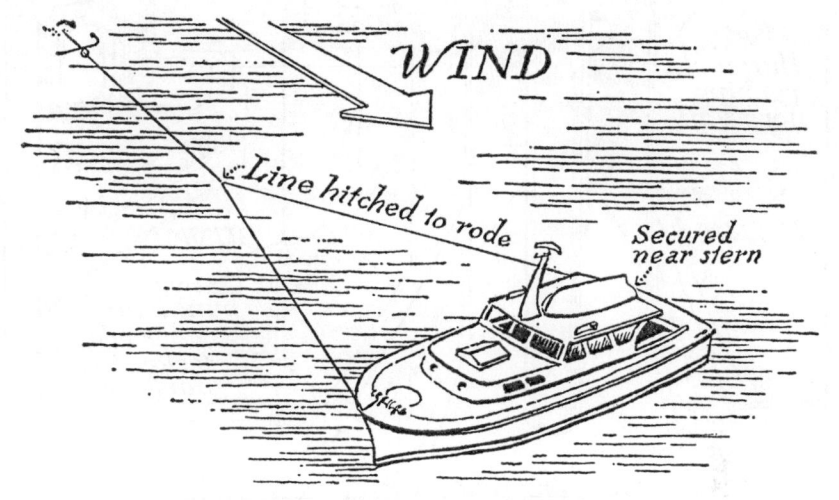

80. *Improving ventilation by anchoring across the wind.*

Lucina had a large sliding hatch in the middle of the cabintop. After some experimenting, I found a simple way to force air below: a squaresail set on the downwind end of the hatch. Even in a gentle breeze it made papers blow around in the cabin.

An awning, rigged not just over the cockpit but over the entire house, will keep the cabin cool. It's not only the shadow it gives; its rippling makes it act as a fan.

Some boats get the best ventilation when the wind comes over the stern. You can try to anchor such boats by the stern. I say try, because some boats get restless when anchored that way. Other boats keep coolest when the wind is abeam. I wouldn't try to anchor one of them fore and aft. It would be sure to be unhappy tethered that way and could get itself into trouble if it should breeze up. I'd anchor it by the bow in the usual manner, then haul her stern around to the anchor rode with another line. When an afternoon squall makes up, you can quickly cast off or slacken that line to make her lie in the orthodox way.

Now that you have a healthy, dry, airy ship, what else can you do to make her a happy one?

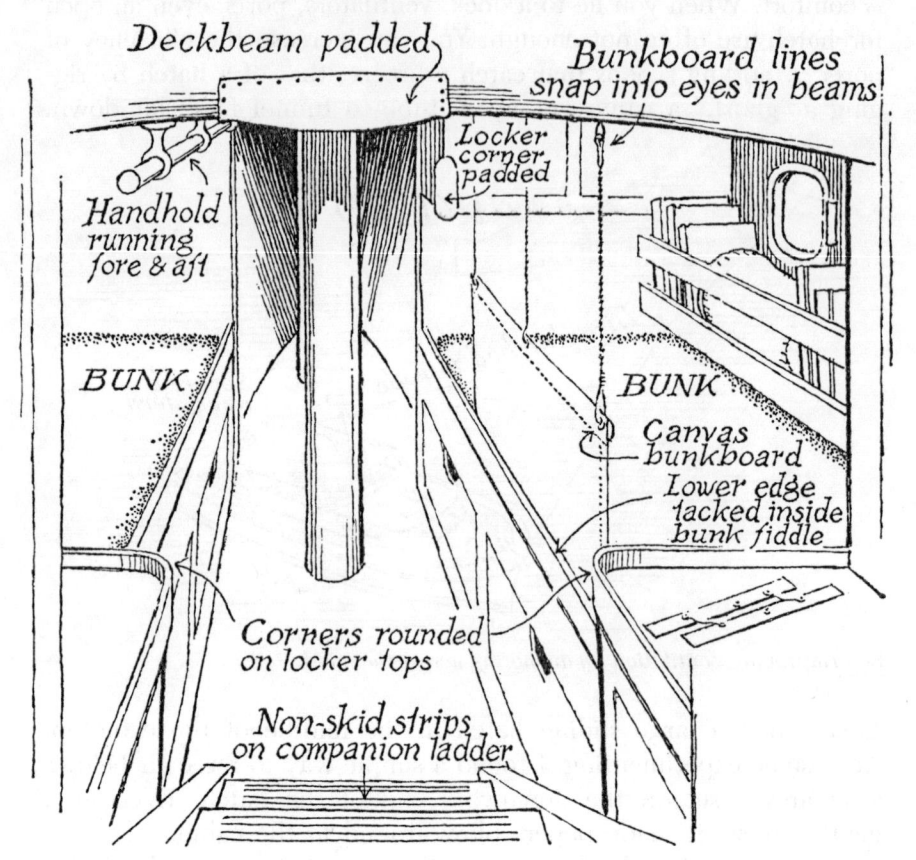

81. *Safety in the cabin.*

Provide for personal safety. A bruised crew is not a happy crew; a burned cook spoils the broth. If the builder or former owner hasn't provided handholds, rig them so that anyone—not just a tightrope walker—can move through her whole length without getting knocked about. Round off all sharp corners; pad places where people knock their heads, that first deck beam, for instance. Make the deck sole slipproof for even wet sneakers—a runner or nonskid paint will do it.

You can't relax in your bunk if you worry about falling out or even about banging your elbow. A sailboat spends much of her cruising life on her ear, so the watch below can't relax unless you give them some support. Even on a powerboat, supposed to be upright most of the time, you may roll a bit, or spend some time aground accidentally or during some maintenance or repair job. Leeboards on all bunks are the answer. They can be hinged, sliding, or fastened in any other way. With sufficient bolsters or pillows they give one the security of a babe in his crib. But you may not use them often enough to make their installation worthwhile. So here is a leeboard I have used; it needs no bolsters and is as comfortable as a hammock, which it resembles. All you need is a piece of canvas, a bit shorter than the bunk and about two feet wide, copper-tacked to the long edge of the bunk. When not in use the canvas lies under the mattress. To rig it for sleep, fasten it to eyes or hooks in the deckbeams. You don't need a sailmaker. If you haven't got the tool to set the grommets, every awningmaker has.

Let me sum up this chapter in one sentence: You don't have to be miserable to have fun.

24 The Gimbaled Cook

The old rule, "One hand for the ship, one for you" may work on deck, even high in the rigging of a windjammer, but how do you peel potatoes with one hand? Simple: Secure the cook so he won't be thrown against the hot stove, and arrange the galley so hot pots won't land in his lap. That's not just for ocean cruisers. In every anchorage, even in a marina, the wake of a passing boat can upset the stew. Then you'll also have an upset cook, if not a scalded one.

The cook should also be gimbaled in another sense: He should swing with the ship's facilities, the available supplies, and the taste of the ship's company. That's what this chapter is about. Then I'll give some pointers on what to do if somehow you find yourself presiding over a galley, although you aren't a cook at all. For that last kind of advice I'm most qualified.

On only a few boats will you find a gimbaled stove. It may be the food processing system on a gold-plater, or—at the other end of the economic scale—the one-burner on a single-hander's craft. More often, especially on sailboats, the stove is slung so as to remain level when the boat heels or rolls, but it tilts when she pitches. These half-gimbaled stoves can bring on seasickness by drawing attention to the wild motions of the boat. So perhaps the solidly anchored stove—solidly is emphasized—with a guard rail to keep the pots from sliding off, will do best for most of us.

On any boat you can physically gimbal the cook and free both his hands for stuffing shrimp. Just give him a comfortable seat, and if possible footrests. On *Boheme* I had a folding seat for the cook, who could hook his legs around the supporting stanchion. *Lucina* had a foam-padded, rump-fitting seat, and the cook could brace his legs against the shelf that supported the stove.

That wood-and-coal burner came with the boat, as did the lack of headroom in the galley which made cooking while seated a necessity. When later, in the warmth of the Islands, I replaced that stove with a pressure kerosene job, I planted a whirling ventilator atop the original deckiron, and so had an exhaust fan just like the girls in *House Beautiful*.

On boats with the galley aft, the companion steps can be made to carry a hinged seat. On a sailboat with a mast running through the galley, it should be easy to build a saddle for the chef.

Don't forget to give the cook a board to hold on his lap; it'll be the most used piece of galley equipment. While you are at it, Cap'n, get yourself one too. It's amazing how many jobs—from nursing a carburetor to preparing baits—you can do more easily while seated with a board on your knees.

On most ship's stoves the rail will keep pots from sliding off. When only one pot is in use on a two-burner stove, that pot can still go adrift. The cook may like a removable center fence, made perhaps from a wire clothes hanger.

A pressure cooker is a useful gadget on a boat. It not only cuts cooking time when used in the recommended way, but in plain cooking (without the jiggling weight) will save your chow when the pot somehow lands on the deck.

Over the years my galley on *Lucina* had become so efficient that now the most elaborate kitchen in a shore apartment seems awful: I can't get the dishes, tools, cans, fresh foods, dry stuffs, spices, and sauces by merely reaching. Unfortunately the galleys on stock boats, seen at boat shows, imitate the luxury of a real estate

82. *Galley with gimbaled cook.*

developer's model rather than the efficiency found in the cuddy cabin of a Nova Scotia fishing boat.

If you have on your boat walk-in freezers, unlimited storage space, and a French chef, you can serve meals fit for a cruise ship. Most of us haven't and can't. But neither are we willing to put up with a bachelor's seaboot stew, meal after meal. The secret of variety in menus is, of course, some plan. The meal planners in shoreside cook books often let you down, especially when you can't keep a lot of fresh meats, and can't run to the nearest gourmet shop for glazed bluebird's tonsils.

I'd start by planning only the main courses. Soups and other starters, and desserts, go on separate lists. First I'd find out what the crew likes. Say someone is crazy about wieners. No problem: They are available in cans. Next: What goes with wieners? Sauerkraut? Another can. Mashed potatoes? Potatoes are carried as staples, regardless of menus; so is canned milk and the butter you'll need for the mashed potatoes. Someone else likes corned beef? Again no problem: cans. With it you'll serve perhaps cabbage. That, like onions and carrots, keeps well outside the ice box. From corned beef you can go on to spaghetti and meatballs, chili con carne, and Chinese dinners (a can, and some rice, the rice a most useful staple anyway). When you make that list of main courses avoid landing on a total of seven or fourteen dishes, for the temptation gets too great to allot a day for each meal, until your people call Thursday "Duffday" and Saturday "Beanday." But get a good number of dishes so you won't repeat too often.

Two lads, who crossed the Atlantic from Cape Cod to Ireland in a twenty-foot boat with neither sail nor engine, and wrote a book about it, had five basic menus—labeled scientifically from A to E. That's hardly enough variety for so long a voyage. Worse, every one of their meals—from A through E—had beef curry, rice, and sultanas for the main course. Ninety days of beef curry, rice, and sultanas.

In my list of main courses I have avoided seafoods. I always treat fish, lobster, and the like as a gift from the sea that saves me a day's worth of cans, but I never really count on catching any. But I always carried extra goodies for Sundays, holidays, and hurricanes weathered. I also stocked mixed pickles, dills, chutney, and other such perker-uppers under which to bury my failures.

The list of menus will help you stock ship for a cruise. Simply work it out in days, or with a large crowd in man-days. Even when you plan to tie up every night, stock the galley for several days to make yourself independent of the shore. Some nights you may want to anchor off. In the Inland Waterway, even at a dock, the store may be miles away. Or you may find a delightful spot where you'd rather stay than go on. Too bad if you had to move on just because there's nothing left but onions, onion flakes, and elbow macaroni.

Stocking ship in Nassau and a few other places in the Islands isn't very different from stateside shopping. In fact you'll find some foods there that are not on the shelves of supermarkets but are useful on a boat—canned butter, for example.

Limes are grown in every settlement and are available the year round. Freshly pressed they make wonderful seasoners, and not only for seafoods. Try them on salads. I only rarely had ice aboard, but found that lime juice made lukewarm rainwater, further flattened in my tanks, quite drinkable. Squeeze only as much juice as you need when you need it; after standing a few minutes it'll taste like brass doorknobs.

Small red peppers, locally called bird peppers, are so hot you can never get little enough of them into a stew. Ground pepper loses its hot quickly, and pepper mills rust. So I cut up a few of the small peppers and kept them in vinegar in a sauce bottle from which I sprinkled a few drops whenever I wanted pepper. Any food that needs pepper can stand a few dabs of vinegar. In another sauce bottle I kept garlic chopped in vinegar. That way my hands would reek of garlic only every other month.

Fresh vegetables were often hard to come by in the Out Islands of the Bahamas. After a summer in the Exumas I blamed the mineral-free rainwater for some complaints that a doctor had diagnosed as iron and calcium deficiencies. Then a wise friend chirped up, "Do you really think the Germans brew their beer with rainwater?" So there went another one of my theories. Anyway, a lot of people who cruise the year round in the Islands supplement their diet with vitamin and mineral capsules. Ask your doctor's advice.

Now what's a fellow to do who gets into a galley and knows practically nothing of cookery? That can happen in a variety of ways. You may be the man with the strongest stomach aboard; if you want to eat you'll have to cook. Or perhaps you are on a boat where chores rotate daily. (That sounds fair, but I don't think it's such a good system. The cook-of-the-day will spend a lot of time looking for things misplaced by the cook-of-yesterday. Tomorrow's cook will accuse him of having hidden the pancake turner.) You can also have talked yourself into the galley. You may have tried to promote a berth on a cruise, and people are always looking for a cook. If you can play sea chanteys on a guitar, the berth is yours. But you'll find you'll have to cook far more than strum. Or perhaps you got into the galley by single-handing. Then you don't even have the hope of getting thrown overboard if the crew doesn't like your cooking.

Cook books are little help. They forever call for ingredients and spices you haven't got, and most of them seem written by people who have nothing to do but cook—one meal a day, that is.

But here are a few tricks that I, a famous non-cook, have found handy.

Take a can and read the label. I don't mean study it, you wouldn't want to read right down to the hydrogenated vegetable oils and the monosodium glutamate. Just the big print. Suppose it says PORK AND BEANS. Anyone but a hopeless optimist knows what this can needs is pork. So fry some bacon, dump it on the beans, and someone is going to compliment the chef—if only so he won't have to take over the cooking. If it says CHICKEN SOUP on the label, you can guess that this soup could use some chicken. Root around until you find a can of boneless chicken (or turkey) solid or jelly pack. Dump the contents into the soup and let it simmer a while. That's all there is to that.

You'll find many variations on this theme. But someday your imagination will boggle. There's just nothing aboard that'll help this can. Whoa! There is on almost every yacht: Alcohol. Dilute the bean soup with sherry, or even rum or Scotch, and watch the growlers beam. This prescription will work wonders on anything from stew to resuscitated prunes.

If you are a single-hander and your cooking is tasted by humans only on rare occasions, you can get by with a repertoire of one spectacular. You may try to produce baked potatoes without an oven of any kind. How? Boil the Irishers in oil.

My bravura piece was potato salad. Now any idiot can boil and slice spuds, add onions—also sliced—salt and pepper, and pour oil and vinegar (or lime juice or pickle drippings) over the hot mess. I acquired the totally undeserved reputation of a cook by making a mayonnaise dressing. Not the stuffing-box grease that comes in jars and that, unrefrigerated, spoils without changing looks or smell, but the kind one's grandmother used to make. In a bowl I worried two egg yolks (a little white doesn't hurt), stirred in a slurp each of mustard powder, salt, delumped sugar, and lime juice. Then still worrying the mess I'd add very slowly about half a cup of oil. Then drop by drop I'd add more oil and more lime juice—licking my fingers to test. If the stuff curdled, I'd rub in another yolk. When I didn't have another egg, I'd pour the concoction over the potatoes anyway. It got so that whenever a picnic threatened, or someone put on a bring-something buffet, I'd be asked to bring a bowl of my salad.

And that gets me to the last of the tricks for eating well, though a poor cook: Get yourself invited often. In my bachelor days I did pretty well, and few of my hosts expected me to retaliate. Some of the charter-boat captains invited me whenever we met at an anchorage. It was a good arrangement: I'd entertain their guests during cocktail hour, and the captain got to bathe the engine, or splice a halyard, without kibitzers.

25 Hints for Boat Living

Living ashore, although we have done it for years, can be difficult enough. Living on a boat has most of the shore problems and some of its own. On boats where I visited, and from living aboard my own boats for several years, I have collected shippy household hints. Some of them are just as useful on a weekend cruise on a lake as on an ocean passage. I have a whole seabagful of them.

The trouble with seabags is that it's hard to keep their contents separate, arranged in some sort of system, and get out just what you want without spilling some other stuff. So don't expect a well-structured essay in this chapter. It's going to be a chowder.

Your house or apartment normally stands still; a boat pitches and rolls. Even if the yard has built drawers that don't slide out, and lockers that don't fly open, we still have to stow everything. That would be simple if we ever had enough storage space on our boats. But how many yachts have, for instance, the shallow drawers that on the hungriest tramp steamer keep the charts flat and neat? So we build holders into the overhead, and put up with rolled charts that snarl at us everytime we look at them. This Heloise keeps his charts, folded once, under his mattress. Or: What do you do with teapot, saucepan, and dishes that have no permanent home? Stack them in a plastic dish drainer that's fastened down but can be removed once in a while for scrubbing.

Where to stow all the canned goods? They belong in the galley, and you'll say I should have talked about them in the last chapter. But on most boats they spill over—often literally—into the living quarters. The most original solution for storing a fleet of cans came to me from Hank, who, stocking his *Ben Gun* for a trip to Tahiti, lined up the cans on the deck sole and lived on top of them. Doris on *Tang* wanted can storage arranged the way baby foods are dispensed in supermarkets: one kind to each bin; take out the bottom can, and the next one slides in place. When that was too much work for her carpenter, she settled for bins accessible from the sink top, and prongs to fish out whatever can took her fancy.

There are two schools of thought when it comes to stowing cans. One captain, or cook, wants them all mixed up so that, wherever he starts digging, he has hope of finding quickly a soup, a vegetable, and a dessert. Another skipper will have all his vichyssoise in one place. Then he risks losing his entire supply if a leak there rusts all the cans. To me that's a small risk; I'd be much more worried about finding myself with nothing but one lockerful of the stuff.

Either way, although you of course know about it, tell any novice friends to make sure the labels can't get into the bilge. Perhaps advise him to remove the labels, and paint some code letters on the cans. Then he'll have to post the code somewhere, or with tastebuds programed for pears open a can of . . . parsnips.

With never enough space for storage, Ken on *Jane Austen* built hinged boxes into the otherwise wasted space between deck beams. He had boxes for silverware, napkins, stationery, and I forget what other small things. A knife rack would go well in such a place in the galley, protect the crew, and keep the knives from dulling their edges on each other.

My bearing compass was a stowage problem until I built a bracket just inside the companion where I could reach it from the cockpit.

For small things a canvas ditty bag with drawstring may be the solution. Sail needles, twine, palm, and related stuff have always been kept that way. The bag can dangle from a hook, or rest under the bosun's pillow. It's so handy, I made another one for the most-used tools. Ditty bags are habit-forming and collect gear faster than an old maid's sewing basket.

Perhaps you can adapt my schooner's stowable table for your own cabin or cockpit. When not in use it buttoned to a bulkhead. In use it dropped one hinged leg and was supported by a small shelf on the mast. Two dowels held it to the shelf. Two other dowels fitted into holes in the deck sole and prevented the leg from getting kicked out from under the table.

Books are a problem. Even when you don't carry a library you'll have light lists, tide tables, coast pilots. Book racks, even those that run athwartships, the better way, need some device to keep the books in place when it gets rough. A batten to be removed when you take out a book will work, or an ornamental rope—nylon flag halyard stuff perhaps—looped into itself and then fastened to cup hooks at the ends.

One piece of gear I don't want stowed on my boat is flashlights. I'd have them hanging in the open near every hatch, next to my bunk, in the head, wherever I might need a light or can grab one on my way on deck.

Now let's talk about water. Fresh water, that is. In your home port it probably comes out of a tap, clear and delicious. Don't let that fool you. When you cruise you'll find taps that spew forth brownish fluids, hoses that give water a taste of old galoshes, and water that smells like graves in a swamp. Sample the stuff before you put it into your tanks. If I had to take some of the doubtful kind—there is no other to be had along some stretches of the Inland Waterway—I'd keep it out of my built-in tanks and just fill some plastic cans or bottles. They are easier to decontaminate than the tanks.

Running water is convenient, but it leads to waste. Even the spring faucets, that shut off when you take your hand off, aren't as economical of water as a pump. You'll be surprised how quickly your guests tire of pumping. And so does your cook. Where water has to be husbanded, as on an ocean cruise, the cook can save a lot of it by using salt water for cooking. Only foods that absorb water—rice and spaghetti, for example—need fresh water. Salt water washes dishes as clean as fresh water. Some detergents work better than others. I have used a liquid kind that removed even cold bacon grease, and made an efficient bilge cleaner when poured into the bilge on a rough day. You can launder in salt water, using fresh water only for the last rinse.

You might get the cook to use more salt water by giving him a pump right in the galley. This pump, unlike the fresh-water pump, should work easily.

Water consumption is hard to predict. If everyone aboard is water-minded one gallon per day per person is enough for drinking, cooking, brushing teeth, etc. Using the ocean for a bathtub I often averaged only one-half gallon a day in the Bahamas. Of course soups, canned fruits, and vegetables added to my total water intake. And I did no hard work, and stayed out of the sun most of the time.

The secret for keeping out of the sun is a well-designed awning. The same awning also makes an efficient water catcher. You can lower one corner, and catch the runoff in a bucket; or gimmick a hose connection patterned on an inner tube valve in the center of the awning, and let the water run through a rubber hose directly into the tank. In either case wash off any salt by letting the first few gallons that fall drain overboard.

One thunder shower will fill your tanks to overflowing besides leaving enough for laundry, a sponge bath, and whatever else your parched heart may desire. But don't chase thunder showers. One dry summer Bob and Marie would look out from their anchorage in Hopetown and seeing towering cumulus build up over Marsh Harbour, six miles away, they'd hoist sail and up anchor. When they were in Marsh Harbour they'd sail to catch rain in Hopetown. They sailed a lot that summer. Both settlements got some rain, but the tanks on *Golden Future* ran dry, and they had to resort to their mermaid locker (a plastic garbage can) to haul water from shore.

Plastic cans and bottles for water storage are old stuff now, but I can't resist saluting some fellows who had an even better idea. They mounted an expedition across the Atlantic. (The difference between a trip and an expedition? In an expedition someone else pays the expenses.) Some institution loaded them with specimen jars to be filled according to some scientific plan. There were so many jars, they hadn't enough room left for water. Then someone came up with this idea: "Let's fill these nice sterile jars with water; as we use it, we can fill the jars with specimens."

Boating is supposed to be fun, but sometimes pests spoil our pleasure. I'm not now referring to the noisy party in the next slip, or the fiend who runs the dry exhaust of his generator into your ears and lungs in what before his arrival had been a pleasant anchorage. I'm talking about animal pests.

One day my little schooner decided to play big ship, and acquired a rat. I borrowed a trap and bought gourmet rat cheese. For three nights the rat had his midnight snack, but didn't get caught. Next day I borrowed a ferocious tomcat from Ed on *Sahara*. To make the cat even more ferocious, Ed didn't feed him for a whole day. The fierce tom slept on the port bunk, while the rat promenaded between the bunks. I next discussed my problem with Romain, on *Olad*. "Scuttle the schooner," he suggested. "The rat will leave the sinking ship. At least he is supposed to."

Before taking his advice, I decided to play ferocious myself. I sat up, armed with a machete. Again the rat strolled over the cabin sole. Of course I missed the blighter, and didn't improve the woodwork one bit. I tried poisoned grain next. He thrived on that diet. Phosphorous paste finally did him in. He was decent enough to die in the cockpit, saving me the trouble of moving a lot of inside ballast before the funeral.

Rats are not a common problem on small boats. Mosquitoes are. Screening helps, but one mosquito always gets through and starts singing in my ear the moment I want to go to sleep. My remedy: I swat him. Even if I miss, I hit myself so hard that I can't hear on that ear for a while. Less drastically, you can rub or spray yourself, or spray the cabin if you can stand the smell. But you know all that. What many people don't realize is how localized these rascals are. I suffered at one cay in the Exumas until I couldn't take it any longer. I shifted my anchorage a few hundred yards, and there wasn't another mosquito.

Sandflies, little biters that devour your ankles ashore around sunset time, will leave you alone if you anchor a little distance from shore, I found. Dockside, try spraying the screens to discourage these pests, which are small enough to get through any screen.

Roaches are a worldwide nuisance in warm climates. Their presence aboard is no reflection on your character. If it makes you feel less like a social outcast, call them "palmetto bugs." They walk aboard when you lie to a dock. Captain Muhlhauser, who sailed around the world in the *Amaryllis* and wrote a book about it, hated these critters so much that he never tied to a dock but always anchored off. The anchor he used was too heavy for his crew to get up, and he had to get help from shore whenever he wanted to leave.

That for my money is carrying cucarachaphobia a bit far. I also wonder if the good captain knew that these rather harmless beasts can fly. If you see one on your boat, don't throw him overboard. I have watched roaches swim back to the boat and climb aboard happily.

You can keep their population down by taking a few precautions. I always took cans and jars out of the cartons in the dinghy, put them aboard, but left the cartons in the dink for later disposal. Also, still in the dinghy, I'd pick over potatoes, onions, and fruit before putting them aboard. I left a few roach pills under the sink and other spots in the galley. With this routine I'd never see more than one or two scuttle off when I turned on the light; sometimes I'd see none for weeks. If I did I'd spray him directly, and that was the end of that one.

Then I mentioned this routine, and its rather pleasing results, in a column I wrote for the Nassau *Tribune*. Before it appeared in print, my boat was overrun by these fellows. (They must have come aboard with a gift of onions from a friend ashore.)

Once they have taken over your ship, massive doses of flying-insect spray in all lockers, behind the ceiling, and in the bilge may control them. In stubborn cases you may have to fumigate. If you do the job yourself, read all the small print in the instructions. If a professional exterminator does it, make sure the stuff he uses isn't the kind that turns brass black.

Apart from ants, which are easily controlled, that's about all the pests that are likely to bother you aboard. If the ants get into your only canister of sugar, don't throw the sugar out. Just pour it into a clean fry pan and heat gently. The ants will leave.

Now let me talk about lights and such. Electricity is without equal, and when you draw shore current, there is no problem. When you anchor off, a few lights will soon run down your battery; then you have to run the generator and listen to its clatter. Shoreside, electric cooking is ideal; from batteries it isn't practical. Butane gas is great for cooking and safe enough in a proper installation if handled with common sense. For lights it's second rate. Alcohol in the galley is great, but expensive compared to other fuels. It's no good for lights. In out-of-the-way places you may not be able to buy alcohol. Wood and coal are great in galley stoves in cold climates. Candles, even shielded from drafts, drip away in no time when the boat is on anything but an even keel. They are friendly and festive but it takes too many candles to give light for reading hour after hour. Gasoline, though popular for stoves and lanterns used in camping, is much too dangerous to be used on a boat.

There is only one fuel that works equally well in galley and lamps, is cheap, and gets more available the farther you get from civilization: kerosene. Or call it coal oil. If you want to go fancy, use mineral spirits, a more refined distillate, still cheap enough.

Riding and anchor lights use kerosene in wick burners. If the wick is adjusted correctly—let it burn for a couple of minutes, then turn it down—the lamps will burn cleanly all night. Once in a while something goes wrong, and your lamp turns into a lampblack factory. When that happens take the lamp ashore to clean, or you may have to repaint and reupholster the cabin. By the way, you can buy navigation and anchor lights that work on either kerosene or battery power. I have used them both ways and like them. The two systems backstop each other. When it's too rough to monkey with lighting the kerosene, I'd use electricity. When my electric system acted up, or I had to baby my batteries, I'd use kerosene.

In the cabin a couple of kerosene wick lamps give a friendly light, brighter than candles, but still on the dim side. For reading or any work that needs good light, I prefer a kerosene pressure lamp. For years I have used Tilley lamps, made in England, but available in the United States and Canada. Like all pressure lamps they hiss and throw a good deal of heat, but if you can put up with that, they are great lights. With a shade, or a milk glass bowl, they give a pleasant light, quite unlike the glare from the usual camping lanterns. You can improvise a gimbal by hanging the lamp from its bail while limiting its swings by two pieces of shock cord pulling in opposite directions.

All open-flame lights need smokebells above them. Even then they heat up the overhead and can dry out a laid deck enough to start a leak. A metal shield backed with asbestos should prevent that.

If you go in for wick-type ship's lamps in the cabin, make sure they are really gimbaled. Many models swing in one direction only, and should be mounted so they'll swing easily athwartships. The setscrew that secures such lamps is prone to work loose, and should be taped. Under way I wouldn't use these lamps below. I'd also remove the chimneys and stow them safe from breakage.

I have cooked many meals on kerosene stoves. They need more

attention when you light them than butane or alcohol stoves. But they are hot, clean, and trouble-free when you treat them correctly. By all means get a model with fuel gauge, and if possible, two separate fuel tanks. Otherwise in the middle of a batch of pancakes you may run out of fuel and patience.

Strain the kerosene to get rid not only of particles but occasional dollops of water. Do the straining, and all other fuel handling, on deck and not in the cockpit, where a spill would run into the bilge and smell up your cabin.

You'll have to carry a few spares (mantles for the lamps, generators for lamps and stoves, and perhaps a pump gasket and leather for either) and the simple tools needed to install them. With occasional replacement of these parts, kerosene appliances will give you many years of good service, if you do a little preventive maintenance.

In my happy cruising I often forgot what day, even what month, it was, but I was always conscious of Sundays. So Sunday had its schedule of chores: cleaning lamps and stove; running the engine if I hadn't used it during the week; winding the seven-day clock.

At sea, garbage disposal is no problem: Over the side it goes. Near shore, and on lakes and rivers, in harbors and anchorages many people thoughtlessly use the same system. There are good reasons against that.

The law is one. In most such places you aren't supposed to drop anything overboard but your anchor. In salt water there is another reason: sharks. They regularly patrol an area where they once have found food. Someday a shark on patrol may mistake the cook, out for his daily dip, for a specially juicy piece of garbage. In skin-diving waters you really can ruin the scenery with your trash. I once took some visitors to a colorful coral head I had discovered on an earlier trip. Between my visits someone had used it for a garbage dump. And how would you like to come to an unspoiled beach to find a mess of rotting grapefruit rinds as a welcome gift? Then also some lucky people own homes on the shore; is it fair to dump refuse in their front yards?

In every marina, and on most public docks you'll find garbage cans. Don't be a waterborne litter bug; carry your stuff until you get there. Yachts anchored in some harbors organize their own informal disposal system. Someone makes a garbage run in his dinghy, and collects stuff from nearby boats at the same time. A perfect stranger may come alongside soliciting your trash business. What a nice way to get to know your neighbors!

Cruising, I'd often pass a cut leading to the ocean. On an ebb tide I found it a good place to liberate garbage in a grocery bag tied with a pipe cleaner. By the time the bag soaks through and spills its contents, it'll be miles out to sea.

83. *Garbage, anyone?*

Now you have had a peek into my seabag of household hints. You can still go ahead and keep your charts rolled, waste all the water you want, breed roaches under the sink, turn up your nose at kerosene, and wind your clock on Mondays. But whatever you do, have fun.

Glossary of Terms

Sailors have their own vocabulary, just as doctors and stock brokers have theirs . . . not to impress the farmers, but to convey quickly a precise meaning, which often would take a string of words in ordinary language.

abeam in line with the beams of a vessel, that is, at right angles to her fore-and-aft line; a light is abeam when it bears ninety degrees from your course

altitude of a celestial body is the angle, measured at the eye of the observer, between the body and the horizon

athwart, athwartships in the direction of the thwarts of a boat, crosswise, across the line of a vessel's course

awash with the sea just washing over, level with the water's surface

aweather toward the weather, that is, the windward side

azimuth bearing of a celestial body, reckoned in degrees (from 0 to 360) starting from true north

back the wind is said to back when it shifts *against* the sun, e.g., from S to E; opposite of veer

backstays rigging wires that lead from mast top aft to the ship's sides

baggywrinkle fuzzy padding, made from rope yarns, used as chafing gear

bail to rid a boat of water by throwing it out with a scoop (bailer) or bucket

beam timber that runs across the width of a ship, e.g., deck beam; hence, also her width at the widest part; beam wind or beam seas come from abeam

bearing direction of an object given in degrees from magnetic or true north, or from ship's heading, e.g., astern

belay make fast a rope; also to cease to talk, or to carry out an order or intention

bend on tie on

bight in line or knot: bend, loop, or slack section of line

bilge where a round-bottom boat (or a barrel) bulges; part of boat where seepage accumulates; also the contents of that space (short for bilge water, which also means piffle) *bitter end* the inboard end of rope or chain; not related to astringent taste but bitts, that is, mooring posts on deck

bobstay wire, or often chain, leading from bow (near waterline) to bowsprit

boom spar, especially one at the foot of a modern sail

bow line rope from bow to dock, etc.; not to be confused with bowline (sounded like bol'n), the useful knot

bowsprit spar that stands out from bow of a sailboat to increase vessel's sail area and give a better lead to forestay

breasts or breast lines, mooring lines leading roughly at right angles from ship's sides

broad on the bow, etc., often used as opposite to "fine" on the bow, etc.; strictly speaking, four points (45°) from dead ahead, while fine means two points (22½°) off

bulkhead nautical equivalent of partition, wall

cabin on a pleasure boat, the living compartment; cabin trunk is the box raised above the deck; cabintop the deck of the house; cabin sole what would be the floor ashore

careen to lay a vessel on her side so her other side will be exposed for work on hull below the waterline

celestial equator line directly above your head if you sailed along the equator

celestial pole point in the sky directly above your head when you stand at one of the poles

chafe a wearing away by rubbing; chafing gear is used to reduce chafe

chainplates metal straps on side of sailboat to which lower ends of shrouds are fastened

Charlie Noble chimney top of the galley funnel, or the whole funnel, on a vessel; supposedly named after a skipper who had crew polish it

chine part of hull where sides and bottom meet at an angle; corresponds to the area of the turn of the bilge on a round-bottom hull

chock a fitting to lead ropes or chain, fair and with minimum of chafe, overboard, as in bow chock, roller chock

cirrus wispy, white, high clouds

cleat wooden or metal fitting, usually two-horned, to which ropes can be fastened

coaming raised boards around cockpit or other deck opening to keep water from flowing in

cockpit on pleasure boats, area aft of the house; usual position for helmsman on sailboats and some powerboats

comb notched contrivance to hold tiller in any desired position, freeing helmsman for other duties *contour lines* lines connecting points of same height or depth, e.g., the ten-fathom line on nautical chart

coral head or coral stack, an *isolated* colony of coral, as distinct from the multitude of colonies of a coral reef

cowl sousaphone-shaped hood of a ventilator, often turnable for maximum air movement

crown area of anchor where arms meet shank

cuddy small forward cabin

cumulus massy, bulging, often flat-based, midlevel clouds

datum reference plane of sea level used on a chart; to get depth of water at any given time, height of tide is to be added to sounding given (or occasional minus tide to be subtracted)

dead reckoning abbreviated DR; position from courses and distances run (not from celestial observations, etc.); supposedly from "deduced" reckoning, but perhaps from rare meanings of dead "unbroken" as in dead run, or "exact" as in dead center

deck iron fitting for cooling galley chimney to prevent scorching where it passes through a wooden deck

degaussing demagnetizing; from magnetic unit gauss, named after German physicist Karl Friedrich Gauss

deviation error of mariner's compass due to magnetic influences on board

dinghy small boat, especially one intended for use as yacht tender; sometimes called "dink," sometimes unprintable names

ditty bag small bag used by a sailor to hold his sewing kit and other personal treasures

dividers instrument for stepping off distances on chart; a landsman might call it a compass with two steel points

dock originally the water between jetties, seawalls, etc.; now the floating or fixed structure to which vessels tie; docking, then, is bringing a boat to such a tie-up place and securing it there

draft the depth of water a vessel draws, that it needs to float; the vertical distance from lowest underwater part (keel, propeller, rudder) to waterline

ebb tidal current moving seaward or down a tide way, opposite of flood

echo sounder device that indicates depth by measuring time between sending a sound signal and receiving its echo from the bottom

equator reference line around the globe at latitude zero, that is, halfway between the poles

equinoxes literally, times of year when lengths of night and day are the same, that is, at the beginning of spring and fall, about March 21 and September 23

estimated position abbreviated EP; probable position of a vessel; especially one based on dead reckoning to which corrections for current, leeway, etc. have been applied

eyesplice a rope looped back and spliced into itself

fathom unit of length equal to six feet, used for depths on charts of English-speaking countries; also the approximate span of a man's arms, which makes it handy for measuring rope

fenders buffers to protect topsides when lying to a dock or against another vessel

fending off pushing a boat clear of a dock or another vessel, e.g., with a boat hook

fetch a vessel fetches a mark when she gets to it; she fetches up when she runs aground; a chain fetches up when it gets under sudden strain

fix point on chart where two or more lines of position, considered reliable, cross; if your fix was wrong you may get into what Webster defines as "a position of difficulty or embarrassment"—a fix

flood tidal current setting toward the land or up a tide way; opposite of ebb

fluke that part of an anchor that's supposed to dig into the bottom

flying bridge light structure above deck house for conning yacht, especially while fishing

fore- prefix indicating toward the bows, as in foredeck, foremast, forehatch

fore-and-aft-rigged carrying all sails more or less in the direction of the center line, rather than athwartships; opposite: square-rigged

forestay wire rope from mast to bow or bowsprit

foul opposite of clear; a fouled anchor is one tangled in its cable; foul ground is bottom obstructed by rocks or wrecks; a foul bottom is the underwater part of a hull on which algae, barnacles, etc., grow; foul-weather gear means oilskins

freeboard the distance between waterline and deck

gaff spar at head of four-sided fore-and-aft sail; gaff-rigged means carrying gaff-headed, as opposed to triangular, jib-headed, sails

gear all-inclusive sailor's term that can mean anything from a ship's guns and appurtenances to his shaving kit

ghosting moving under sail in what seems like a calm

gimbals system of suspension that keeps compass, stove, etc. horizontal regardless of rolling and pitching of vessel

ground tackle anchors, ropes, chain, etc. used for anchoring vessel; some authorities include towing gear and dock warps

grounding a vessel's unintentional touching of bottom

guys ropes used to keep a boom from swinging in horizontal plane

halyard rope for hoisting sails, flags, etc.

hand one of the crew, paid or unpaid; the order "All hands," given, e.g., when the watch below is needed for a sail change, brings the entire crew on deck; the cook can stay in his bunk, unless the order is "All hands and the cook"

haul to pull, especially on a rope; to haul out is to slip a yacht, as on a marine railway. The wind hauls when it changes direction

hawser a stout rope, usually a large one; in some areas any anchor rode, regardless of size

head bows of a vessel; since that was the place for seamen's relief it has come to mean the toilet; the heading is the direction in which a vessel points; to be headed in a sailboat is to be thwarted by the wind blowing from your intended direction

heel to incline, list, under sail

helm steering mechanism of a vessel including either wheel or tiller; the helmsman is the man at wheel or tiller

high water the highest level, or the time of high tide; opposite of low water

horizon line where at sea or on a large lake sky and water seem to meet

isobar line drawn through points of equal atmospheric pressure, e.g., through all stations that report barometer readings (reduced to sea level) of 30.00 inches; isobars are called closed when they curve back on themselves in small area of weather map, as they do, for instance, around the "LOW" of a hurricane

jackstaff flagstaff at bow of a vessel

jib triangular sail set in forepart of vessel; jib-headed means like a jib, not gaff-headed

jibe to bring a boomed sail from one side to the other, under control and on purpose in wearing ship, or accidentally

joker valve no-return value of marine toilet

jury-rig a temporary device, such as a mast or rudder, to replace one that has carried away

kedge to a yachtsman a stocked two-fluked anchor such as a fisherman's, yachtsman's, or Hereshoff; to kedge is to move a vessel—aground or otherwise—by laying out an anchor and pulling

ketch two-masted sailboat, with taller mast forward, and a fairly good-sized sail, the mizzen, aft; a yawl, which a ketch resembles, usually has a small sail aft, and her mizzen is stepped farther aft than in a ketch

knot abbreviated kn; nautical measure of speed; one nautical mile (6076 feet) per hour, about 100 feet per minute, or 1.15 statute miles per hour

lagoon body of water separated from ocean by a sandspit, coral reefs, or low islands

laid deck unlike a plywood deck, is made of individual planks caulked and stopped, either kept bright (natural) or painted, but not covered with canvas or fiberglass

lampblack   fine, bulky, almost weightless soot made of carbon by a flame short of oxygen

lanyard   a small line used to attach anything, e.g., a knife or a bucket

lay and lie   to place and to be in a place, and all their forms, are used almost interchangeably by sailors, more often incorrectly than correctly by shore usage

lee   side away from wind, downwind; opposite of weather, windward; making a lee is giving protection, as to a man about to be rescued from the water; getting a lee is being sheltered from the wind, as under a high shore; leeway refers to a vessel's sagging downwind of her intended course, especially under pressure of wind; the lee rail is the downwind rail, where you'd empty a bucket (or your stomach) to have the contents blow away from you

leeward   sounded as "lured," is downwind; the Leeward Islands of the West Indies are (don't ask why) the Lesser Antilles from the Virgin Islands south to Dominica, at the north side of the Martinique Passage

limb   outer edge of disk of celestial body; the lower limb, referred to in celestial navigation, is the point of sun (or moon) nearest the horizon

list   tilt of a vessel to port or starboard

log   patent log, or taffrail log, is a device that measures distance run, and directly or by calculation, the speed through the water

low water   the lowest level, or the time of low tide; opposite of high water

lubber   clumsy, unseamanlike character

lubber's line   index mark on mariner's compass

lunar   sight, based on apparent movement of moon against background of stars, to get a longitude without knowledge of exact time; inexact and tedious, now obsolete

magnetic   abbreviated mag; based on magnetic north as opposed to true north; a magnetic bearing is one shown by a (corrected) compass; a magnetic course is the course to steer with a (corrected) compass

magnitude   apparent brightness of a celestial body; the smaller the number, the brighter the object

mainsail   sounded like mains'l; or main, the largest regular sail on a modern sailboat

MAYDAY   internationally agreed distress call for use on radio telephone. Transliteration of French *m'aider*, "to help me"

miles per hour   abbreviated mph; unit of speed on land and on inland waters; statute miles (5280 feet) per hour, about 0.87 knots *mizzen*   sail at stern of ketch or yawl

monkey fist   ball-shaped, ornamental knot formed at outboard end of a heaving line to help in aiming it

monkey island   open platform atop the bridge of a freighter

motorsailer   a yacht specially designed for efficiency under power, yet able to sail; a sailboat with an auxiliary engine (usually small) is a sailboat with an auxiliary engine (or an auxiliary, if you will) but *not* a motorsailer

nautical mile   abbreviated nm; universally accepted unit of distance at sea based on one minute of latitude, exactly 1852 meters, about 6076 feet (roughly 2000 yards), about 1.15 statute miles

nose   stem of a vessel; the wind is on the nose when it blows directly from where you want to go in a sailboat; remedy: go somewhere else

offing   distance from shore which you gain (get) or lose; something is in the offing, strictly speaking, when it seems nearer the horizon than the shore

painter   rope at bow of a small boat, such as a dinghy, for tying her up

part   rope or cable parts when it carries away, that is, breaks

pin rail   rack fitted with belaying pins to which ropes, such as halyards, can be secured

pitching   motion of a vessel that plunges now her head, now her stern

Plimsoll marks   indicators of waterline to which a ship may be loaded; named after S. Plimsoll, M.P., sponsor of British Merchant Shipping Act

point   unit of angle; compass card was divided into thirty-two points; now degree scale (0°–360°) has largely displaced points except in Rules of the Road, and a few simple angles, e.g., eight points (90°), four points (45°), etc.; a boat points high when she sails close to the wind, say within four points or less

Pointers   the two stars farthest from the handle in the Big Dipper, which point roughly to Polaris, the star nearest the celestial North Pole

popple   a choppy sea, especially short cross-seas in shallow water

preventer   any one of several ropes used on sailboats in rough seas or storms; especially the line rigged to keep the boom of a sail from slamming across accidentally

quarter   the area of a vessel between midships and astern, port or starboard; on the quarter means, strictly, four points (45°) abaft the beam—sometimes extended to mean four points off either side of her stern

range   two objects, such as lights, in line (in transit) form a range; when ahead they serve as leading marks for the helmsman, when astern as gauge of leeway; range of a tide is the difference in height between high and low water; range of visibility, say of a light, is the maximum distance from which it can be seen

ratlines sounded ratlins—lashings between shrouds to form rungs of a ladder for going aloft; on yachts a good temporary station for lookout

reciprocal course the one that'd get you back where you came from; when you have steamed east (90°), the reciprocal course is obviously west (270°); a common mistake in plotting courses and bearings is to take, or forget to take, the reciprocal

refit after first fitting out, a yacht is always in state (or need) of a refit, consisting of minor repairs, painting, renewal of cordage, etc.

revolutions per minute abbreviated rpm; measure of engine speed, or propeller turns; an indirect approximate measure of speed of vessel under power

rigging ropes (usually wire ropes) that support the masts of a sailboat (shrouds and stays), *the standing rigging*—and the ropes (usually fiber ropes) that hoist and lower the sails (halyards), or trim them (sheets), *the running rigging*

roadstead anchorage with little protection, except perhaps from the prevailing winds

rode to confuse lubbers, an anchor rope is called rode

rolling side-to-side motion of a vessel

runabout a small, open motorboat

Samson post vertical timber on foredeck serves as mooring post, strong as the Biblical character

schooner fore-and-aft-rigged sailing vessel with two or more masts; when two-masted, taller mast is aft (in ketch and yawl the mast nearest stern is the shorter)

scope length of anchor cable paid out

scuppers openings at deck level for draining water overboard; in a self-draining cockpit, the pipes for that purpose

sea buoy outermost of a string of buoys that mark entrance to a harbor

seacock shut-off valve on through-the-hull connections below the waterline

seas waves; when a sea is running, it's rough; short seas make it choppy; swells are long seas

secure make fast

semidiameter fancy word for radius; in celestial navigation, apparent angular distance from center of body to its limb

shackle link for joining chain, etc., usually U-shaped with removable pin

shock cord cotton-covered elastic like that used in round garters

shrouds wire ropes from mast to ship's sides

single-hander sailor who needs no other hands to get him into trouble *slack water*   absence of current at change from flood to ebb, or ebb to flood

smackboat   or smack, fishing vessel propelled by sails

springs   lines leading from bow aft to the dock, or from stern forward; also short for spring tides, the twice-monthly highest tides after new and full moon

squall   sudden violent blast of wind; a white squall hits out of the blue, cloudless sky

square rigger   sailing vessel that carries most of her sails on athwartship yards rather than fore-and-aft booms

stand   of the tide, the height or time of unchanging level at high and low water

standing off and on   sailing to and fro, e.g., to maintain approximate position without anchoring

standing on   maintaining one's course and speed

steam   to proceed under power; to sail does not necessarily mean doing it under sail; also, a ship sails at noon (or any hour) even when propelled by atomic energy

step   timber that holds the lower end (the heel) of a mast

sternfast   mooring rope leading aft

sternstaff   flagstaff aft

stops   lashings around boom and sail for stowing sail

stores   all-inclusive sailor's term that can mean anything from rum to salt horse to paint; unlike gear, stores are usually to be consumed in one way or another

stranding   grounding on or near shore; when intentional it's called beaching

strapping in sail   bringing fore-and-aft sails close to the center line of vessel

stratus   sheet-like, low clouds

stuffing box   device that keeps water out while it lets propeller shaft turn freely

swells   long, regular, rounded waves

tacks   zigzag course of a sailboat that tacks, comes about, by changing course to bring the wind on the other side of her sails after having headed directly into the wind; onshore (or inshore) tack brings her closer to land, offshore tack takes her away

teredo   wood-gnawing ship worm

thwart   oarsman's seat

tide   the periodic rise and fall of sea level under the influence of moon and sun; tidal current is the horizontal movement of water caused or influenced by tide

tide rip swirling or breaking water caused by the clash of opposing tidal currents

topping lift rope from mast to outer end of boom to support or raise it

topsides part of yacht's hull above the waterline

transom originally, athwartships timbers at the stern post; now practically synonymous with the flat, or slightly curved part of the stern

trim fore-and-aft balance of a vessel; trimming is to change ballast, etc. to bring her head up or down; trimming sails is to adjust them to take best advantage of the wind

trough hollow between one wave and the next

true abbreviated T; direction referred to geographic north, as opposed to magnetic north

variation angle between true north and magnetic north; changes with geographic location, is called easterly when (corrected) compass points east of true north, otherwise westerly

veer the wind veers when it gradually changes direction *with* the sun, e.g., from E to S, opposite of back

way motion of vessel through the water; to have way on means to be moving; under the Rules of the Road a vessel is "under way" when she is not at anchor, or made fast to the shore, or aground

ways the place where a vessel is being built, launched, or hauled out for repairs, etc.

weather the weather side is the windward side of a vessel; to weather a headland is to get around it; to weather a storm is to get through it safely

wildcat sprocket wheel on windlass that receives the links of a chain; the drum used for rope should be called gypsy

windlass winch used to weigh anchor

windward toward the wind, opposite of leeward; to work to windward in a sailboat is to make progress toward the direction from which the wind blows; the Windward Islands of the West Indies are (don't ask why) the Lesser Antilles south of Martinique Passage, Martinique to Grenada

yaw under way: to deviate from course; at anchor: to swing

Index

Abandoning ship, 192–95
  kit for, 221
  life rafts, 193
  lowering the dinghy, 193
  supplies, 195
  swimming, 194
  See also Wrecking
ACRUX, 144
Alcohol as fuel, 248
Alden, John, 21
Anchor chain, 10–13
  advantages of, 10
  calibrated, 12
  chain locker, 12
  depth markers, 12
  devil's claw, use of, 13
  fastening of, 13
  fetching-up strains, remedying, 10–11
  ground tackle, *ill.* 14
  hauling in, 12
  inexpensive, 11
  length, desirable, 11–12
  nylon, bright-bridging with, 10, 11, *ill.* 11
  rope compared with, 10
  selection of, 11–12
  shackles, defined, 11–12
  short-link, 11
  size, choice of, 12
  sliding weights, use of, 10–11, *ill.* 11
  stretch, 11
  stud-link, 11
  types of, 11–12
  weight of, 10–11
  windlass, use of, 12
Anchor dragging
  indicators of, 15–16
  prevention of, 16–18, *ill.* 17
  types of, 13–16
Anchoring, 3, 8–20
  breaking out, causes of, 10
  grapnels, 18–19
  kedging off, 178–82, *ill.* 181
  lashings for depth measurement, 12
  nylon rope, 13
  rope, 10
  scope-to-depth-ratio record set, 8–10
  selection of anchors, 18–19
  signals, 19–20, *ill.* 20
  skindiving and, 71, 72
  system for, 19–20
  two anchors, use of, 16–18, *ill.* 17
Animal pests, extermination of, 247
Ants, 248

Barometric readings, 40
Batteries, 212–13
Beaching, 59–61, 66
Bearings. *See* Lines of position
Big Dipper, 143, *ill.* 144
Binoculars, 80–81, *ill.* 81
Boat speed measurement, through the water *vs.* over the bottom, 191
Bobbing a light, 100
Books, storage of, 245
Bowditch, Nathaniel, 133
Bubble sextants, 169
Bunkboards, building, 237, *ill.* 236
Buoys, 104–6
Butane gas, 248

Cabin, safety in, 236–37, *ill.* 236
Candles, 248
Cans, storage of, 244
Careening, 61, *ill.* 62
Celestial navigation, 96, 163–75
  altitude measurement, 169
  chart work, 166–68, *ill.* 168
  circle of position from sun, 165–67, *ill.* 167
  cocked hat, 173
  crossing lines of position, 173
  fix, getting a, 173
  horizon, 169–70

Celestial navigation (*cont'd*)
  line of position from angles, 164–65, *ill.* 166
  at night, 169–70
  recognizable celestial body, obtaining, 170–71
  "round" of stars, shooting a, 173
  sextants, 164, *ill.* 165, 169
  sight reduction tables, 171
  simplicity of, 164
  single lines of position, 171–73
  star sights, 169–70
  subsolar point, 166, *ill.* 167
  three lines of position, 173
  time, importance of, 171
  uses of, 163–64
  working up the sight, 171–72
Chart
  in celestial navigation, 166–68, *ill.* 168
  compass course, plotting a, 85–87
  courser, use of, 85–86
  distance measurements, 84
  dividers, single-handed, 84–85, *ill.* 84
  magnetic course, finding of, *ill.* 86
  pencils, use of, 83–84
  protractor for coursing, 85
  rangefinder, need for, 87
  spares, 215
  speed problems, 84–85
  weights for, 86
Chip log, 78
Close-hauled sailing, 106–7
Coal as fuel, 248
Coal oil, 249–50
Coast and Geodetic Survey, 130
Cocked hat, 173
Compass
  degree markings, 118
  hand bearing-type, 87, 115–16, *ill.* 116
  interference, example of, 140
  need for, 114–15
  roses, 89
  sailboat heeling and, 119–20
  spares, 215
Compass adjustment, 116–26
  magnetic influences and, 116–17
  magnetic field and, 125–29
  memory aid for, 127–28, *ill.* 128
  second lubber's line, 126, *ill.* 127
  by the sun, 120–25

true courses converted to magnetic, 126–27, *ill.* 127
Consolan bearings, defined, 92
Cook, James, 108–9
Cooks and cooking, 237–43
  alcohol, use of, 242
  board for lap, 238
  cookbooks, 242
  dinner invitations, obtaining, 243
  gimbaling of, 237–38
  potatoes, preparation of, 242
  potato salad dressing recipe, 242–43
  pressure cookers, 238–39
  rotation, 241
  seat for, 238
  single-hander and, 242
  supplementing canned foods, 242
  See also Food; Galley
Copper tubing, uses of, 211–12, *ill.* 212
Coral waters, piloting in, 75, 107–14
  depth, color of water and, 112
  depth at which coral found, 107–8
  lookout, 110
  at night, 110, 111
  plant growth, 113–14
  range of coral, 107
  reefs, growth of, and, 111
  reefs, locating, 108, *ill.* 109
  sandbanks, 112–13, 114
  shadow of boat, use of, 112, *ill.* 113
  single-handers and, 110
  sounding poles, use of, 110
  stacks and heads, locating, 108–11, *ill.* 109
  storms, effects of, 114
  sunglasses, 110–11
  sunlight factors, 110
  visibility of coral, 108
Coursers, 85–86
Current, distinguished from tide, 129
  See also Tidal currents; Tides

Dead reckoning (DR), 89, 95–96, *ill.* 96
Deck beam, padding of, 237, *ill.* 236
Declination (DEC), 170
Depressions, in tropical summer weather, 43
Dinghy, 21–29
  adrift, recovery of, 26–27
  identification markings, 26
  instability of, 194

Dinghy (cont'd)
  lashing, 23-24
  lowering, 23 *ill.*
  raising, 23 *ill.*
  stowing, 23-25, *ill.* 24
  uses of, 21, *ill.* 22
Dinghy, towing of, 25-28
  curbing in an anchorage, 28-29, *ill.* 29
  cutting adrift, 27
  filled dinghy, 26-27
  floats for towline, 28, *ill.* 27
  "lazy" painter for, 26, *ill.* 27
  length of towline, 26
  rig, *ill.* 27
  stopping, method for, 27-28
  tow rope, 25-26
  tow rope, floating, 28
Dinner Key Teak, 232
Distance of Visibility tables, 97
Dividers, single-handed, 84-85, *ill.* 84
Docking, 3, 61-66, *ill.* 62, 63, 64
Doglegs, 105
DR. *See* Dead reckoning
Drills, 192-200
  appropriate timing for, 200
  children, dealing with, 200
  on runabouts, 192
Drills, abandon ship, 192-95
  life rafts, 193
  lowering the dinghy, 193
  staying aboard, importance of, 194
  supply checking, 195
  swimming, 194
Drills, fire, 198-200
  alcohol fires, 198-99
  classes of fires, 198
  electrical fires, 199
  for engine hatch safety, 200
  extinguishers, use of, 199
  for galley safety, 200
  for gas explosions, 199-200
  liquid fuel fires, 198
  water, use of, 198-99
Drills, man overboard, 195-98
  announcement of, 196
  approaching victim, 196-97
  boat maneuvers during, 196
  bringing victim aboard, 197
  life preservers, 196
  objects of rescue, suitable, 196
  on sailboats, 196
  for single-handers, 197, *ill.* 198

Drinking water. *See* Water
Drowning. *See* Floating
Dry rot, 233

Easterly waves, 40-43, *ill.* 42
Echo depth finder, 78
Electricity, 248
Estimated position (EP), 89

Fires
  alcohol, 198-99
  burning themselves out, 194-95
  classes of, 198
  controllability of, 194
  electrical, 199
  extinguishers, use of, 199
  in galley, 200
  gas explosions, 199-200
  liquid fuel, 198
  water, use of, 198-99
Fix, 89, 91, *ill.* 91, 92
  in celestial navigation, 173
Fixing position, rudiments of, 88-90
  See also Lines of position
Flares, 223-24, 225
Flashlights, 245
Floating
  on back, 202
  coughing, 206
  extra lift, stroke for, 207
  face mask, use of, 204-5, *ill.* 206
  method delineated, 203
  natural position of man, 202, *ill.* 203
  physical condition and, 204
  public demonstration given, 201-2
  in rough water, 207
  snorkel, use of, 204-5, *ill.* 206
  stroke, 205, *ill.* 206
  swimming, technique for, 203-4
  teachers, finding, 204
  teaching oneself, 204-7
Food
  emergency supply, 221
  limes, use of, 241
  nutrition supplements, 241
  rainwater, use of, 241
  red peppers, 241
  spices, 241
  stocking ship, 240-41
  vegetables, 241
  See also Cook; Water

Fore-and-aft-rigged sailboat, 48–50, *ill.* 49
Fuel for galleys and lamps, 248–50

GACRUX, 144
Galley, *ill.* 239
  as fire hazard, 200
  fuel for, 248–50
  See also Cooks and cooking
Garbage disposal, 250–51, *ill.* 251
Gaskets, 211
Gasoline, 249
  explosions, 199–200
GHA (Greenwich Hour Angle), 170
Gimbaling
  of cook, 237–38
  of lamps, 249
  of stoves, 238
Grapnels, 18–19
Greenwich Hour Angle (GHA), 170

H.O. Publication tables, 171
Hand bearing-compass, 87, 115–16, *ill.* 116
Handholds, 236
Heating, 234–35
Hermit crabs, 225
Hopetown, Elbow Cay, Bahamas, *ill.* 6
Hopetown–Nassau Course 195°, *ill.* 141
Horizon, distance to, 97–104
  in celestial navigation, 169–70
  formulas for, 101, 103, *table* 102
Hull work between tides, 59–66
  beaching, 59–61
  beaching, emergency, 66
  careening, 61, *ill.* 62
  complete-haulout method, 65–66, *ill.* 64
  docking methods, 61–66, *ill.* 62, 63, 64
  drydocking against seawall, 61–63, *ill.* 63
  giving boat a list, 65
  gouges, filling of, 64
  grids, building of, 63
  range of tides and, 60–61
  shortcuts, 64
  on soft bottom, 63
  suggested types, 59
  tide interrupts, 64–65
  trimming with water-filled dinghy, 65, *ill.* 66

weather considerations, 61
See also Skindiving
Hurricanes, 43–46

International Rules of the Road, The, regarding sailboat protection, 47–48

Jury-rig sailing, 56–57, *ill.* 57

Kedging off, 180–82, *ill.* 181, 183
Kerosene, 235, 248–50
Knot, defined, 90

Lamps, fuel for, 248–50
Lanoue, Fred, 201–5
Latitude, 89–90, 146–49, *ill.* 148, 153
"Leading" star, defined, 144
Leads, use of, 77–78
Leaks, 208–10
  oil, 211–12
  patching, 194
  patching materials, 210
  See also Waterproofing
Life preservers, 196
Light, bobbing a, 100
Lighthouses, charted range of, 97–104 *passim*
Lights
  fuel for, 248–49
  spare, 213
Lines of position, 88–96
  areas of uncertainty, 94–96, *ill.* 94, 95, 96
  in celestial navigation, 164–75
  circular, 92, *ill.* 94
  consolan bearings, 92
  curved, 92, *ill.* 94
  dead reckoning, 95–96, *ill.* 96
  defined, 90
  from known distance of an object, 92
  loran bearings, 92
  odd, 92–93
  parallels of latitude, 92
  RDF bearings, 92
  single, 92
  straight, 92, *ill.* 94
  visual bearings, 92
  width factor, 93–96, *ill.* 96
Logs, 78–80
  engine revolutions, use of, 79
  odometers, 80

Logs (*cont'd*)
   speedometers, 80
   throttle setting, 79–80
Longitude, 89–90, 153
Lookout, the, 80–83
   binoculars for, 80–81, *ill.* 81
   direction of looking, 81–82
   looking aft, importance of, 82
   current effects and, 82–83
Loran bearings, defined, 92

McAuley, Herb, 205
Magnetic course, finding of, *ill.* 86
Marine sextant, 164, *ill.* 165, 169
Master mariner's compass. *See* Compass
MAYDAY, 90
Medical supplies, 221
Menu planning, 240
   See also Food
Moon, navigation by, 142
Mosquitoes, 247
Motion sickness, 227–31
   chronic sufferers, 228
   drugs for, 230–31
   ear, role of, 227–29, *ill.* 229
   fear affects, 227
   home remedies, 230
   illness affects, 228
   incidence of, 227
   masks more serious symptoms, 230
   medical knowledge of, 228
   resistance to, development of, 228
   smell, sense of, and, 229
   symptoms of, 229–30
   vehicle characteristics and, 230
   visual factors in, 229
Mulhauser, Captain, 247

Nassau Tribune, 248
Nautical miles, 167
   statute miles and, 84
Navigation and pilotage
   alternate plans, importance of, 1–5
   length-of-day method, 153
   mental practice for, 7
   by moon, 142
   pig, use of, 153–54
   pilotage distinguished from, 77
   planets, use of, 142
   skew course, 149
   swells, steering by, 141–42
   without instruments, 140–54
   See also specific entries
Navigation by stars, 143–49
   ACRUX, 144
   Aquila, *ill.* 146
   Big Dipper, 143, *ill.* 144
   Cassiopeia, 143, *ill.* 144
   east and west, locating, 144–46, *ill.* 146
   GACRUX, 144
   Kochab, 153, *ill.* 154
   latitude, finding, 146–49, *ill.* 148
   "leading" star, defined, 144
   north and south, locating, 143–44, *ill.* 145
   Orion, 145, *ill.* 146
   Pole Star, 143–44
   "sacred calabash," 147
   Sigma Octantis, 143
   Southern Cross, 144
   star-overhead method, 146–47
   stars as clock, 153, *ill.* 154
   stick method for finding latitude, 146–48, *ill.* 148
   Theta, *ill.* 146
   "trailing" star, defined, 144
   Virgo, 145–46, *ill.* 146
   Zeta, 145–46, *ill.* 146
Navigation by sun, 149–53
   hourly change in bearing, 152
   latitude, locating, 153
   longitude, locating, 153
   noon, time of, finding, 150–52
   "sunstone," use of, 153
Nelson, Lord, 227
Non-skid devices, 237, *ill.* 236
Northers, 31–32

Odometers, 80
Oil leaks, 211–12

"Palmetto bugs" (roaches), 247–48
Patent log, 78–79
Pen gun, 224
Pilotage
   navigation distinguished from, 77
   See also Navigation and pilotage; specific entries
Planets, 142
   distinguished from stars, 160–62
Pole Star, 143–44, 170
Position lines. *See* Lines of position

268 INDEX

Propeller
   changing, 70–71
   freeing, 70, *ill.* 73
Pump failure, 209, 210–11

Radio, need for, 225
Rangefinders, 87
Range of lights, 97–104 *passim*
Rats, 247
RDF bearings, defined, 92
Reefs. *See* Coral waters, piloting in
Refraction effects, 99
Repair. *See* Hull work between tides; specific entries
Roaches, 247–48
Rodman, Admiral, 147
Rope, raveling of, preventing, 211–12
"Round" of stars, 173
Rude, E. B., 155
Rude star finder. *See* Star finder
Running aground, 71, 177–84
   anchor, use of, 178, 182, *ill.* 183
   anchor, getting out the, 180, *ill.* 181
   anchor, kedging off with, 179
   changing fore-and-aft trim, 179
   checking bilge for leaks, 179
   dinghy, use of, 180, 181–82
   first steps after, 178
   incidence of, 177
   kedge, *ill.* 183
   kedging off, 180–82, *ill.* 181
   last resort, 183–84
   lightening the ship, 179–80
   in mud, 179
   reducing draft, 182
   on reef, example of, 215–25
   running the engine, 181
   sailboats, 178, 179, 182, 183
   skindiving and, 178
   sounding with boathook, 178
   tide considerations, 178
   turning her head, 179–80
   undesirable reactions to, 177–78
   with wind or current toward deep water, 178–79

"Sacred calabash," the, 147
Sailing, 47–58
   attitudes toward, 47
   basic principle of, 48–50
   beating, 50–53, *ill.* 51, 52, 53
   before the wind, 54–55
   broken boom, 214
   built-in top speed of sailboats, 190–91
   close-hauled, 50–53, *ill.* 51, 52, 53, 106–7
   compass adjustment, 119–20, *ill.* 119
   downhill in following breeze, 54–55
   entering harbor, 4–6
   fore-and-aft-rigged boats, 48–50, *ill.* 49
   halyard parting, 214–15
   in irons, solution for, 53–54
   a jibe all standing, 54–55
   jury rigs, 56–57, *ill.* 57
   laws protecting, 47–48
   during lulls, 52
   missing stays, 53–54
   motor sailing, 55–57, *ill.* 57
   in narrow channels, 52
   off the wind, 54
   on the wind, 49, 50–53, *ill.* 51, 52, 53
   points of, *ill.* 51
   powerboats and, 55, 56–58
   in puffs, 52
   reaching with the sheet, 54
   rigging repair, 214
   running, 54–55
   running aground, 178, 179, 182, 183
   sail patching, 213
   sloops, 49–50, *ill.* 49
   square-riggers, 49–50, *ill.* 49
   tacking, 52, *ill.* 53
   to windward, 52, *ill.* 53
Sandflies, 247
Sea cucumbers, 113
Seasickness. *See* Motion sickness
Sea urchins, 75
Sextants, 164, *ill.* 165, 169
Sharks, 74, 79, 250
Shelter, emergency, 221
Shipwrecking. *See* Wrecking
Sight reduction tables, 171
Signal supplies, 221
Single-handers
   celestial navigation and, 163
   cooking and, 242
   in coral waters, 110
   falling overboard, 197, *ill.* 198
   hyperventilation and, 72
   skindiving and, 69
   as teachers, 6
Skidproofing devices, 237, *ill.* 236

Skindiving, 67-75
  in anchor work, 71, 72
  checking hull damage, 71
  cleaning waterline, 69-70
  coral, injurious, 75
  in coral waters, 108
  face mask, 67
    with built-in snorkels, 68
      oval type, 68, *ill.* 69
      goggle type, 68-69, *ill.* 69
  flippers, 72-74
  hyperventilation, use of, 72
  injuries, underwater, 74
  knives, use of, 74
  for pleasure, 74-75
  propeller, changing the, 70-71
  propeller, freeing the, 70, *ill.* 73
  retrieving objects lost overboard, 71, *ill.* 73
  when run aground, 71, 178
  sea urchins, 75
  shallow diving, 71-72
  sharks, 74
  for single-handers, 69, 72
  smoking and, 72
  snorkel, 67, 69, *ill.* 69
    clearing of, 70
    valves, 68
  stuffing-box leaks, repairing, 70
  weed removal, 70, *ill.* 73
  weights and weight belts, 72, *ill.* 73
  wet suits, 67-68, *ill.* 69
  See also Floating
Sleeping conditions, 3-4
Slocum, Joshua, 2, 215
Sloops, 49-50, *ill.* 49
Sounding pole, 78
Southern Cross, 144
Spares, 208-15
Speedometers, 80
Square-rigged sailboats, 49-50, *ill.* 49
Star finder, 155-63
  altitude ovals, 156
  compass bearing of known star for setting, 157-58, *ill.* 157
  degrees of azimuth, 156-57
  described, 155-56
  distinguishing between stars and planets, 160-62
  hand measurement of altitudes, *ill.* 156
  horizon oval, 155-56

  miscellaneous features of, 162-63
  Nautical Almanac for setting, 158-59
  overlay, 155-56
  Rude, 155
  "Rule of Sixty-Eight" for setting, 159, 161
  stars shown on, 159
  table for setting, 159, 160-61
  types of, 155
  zenith, 156
Stars, distinguishing planets from, 160-62
  See also Navigation by stars
Steering mechansim, 213
Storage, 243-45, 246
Storms. *See* Weather
Stove
  gimbaled, 238
  kerosene, 249-50
  spares for, 250
Stuffing-box leaks, repairing, 70
Subsolar point, 166, *ill.* 167
Sun. *See* Navigation by sun
"Sunstone," 153
Survival kit, 221
Swells, steering by, 141-42

Tables, stowable, 245
Taffrail log, 78-79
Teachers, single-handers as, 6
Thrumbox, 211
Tidal currents
  at angle to channel, 138
  at high and low water, 135, 137, *ill.* 136
  misconceptions about, 134-35
  near shore, 138
  rotary, 138, *ill.* 139
  slack periods, predicting, 137
  speed of, predicting, 137-38
  strong, effects of, 136-37
  strong, locating, 137-38
  strong through passage, approach for, 139
  tables, 139
  westward flood current concept of, 134-35
  where two bays meet, 138
  wind affects, 138
Tides, 129-40
  barometric pressures affect, 131
  causes of, 129-30

270 INDEX

Tides (cont'd)
  current distinguished from, 129
  dockmaster's information on, 131–32
  height of, calculating, 132
  hours after morning as indicator of, 133
  moon, age of, as indicator of, 133–34
  moon, position of, as indicator of, 133
  prediction of, 130–34
  range of, predicting, 60–61
  river stages affect, 131
  tables, use of, 131–34
  tide mark as guide to height of, 133
  winds affect, 131
Tilley lamps, 249
Towing, 184–92
  dropping off at dock, 191–92
  preliminary investigation, importance of, 184–85
  without a rope, 184–85
Towing, alongside, 189–90, *ill.* 190
  fenders, 189, *ill.* 190
  size of boats and, 190
  spring lines, 189, *ill.* 190
  thwartship line, 189, *ill.* 190
Towing, astern, 187–89
  bridle, use of, 187–88, *ill.* 188
  code of signals for, 187
  length of tow rope, 188, *ill.* 189
  lights for nighttime, 191
  line, choice of, 187, 188–89
  sailboats, 190–91
  securing line, 187–88, *ill.* 188
  starting the tow, 188
  weights for line, 189
  yaw, curbing of, 189
Towing, getting a line out, 185, *ill.* 186
  by dinghy, 185
  floating line, use of, 185, *ill.* 186
  relative drift technique for, 185, *ill.* 186
  wind or current floats, 185, *ill.* 186
"Trailing" star, defined, 144
Tropical weather. See Weather, tropical

Ventilation, 233–36, *ill.* 234
  anchoring across the wind improves, 235–36, *ill.* 235
  awnings and, 235
  in cabin when using flame, 234
  condensation, 233–34
  devices for improving, 235, *ill.* 234
  dry rot and, 233
Very pistol, 223, 225
Visibility, 97–104
  bobbing a light, 100
  geometry of, 97–99, *ill.* 98, 99
  horizon, distance to, formulas for, 101, 103, *table* 102
  lights, problems with, 99–100
  refraction effects, 99, 100
  seas and swells affect, 100
  sky, height of, 103–4
  table, 102
Voss, J. C., 142, 215

Water
  clean, difficulty in getting, 245
  consumption, prediction of, 246
  for emergencies, 221
  rainwater, reliance on, 246
  running, 245
  salt, uses of, 245–46
  storage, 246
Waterproofing, 231–33, *ill.* 233
  Dinner Key Teak, 232
  drip-leak relationship, 231
  dry rot, 233
  hatches and coamings, 232, *ill.* 233
  mildew, 233
  pinhole leaks, tracing, 231–32
  port gaskets, 232
  splash-proofing a drawer, 232, *ill.* 233
  See also Ventilation
Weather, tropical, 29–46
  annual mean temperatures, 30
Weather, tropical, summer, 38–46, *ill.* 39
  barometric readings, 40
  calms, 38
  depressions, 43
  easterly waves, 41–43, *ill.* 42
  hurricanes, 43–46
  hurricanes, wind strength during, 46
  lightning, 40
  storms, tropical, 43–46
  temperatures, 38
  thunderheads, 38
  thunderstorms, 38–40
  winds, 38
Weather, tropical, winter, 31–38, *ill.* 33
  cumulus cloud cover, 35
  dewpoint, 36

Weather, tropical, winter (*cont'd*)
  fog, 36–37
  humidity percentages, 36
  land-and-sea breezes, 37–38
  Northers, 31–32
  pressure distribution, 34
  rainfall, amount of, 36
  seas and swells, 37
  squalls, 37
  sunshine, average hours of, 35–36
  wind directions, 33–35
  wind directions, Rule of Thumb for predicting, 34
  wind speeds, 32
Windlasses, 12
Wood as fuel, 248
Wrecking, 215–25
  emergency supplies, 221
  examples of, 215–20, 222–25
  successful, defined, 215
  See also Abandoning ship
Wrenches, 211